Speed Up Your Spani

CW00411085

'Excellent book. The chapters put together and systematise a lot of material that is often taught in an anecdotal or haphazard sort of way, if at all. Students will learn a great deal from the book and have their confidence in using Spanish considerably boosted as a result.'

Jonathan Thacker, *Merton College, University of Oxford, UK*

'An invaluable, highly original and methodically sound approach to correcting and eliminating common, yet difficult-to-eliminate errors.'

Manuel Delgado, *Bucknell University, USA*

'The user-friendly format and page layout makes *Speed Up Your Spanish* a highly practical reference source for students and teachers.'

Mª Victoria García Serrano, *University of Pennsylvania, USA*

Speed Up Your Spanish is a unique and innovative resource that identifies and explains the common errors which cause confusion for students of Spanish.

From false friends to idiomatic expressions, each of the nine chapters focuses on a grammatical category where English speakers typically make mistakes. Full explanations are provided throughout with clear, comprehensive examples enabling students to learn from their mistakes and gain an in-depth understanding of Spanish grammar and usage.

Key features:

- carefully selected topics and examples based on the most common errors
- exercises throughout to reinforce learning
- shortcuts and mnemonic devices providing vital learning strategies
- a companion website available at www.speedupyourspanish.com providing supplementary exercises as well as audio files

Suitable both for classroom use or self-study, *Speed Up Your Spanish* is the ideal resource for all intermediate learners of Spanish wishing to refine their language skills.

Javier Muñoz-Basols is an Instructor in Spanish at the University of Oxford.
Marianne David teaches Spanish at the Trinity School in New York.
Olga Núñez Piñeiro is Senior Lecturer in Spanish at the University of Westminster.

Speed Up Your Spanish

Strategies to avoid common errors

Javier Muñoz-Basols
Marianne David
Olga Núñez Piñeiro

Routledge
Taylor & Francis Group

LONDON AND NEW YORK

First published 2010
by Routledge
2 Park Square, Milton Park, Abingdon, Oxon OX14 4RN

Simultaneously published in the USA and Canada
by Routledge
270 Madison Ave, New York, NY 10016

Routledge is an imprint of the Taylor & Francis Group, an informa business

© 2010 Javier Muñoz-Basols, Marianne David and Olga Núñez Piñeiro

Illustrations by Sofia Kaba-Ferreiro

Typeset in Univers and Palatino by
HWA Text and Data Management, London
Printed and bound in Great Britain by
MPG Books Group, UK

British Library Cataloguing in Publication Data
A catalogue record for this book is available from the British Library

Library of Congress Cataloging-in-Publication Data
Muñoz-Basols, Javier.
  Speed up your Spanish : strategies to avoid common errors /
  Javier Muñoz-Basols, Marianne David, Olga Núñez Piñeiro.
      p. cm.
  Includes index.
  1. Spanish language—Textbooks for foreign speakers—English.
  2. Spanish language—Grammar. 3. Spanish language—Errors of usage.
  I. David, Marianne. II. Núñez Piñeiro, Olga. III. Title.
PC4129.E5M86 2009
468.2'421—dc22   2009009276

ISBN10: 0-415-49333-1 (hbk)
ISBN10: 0-415-49332-3 (pbk)
ISBN10: 0-203-87121-9 (ebk)

ISBN13: 978-0-415-49333-8 (hbk)
ISBN13: 978-0-415-49332-1 (pbk)
ISBN13: 978-0-203-87121-8 (ebk)

A mis padres, Miguel Muñoz Osta y Carmen Basols Tena, por enseñarme a ser persistente en la vida

Javier Muñoz-Basols

To my son Walter

Marianne David

To my son Benjamin Alexander and my husband Andrew

Olga Núñez Piñeiro

Contents

Introduction

This book focuses on common errors frequently made by English-speaking students who have attained an intermediate level of Spanish. Once identified, classified and explained, these errors can be tackled and eliminated to enhance spoken and written fluency in the language.

Learning a foreign language can be likened to a journey through a maze of errors. *Errare* (to err in Latin) is what the student must do in order to learn. Like a knight errant, riding through a dark forest full of wrong turns and dead ends before finally coming out into a clearing, the willing learner confronts error in order to become free of it. There is no learning without making mistakes. Mistakes are a key element on the road to mastery since they lead to correction, understanding, and ultimately self-correction.

Some of the common errors we have identified in this book deal with gender and number, accentuation, spelling and capitalization; others highlight false cognates, idiomatic expressions and non-existent words. These errors all reflect misconceptions about the structure of the Spanish language in contrast to English. To help English-speaking students, we have highlighted similarities and differences between English and Spanish, and set down some simple rules. By following these rules, the student will make better connections and associations, and thus gain a deeper knowledge and understanding of both languages.

In order to assist students in achieving mastery in Spanish, we also offer a variety of mnemonic devices and practical shortcuts for remembering both grammar rules and vocabulary. We hope that they will add enjoyment to the process and encourage the development of personal learning strategies.

To effectively practice and drill the material presented, each chapter contains a variety of exercises as well as an answer key in the appendix. To ensure that students also receive the benefits provided by new technologies and interactive learning, the book is accompanied by audio files and supplementary exercises made available on the *Speed Up Your Spanish* companion website, www.speedupyourspanish.com.

Chapter 1 deals with the number and gender of nouns, stressing the importance of gender in Spanish in contrast to English. It indicates numerous exceptions and suggests strategies for remembering the gender of words that tend to cause problems for English speakers. The purpose of this chapter is to show how correct usage of gender will enable the student to make the proper agreement among the different elements of a sentence, thus leading to improved accuracy both in writing and speaking. This chapter also teaches how to distinguish between words that look similar, but have very different meanings due to their gender, e.g., *el puerto* (port) and *la puerta* (door); *el capital* (money) and *la capital* (capital of a country), etc. Examples of gender affecting meaning are not usually covered by Spanish textbooks, but they are required knowledge for intermediate-level Spanish students.

The next three chapters deal with 'false friends,' also known as false cognates. Given the relevance and breadth of this linguistic phenomenon, we have subdivided it into categories and chapters that deal separately with verbs, nouns, and adjectives and adverbs. Our method is to create awareness of the similarity in form between an English and a Spanish word, while demonstrating the difference in meaning. From our experience of teaching English speakers, we know that this is a key area of misunderstanding, and one that has been neglected by traditional grammar texts. Therefore students will find it of particular value.

Chapter 2 highlights false cognate verbs by demonstrating and explaining their different meanings. This is complemented, where appropriate, with useful expressions that help to reinforce the meaning of these verbs.

Chapter 3 presents false cognate nouns and their usage. It complements the explanations with related expressions. In addition to learning which nouns to use, students will benefit from learning related nouns and synonyms, thereby expanding their vocabulary.

Chapter 4 deals with false cognate adjectives and adverbs, and also includes related expressions to help emphasize the meaning of each word. Synonyms are also presented to help broaden students' vocabulary.

Chapter 5 clarifies the variations and shades of meaning of certain Spanish verbs, as well as other words that appear to be similar yet have different meanings. Some of these verbs are differentiated by their prefixes, e.g., *seguir - conseguir - perseguir - proseguir*.

Chapter 6 contains expressions organized by semantic field, e.g., *caer*, *haber*, *tener*, etc. We stress how important it is for students to master an array of such expressions that cannot be translated literally, but are an essential element of everyday communication.

Chapter 7 covers non-existent words, words with double meanings and other misused expressions that are often a result of linguistic transfer from English. The aim of this chapter is two-fold: to eliminate such non-existent words or expressions from the student's repertoire; and to highlight words with double meanings. Thus by learning correct usage, students can consolidate their knowledge of the language while expanding their vocabulary.

Chapter 8 deals with rules of tonic and written accentuation. This is an important aspect of the language, not often taught in a focused manner, but very relevant to both written and spoken Spanish. Students can practice Spanish accentuation on the companion website and listen to interactive exercises designed for this purpose.

Chapter 9 deals with spelling, punctuation and capitalization. These aspects of the language are not easily mastered, yet are very important in written Spanish. Contrary to popular opinion, Spanish is not a simple phonetic language that is written as it is spoken. This chapter identifies letter combinations that do not exist in Spanish, while highlighting those that are frequently used. Once students become aware of the writing conventions in Spanish (in some cases considerably different from English), they are able to enhance their writing skills. This chapter comes with audio files on the companion website, so that students can listen to audio clips and put into practice what they have learned.

Answers to the exercises contained in each chapter can be found in the Appendix.

It is our conviction, as authors of *Speed Up Your Spanish*, that we are providing students with a rich and invaluable repertoire of words and expressions that will facilitate, if not ensure, a mastery of Spanish. Our hope is that by focusing on the content of each chapter and doing the exercises, students will feel empowered not only to tackle their own common errors and the difficult aspects of the language, but to immerse themselves in the rich and diverse Hispanic culture.

Acknowledgments

We would like to thank the following people: Pawel Adrjan for his continuous support, for reading every page of the manuscript and also for his insightful and valuable comments on both the English and Spanish portions of the text; Yolanda Pérez Sinusía and Dr. María Rox Barasoain for their advice on the design of the exercises; and Andrew Ellis for his input and advice. We would also like to thank the teachers from the Modern Languages Department of the Trinity School in New York, most especially Óscar Cerreño for his feedback and help in the initial steps of this project, as well as Laura Gordon and Janet Kehl for our numerous conversations on language teaching and learning that have enriched this book. At Routledge, we would like to thank Anna Callander, Sarah

Mabley and Samantha Vale Noya for their guidance and patience throughout the publication process. We are also grateful to Nahade Olivia Castro Alva, Alejandro David Muñoz-Basols and Pawel Adrjan for their help with recording exercises for the companion website, and to our students at the University of Oxford, Trinity School and the University of Westminster, who often, unknowingly, have provided us with valuable feedback in identifying areas of special relevance or difficulty for learning Spanish.

Website

The book is accompanied by audio files and supplementary exercises for all the chapters through the *Speed Up Your Spanish* companion website, www.speedupyourspanish.com

Authors

Javier Muñoz-Basols is an Instructor in Spanish at the University of Oxford. He has taught at the University of Pennsylvania, Bucknell University, Université de Bourgogne, Royal Holloway – University of London, Instituto Cervantes and Trinity School in New York. He holds an MA in Romance Languages from the University of Pennsylvania, and a DEA in translation studies from the University of Zaragoza. Javier has published articles on applied linguistics, translation studies and Spanish and Latin American literature. He has served as editorial assistant at the *Hispanic Review* and as bibliographer at the Modern Language Association of America (MLA). He is also a member of the editorial team of the www.todoele.net website.

Marianne David holds a PhD in comparative literature from Yale University. She has taught Spanish and French at Trinity School in New York for 27 years and has also taught at Yale University, University of New Haven, Dartmouth College and Faculté d'Amiens in France. She has also served as gallery educator at the Guggenheim Museum in New York.

Olga Núñez Piñeiro is Senior Lecturer and Head of Spanish at the University of Westminster, where she co-ordinates the undergraduate Spanish language modules. She holds master's degrees in bilingual translation, cinema studies, and teaching Spanish as a foreign language, and a DEA in translation studies from the Universitat Rovira i Virgili. She is also chief examiner in Spanish for the British Ministry of Defence Languages Examination Board.

1 Gender and number

The aim of this chapter is to teach the correct usage of gender and number so that you can make the proper agreements among the different elements of a sentence. Numerous exceptions are shown, as well as strategies for remembering the gender and number of words that tend to cause problems for English speakers.

Gender

Spanish articles and adjectives agree in gender with the nouns they modify. All nouns, whether animate or inanimate, have gender. While it is logical that humans and animals should be either feminine or masculine, with objects gender is purely an inherent grammatical feature.

Gender of inanimate nouns

1 Most nouns ending in **–o** are masculine and most nouns ending in **–a** are feminine:

> el cielo, el carro, el suelo
> la casa, la silla, la mesa

There are some irregular nouns that end in **–o** and are feminine:

> la dinamo, la foto (or la **foto**grafía), la libido, la mano, la moto (or la **moto**cicleta), la radio (used as a feminine noun in Spain and most of Latin America; however, el radio is also used in some Latin American countries)

Likewise there are also many irregular nouns that end in **–a** and are masculine:

 The list below shows the frequency of the irregularity according to the ending (**–ama, –ema, –ima, –oma, –uma**). Note that many of these irregular masculine nouns are of Greek origin and also exist in English. While a lot of them are part of medical jargon, many are also of everyday use.

–ama / –ma

> el caligrama (calligram), el crucigrama (crossword puzzle), el diagrama (diagram), el drama (drama), el electrocardiograma (electrocardiogram), el epigrama (epigram), el fotograma (in cinema: still or shot), el holograma (hologram), el melodrama (melodrama), el monograma (monogram), el panorama (panorama), el pentagrama (music stave), el pijama (pajamas; also feminine in some Latin American countries), el programa (program), el telegrama (telegram), el carisma (charisma), el cisma (schism), el diafragma (diaphragm), el dogma (dogma), el enigma (enigma), el fantasma (ghost), el karma (karma), el magma (magma), el sintagma (sintagma), el sofisma (sophism), el zeugma (zeugma)

–ema

> el dilema (dilemma), el edema (edema), el eccema (eczema), el emblema (emblem), el esquema (diagram, outline), el estema (stem), el fonema (phoneme), el lema (motto, slogan), el morfema (morpheme), el poema

(poem), el problema (problem), el sistema (system), el tema (topic, theme), el teorema (theorem)

–ima

el clima (climate) (and very few more)

–oma

el aroma (aroma), el axioma (axiom), el coma (coma), el cromosoma (chromosome), el diploma (diploma), el genoma (genome), el idioma (language), el melanoma (melanoma), el mioma (myoma), el síntoma (symptom)

–uma

el puma (puma), el reuma (rheumatism), el trauma (trauma) (and very few more)

 However, in spite of the examples above, there are just as many words that end in **–ma** and are feminine, even though some of them have the same etymology as in English. These words essentially follow the basic rule that words ending in **–a** are feminine:

la alarma (alarm), la broma (prank), la calma (calm), la cama (bed), la cima (summit), la crema (cream), la diadema (hairband), la esgrima (fencing), la espuma (foam), la estratagema (stratagem), la firma (signature), la flema (phlegm), la gama (range), la gema (gem), la goma (rubber), la lágrima (tear), la lima (lime fruit; file or rasp), la norma (rule), la palma (palm), la paloma (dove, pigeon), la rama (branch), la rima (rhyme), la víctima (victim), etc.

 There are also other masculine words that end in **–a**. Some of these nouns may also be feminine when they refer to a woman. In those cases the noun is invariable for both genders:

el/la azteca (male Aztec/female Aztec), el/la albacea (executor of a will), el/la alienígena (alien), el/la camarada (comrade), el cava (Spanish sparkling wine), el chachachá (cha-cha dance), el cometa (comet), el/la dálmata (Dalmatian), el delta (mouth of a river), el día (day), el druida (druid), el/la inca (Inca), el insecticida (insecticide), el koala (koala bear), el málaga (a type of wine), el mapa (map), el/la maya (Mayan), el planeta (planet), el/la poeta (poet) (also: la poetisa), el quechua (Quechua language), el telesilla (chair lift), el tequila (tequila), el tranvía (streetcar), el SIDA (AIDS), el sofá (sofa), el tanga (thong), el vodka (vodka; also feminine in some Latin American countries), el yoga (yoga), etc.

2   Interestingly, in some cases, the use of **–a** vs. **–o** signifies a difference in **size or shape** as in:

el barco (boat)/la barca (dinghy), el bolso (handbag)/la bolsa (bag), el cesto (large basket, laundry basket)/la cesta (basket), el cuchillo (knife)/la cuchilla (razor blade), el charco (puddle)/la charca (pond), el huerto (vegetable garden, orchard)/la huerta (a large orchard), el jarro (pitcher)/la jarra (jug, tankard, beer glass), el saco (sack)/la saca (a large bag made of coarse fabric), etc.

In other cases it serves to distinguish **a tree** (masc.) from **its fruit** (fem.):

el almendro (almond tree)/la almendra (almond), el avellano (hazel tree)/la avellana (hazelnut), el castaño (chestnut tree)/la castaña (chestnut), el cerezo (cherry tree)/ la cereza (cherry), el ciruelo (plum tree)/la ciruela (plum), el manzano (apple tree)/la manzana (apple), el naranjo (orange tree)/la naranja (orange), el olivo (olive tree)/la oliva (olive), etc.

3   Nouns ending in **–aje**, **–or**, **–án**, **–ambre** or a **stressed vowel** are **masculine**:

el equipaje (luggage), el paisaje (landscape), el amor (love), el tambor (drum), el mazapán (marzipan), el refrán (proverb), el enjambre (swarm), el calambre (electric shock; cramp) (but not el hambre, las hambres; see later in the chapter), el colibrí (hummingbird), el champú (shampoo), etc.

4   Also **masculine** are:

- **Mountains, rivers, lakes, seas and oceans:** los Pirineos, el Everest, el Ebro, el Amazonas, el Mediterráneo, el Atlántico, etc.
- **Numbers:** el uno, el dos, el tres, etc.
- **Colors:** el blanco, el negro, el rojo, el amarillo, el azul, el marrón, el gris, el violeta, etc.
- **Days of the week:** el lunes, el martes, el miércoles, el jueves, etc.
- **Sports teams:** el Madrid, el Barça, el Real Zaragoza, los Lakers, etc.
- **Wines:** el rioja, el albariño, el málaga, el borgoña, etc.

5   By contrast the following categories are **feminine**:

- **Islands:** las (islas) Canarias, las Baleares, las Antillas, etc.
- **Roads;** la (carretera) N-342, la A-91, etc.
- **Letters of the alphabet:** la (letra) "a", la "b", la "ñ", la "z", etc.

6 Nouns ending in **–cia, –ción, –dad, –eza, –ie, –itis, –nza, –sión, –sis*, –tad, –tud, –umbre** are **feminine**:

> la paciencia (patience), la celebración (celebration), la ciudad (town, city), la cabeza (head), la serie (series), la gastritis (gastritis), la bonanza (prosperity), la decisión (decision), la hipótesis (hypothesis), la dificultad (difficulty), la actitud (attitude), la costumbre (custom, habit), etc.

> *Except: el análisis, el énfasis, el éxtasis and el paréntesis.

7 A few nouns have **ambiguous** gender, the only difference being one of style, usage or register:

> el mar/la mar (more poetic), el maratón/la maratón, el azúcar moreno/la azúcar blanquilla

Sometimes this ambiguity lies in the use of the noun in question in singular or in plural:

> el arte (art)/las artes (the arts)

8 Some nouns have a different meaning depending on whether they are used in their masculine or feminine form:

> el puerto (port)/la puerta (door)

For these words, see the sections within this chapter: "Similar Word – Different Gender – Different Meaning" and "Same Word – Different Gender – Different Meaning"

Gender of animate nouns

Many nouns that refer to human beings or animals take different endings to indicate gender or sex.

1 To form the **feminine** of nouns ending in **–o, –e** or **–Ø** (a consonant), change **o** ⇨ **a** or **e** ⇨ **a**, or add an **a** to the final consonant.

Masculine	Feminine
–o, –e or **–Ø**	**–a**
niño (boy)	niña (girl)
gato (cat)	gata (she-cat, puss)
jefe (boss)	jefa (female boss)
señor (Mr.)	señora (Mrs.)

2   Other possible **feminine** endings for animate nouns are: **–esa, –isa, –ina, –triz**:

Masculine	Feminine
	–esa, **–isa**, **–ina**, **–triz**
abad (abbot)	abadesa (abbess)
alcalde (mayor)	alcaldesa (mayoress)
barón (baron)	baronesa (baroness)
conde (count)	condesa (countess)
diablo (devil)	diablesa (or diabla) (a she-devil)
duque (duke)	duquesa (duchess)
príncipe (prince)	princesa (princess)
tigre (tiger)	tigresa (tigress)
vampiro (vampire)	vampiresa (vamp)
poeta (poet)	poetisa (or poeta) (female poet)
sacerdote (priest)	sacerdotisa (priestess)
gallo (rooster)	gallina (hen)
rey (king)	reina (queen)
héroe (hero)	heroína (heroine)
actor (actor)	actriz (actress)
emperador (emperor)	emperatriz (empress)

3   Other times gender is indicated with a **different word**:

> varón/hembra (male/female), padre/madre (father/mother), yerno/nuera (son-in-law/daughter-in-law), toro /vaca (bull /cow), caballo/yegua (horse/mare), etc.

4   But there is another category of animate nouns that **stay the same**, while only the article change. These may end in:

- **–a**: el/la atleta, el/la colega, el/la burócrata, etc.
- **the suffix –ista**: el/la artista, el/la budista, el/la comunista, el/la periodista, el/la pesimista, el/la pianista, el/la protagonista, el/la socialista, el/la terrorista, el/la turista, (*exception: el modisto/la modista), etc.
- **–e**: el/la amante, el/la cantante, el/la conserje, el/la estudiante, el/la representante, etc.
- **–o**: el/la soprano, el/la testigo, etc.
- **a consonant**: el/la joven, el/la mártir, etc.

Note that a number of nouns in this category also have a commonly used standard feminine form:

> abogado/abogada, ingeniero/ingeniera, médico/médica, ministro/ministra

5   Certain animals are **inherently masculine or feminine** irrespective of sex:

> la rata, la serpiente, la ballena, el lince, la pantera, el caracol, la hormiga, la liebre, el mosquito, el ruiseñor

6   Other unisex words use a feminine article, but are used for either gender:

> la pareja, la persona, la víctima, la criatura

7   In general, nouns that end in **–e** (whether animate or inanimate) can be masculine or feminine (see the mnemonic device at the end of this section).

> el padre, el traje, el bebé/la madre, la leche, la carne

8   Nouns that end in **–i** (whether animate or inanimate) are normally masculine:

> el alhelí, el colibrí, el rubí, el zahorí

9   Nouns that end in **–u** (whether animate or inanimate) can be either masculine or feminine:

> el menú, la tribu

10   Nouns that end in a consonant can be either masculine or feminine, although as already mentioned above, some of them can be identified because of their ending:

> el almacén, la flor, la razón, el mes, el baúl, la mujer

Mnemonic Device

Designing your own strategy for associating nouns with their gender can help you to remember them, like in the following example:

> ¿Por qué la palabra 'la leche' es femenina en español? Porque **la** leche viene de **la** vaca.
> (Why is milk a feminine word in Spanish? Because cows give milk)

Similarly, this learning strategy can be expanded into an entire scenario. For instance, you may create a short paragraph to remember the gender of the following problematic nouns:

> la leche – la sangre – la parte – la sal – la carne – la llave – la calle – la piel

> La vaca es un animal que da **leche**. También **la carne** es **una parte** de la vaca que comemos y que tiene **sangre**, pero que cuando cocinamos le ponemos **sal**. **La piel** de vaca también es útil para fabricar ropa y zapatos. En la India las vacas están en **la calle** porque son animales sagrados, pero en otros países están en un establo bajo **llave**.

(A cow gives milk. Also, meat is the part of the cow that we eat and it has blood; as we cook it we add salt. The cow's skin is also useful for making clothes and shoes. In India cows are on the street because they are sacred, but in other countries they are locked in a stable with a key.)

Other important aspects related to the gender of nouns

Feminine nouns that begin with a stressed **a** or **ha** take the masculine form of the definite and indefinite article (**el** or **un**) in the singular:

el/un agua	las/unas aguas	el/un aula	las/unas aulas
el/un águila **but**	las/unas águilas	el/un hambre **but**	las/unas hambres
el/un hada	las/unas hadas	el/un hacha	las/unas hachas

The same is applicable when these nouns are combined with adjectives:

el/un área libre		las/unas áreas libres
el/un águila blanca		las/unas águilas blancas
el/un arca llena		las/unas arcas llenas
el/un arpa sonora		las/unas arpas sonoras
el/un aula limpia	**but**	las/unas aulas limpias
el/un agua fría		las/unas aguas frías
el/un ala rota		las/unas alas rotas
el/un arma pesada		las/unas armas pesadas
el/un hacha afilada		las/unas hachas afiladas
el/un hada madrina		las/unas hadas madrinas

However, these nouns will take the singular feminine article if an adjective comes between the article and the noun: la fría agua.

Note that the above-mentioned rule is applicable only to definite or indefinite articles, and not to other parts of speech such as demonstrative adjectives (esta, esa, aquella, etc.):

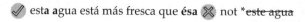 esta **agua** está más fresca que **ésa** not *~~este agua~~

esa arma/esas armas, aquella aula/aquellas aulas, toda hacha/todas las hachas

 *Exercises*

EXERCISE 1. Choose the correct gender for the following words.

1 ¿Me puedes ayudar a resolver (este/esta) problema de matemáticas? No entiendo (el/la) teorema.

2 Hay (un/una) serie en (el/la) televisión que explica (el/la) actitud de (los/las) ballenas ante el peligro.

3 (El/La) café que vendían en (el/la) cafetería desprendía (un/una) aroma inconfundible.

4 Será mejor que no pongas (el/la) mano allí, o igual (el/la) televisor te da (un/una) calambre.

5 Vimos cómo (un/una) águila cayó en (el/la) agua mientras luchaba con (un/una) serpiente.

6 (El/la) investigador encontró (un/una) rubí, pero fue incapaz de resolver (el/la) enigma.

7 (Este/esta) axioma no concuerda con (el/la) tesis principal (del/de la) esquema.

8 Pudieron llegar hasta (el/la) cima (del/de la) Aneto porque (el/la) clima se lo permitió.

9 (El/La) rima de (este/esta) poema no tiene (los mismos/las mismas) fonemas que (ése /ésa).

10 Me parece que (el/la) clase no es en (este/esta) aula sino en (aquél/aquélla).

11 No te comas (ese/esa) chocolate. Ya sé que es (un/una) tentación, pero si lo haces te va a producir (un/una) gastritis crónica.

12 Llevaba (un/una) tanga rosa debajo (del/de la) bañador que se le transparentaba a simple vista.

EXERCISE 2. The following nouns take either a feminine article or a masculine one. But some take both a feminine and a masculine article. Write the article or articles that fit each noun.

1	(**el/la**) dentista	10	_____	rima
2	_____ suelo	11	_____	mano
3	_____ aguafiestas	12	_____	mártir
4	_____ motocicleta	13	_____	carisma
5	_____ barril	14	_____	guía
6	_____ agua limpia	15	_____	paisaje
7	_____ dilema	16	_____	tigre
8	_____ estudiante	17	_____	naranjo
9	_____ dogma	18	_____	barca

19	_____ hada madrina		30	_____ muchedumbre
20	_____ problema		31	_____ serpiente
21	_____ testigo		32	_____ delta
22	_____ víctima		33	_____ tranvía
23	_____ Mediterráneo		34	_____ yegua
24	_____ colega		35	_____ socialista
25	_____ poeta		36	_____ serie
26	_____ do		37	_____ ordenanza
27	_____ actitud		38	_____ miércoles
28	_____ amante		39	_____ área
29	_____ martes		40	_____ análisis

EXERCISE 3. In each of the following examples, either the masculine or the feminine form of a word is given. Complete the exercise by giving the other form of each noun.

	Masculine	**Feminine**
1	el gallo	_____
2	_____	la abadesa
3	el león	_____
4	_____	la poetisa
5	el toro	_____
6	_____	la princesa
7	el emperador	_____
8	_____	la yegua
9	el héroe	_____
10	_____	la nuera
11	el taxista	_____
12	_____	la madrastra
13	el joven	_____
14	_____	la modista
15	el conserje	_____
16	_____	la ballena
17	el vampiro	_____
18	_____	la serpiente
19	el soprano	_____
20	_____	la baronesa
21	el zar	_____
22	_____	la institutriz

EXERCISE 4. Choose the word whose gender is different from the rest.

1   púrpura / lunes / cabeza / rojo
2   carro / barro / hermano / mano
3   cura / profesora / abogada / actriz

4   sistema / planeta / cama / problema
5   sabor / oleaje / parte / calambre
6   llave / carne / leche / café
7   diadema / cima / puma / lima
8   transparencia / rubí / libertad / colitis
9   día / salida / mapa / insecticida
10   análisis / crisis / síntesis / simbiosis
11   agua / aroma / hada / arma
12   clima / idioma / víctima / fantasma

Similar word – different gender – different meaning

The following words have different meanings depending on their gender. Many of them are related semantically, e.g., *el cuchillo* (knife) vs. *la cuchilla* (razor blade), which helps in remembering them. In these cases the difference in size of the two objects can be a helpful strategy to remember their respective meanings. But other words are not at all related even though they share the same root, e.g., *el barro* (mud) vs. *la barra* (bar).

> **Mnemonic device**
> Think of the phrase: **No es lo mismo el pimiento que la pimienta**. It will help you remember the existence of these similar words with different meanings.

el acto	act (action); act (in a play); in plural: cultural events (*actos culturales*); on the spot (*en el acto*)
el acta (las actas)	minutes; proceedings (of a conference); affidavit (*el acta notarial*)

La obra se pone interesante en el tercer acto. ¿Puedo leer el acta de la reunión?
(The play becomes interesting in the third act. Can I read the minutes of the meeting?)

el americano	American male; a type of coffee (prepared by adding espresso to hot water)
la americana	American female; a suit jacket (in Spain)

El americano y la americana se encontraron en Madrid. Él llevaba una elegante americana.
(The American man and woman met in Madrid. He was wearing an elegant jacket)

el apuesto   good-looking man
la apuesta   a bet or wager

Me gusta ese hombre apuesto. Te hago una apuesta a que salgo con él este sábado.
(I like that handsome man. I'll make you a bet that I'll be going out with him this Saturday)

el banco   a bench; a bank; a school of fish
la banca   banking (activity); the banking institution; bank (in a game of chance)

Han puesto bancos nuevos en el parque. La banca atraviesa un mal momento.
(They have put new benches in the park. The banking profession is not doing well)

el bando   a faction; side; edict
la banda   musical band; gang; sash; cushion (in billiards)

Romeo era del bando de los Montesco. Llevaba una banda azul en el brazo.
(Romeo was from the Montague faction. He wore a blue sash on his arm)

el barco   boat; ship; sailing ship (*barco de vela*)
la barca   dinghy, small boat; rowing boat (*barca de remos*)

La barca chocó con el barco pero no hubo heridos.
(The dinghy crashed into the ship but there were no casualties)

el barro   mud, clay
la barra   a bar; café bar; baguette (*una barra de pan*); lipstick (*una barra de labios*)

Había mucho barro en las calles después de la tormenta. Te esperaré en la barra del café.
(There was a lot of mud on the streets after the storm. I will wait for you at the café bar)

el bolero   a Spanish dance and musical rhythm; a lady's short jacket; a bootblack (Mexico) (*un limpiabotas*, in Spain)
la bolera   a bowling alley

Esta noche tocan el "Bolero" de Ravel en la bolera.
(They are playing Ravel's "Bolero" at the bowling alley tonight)

el bolso	a handbag (for a woman); or travelling bag
la bolsa	a bag (plastic, paper); the stock market; a pocket (in Central America and Mexico)

Cuando miró dentro de la bolsa, se dio cuenta de que no tenía su bolso.

(When she looked inside the bag, she realized she didn't have her handbag with her)

el conducto	pipe; channel; duct (anatomy)
la conducta	behavior; conduct

Tienen que operarle el conducto lacrimal. La conducta de tu primo es inaceptable.

(He needs an operation on his tear duct. Your cousin's behavior is unacceptable)

el cuadro	square (also *un cuadrado*); painting (also *una pintura*); a scene; control panel (*cuadro de mandos*), fuse box (*cuadro de fusibles*); symptoms (*cuadro clínico*).
la cuadra	a street block (Latin America) (*la manzana*, in Spain); a stable (for horses)

Ese cuadro es de Picasso. Tenemos que caminar dos cuadras más.

(That's a painting by Picasso. We have to walk two more blocks)

el cubierto	a piece of cutlery; place setting at a table
la cubierta	a cover; the cover of a tire, carcass; the deck of a ship, promenade deck

Pongamos los cubiertos en la mesa. El marinero subió a la cubierta del barco.

(Let's set the table with the cutlery. The sailor went up on deck)

el cubo	a bucket; a cube (geometry); a hub (of a wheel); garbage can (*el cubo de la basura*)
la cuba	a barrel; a cask

Tenemos que comprar un cubo nuevo para la basura. Pepe estaba borracho como una cuba.

(We have to buy a new garbage can. Pepe was completely drunk)

el cuchillo	a knife
la cuchilla	a razor blade

¿Tienes un cuchillo para cortar la cuerda? No, pero tengo una cuchilla para que te afeites.

(Do you have a knife to cut the string? No, but I have a razor blade so that you can shave)

el cuento	a tale, a fairy tale (*el cuento de hadas*); story, lie, a tall story (*un cuento chino*)
la cuenta	a bank account; a calculation; restaurant check, bill (*ila cuenta, por favor!*)

Cuéntame un lindo cuento. Tenemos que pagar la cuenta del restaurante.
(Tell me a nice story. We have to pay the restaurant check)

el derecho	the law; a right
la derecha	the opposite of left (*la izquierda*); right-wing in politics; right-hand side

Tenemos el derecho de ser felices. Gira a la derecha en el semáforo.
(We have the right to be happy. Turn right at the lights)

el fallo	a mistake; a fault, an error or defect (Spain); a veredict
la falla	a geological fault; a fault, error or defect (Latin America)

No sabía que para decir 'mistake' en España se dice 'el fallo' y en Latinoamérica 'la falla'.
(I didn't know that to say 'mistake' in Spain one says 'el fallo' and in Latin America 'la falla')

el fondo	the bottom; the back of a room; the background (of an image); a fund (finance); catalog or collection of a library
la fonda	an inn; a boarding house; a refreshment stand (Chile)

El fondo del lago es profundo. Pasemos la noche en esta fonda.
(The bottom of the lake is deep. Let's spend the night at this inn)

el fruto	fruit (result); profit or benefit; dried fruit and nuts (*los frutos secos*)
la fruta	fruit; seasonal fruit (*fruta del tiempo*)

Esta novela es el fruto de mi trabajo. El melocotón es una fruta riquísima.
(This novel is the result of my labor. The peach is a delicious fruit)

el gorro	a tight-fitting cap; to be fed up with (*estar hasta el gorro de*)
la gorra	a cap (with peak)

Necesito un gorro de lana para este invierno. Me regalaron una gorra de los Lakers.
(I need to buy a wool hat for this winter. I received a Lakers cap for my birthday)

el labio	lip (of a mouth)
la labia	smooth talk; to have the gift of the gab (*tener mucha labia*)

No despegó los labios en toda la comida. Tiene mucha labia, le encanta hablar.

(He didn't utter a single word during lunch. She's got the gift of the gab. She loves to talk)

el leño	a log (of wood); a blockhead (person)
la leña	firewood

Duerme siempre como un leño. Necesitamos leña para el picnic.

(He always sleeps like a log. We need firewood for the picnic)

el libro	a book
la libra	a pound; a pound sterling (*libra esterlina*)

Este libro me pareció interesantísimo. ¿Cuánto cuesta una libra de cerezas?

(This book was very interesting. How much is a pound of cherries?)

el lomo	a pork loin; the spine of a book; back of an animal
la loma	a little hill or hillock

El lomo de cerdo estaba rico. Vamos a subir la loma para ver la ciudad.

(The pork loin was delicious. Let's go up the hill to see the city)

el llanto	crying, sobbing
la llanta	the rim of a wheel; a tire (in Latin America) (*el neumático* in Spain)

En el castillo se podía oír un llanto por la noche. Tenemos que cambiar la llanta antes del viaje.

(Inside the castle, one could hear someone crying at night. We have to change the tire before the trip)

el madero	a piece of wood; a log; a piece of lumber, timber; a cop (in Spain, informal)
la madera	wood

Necesito ese madero para el fuego. Cortan árboles para obtener madera.

(I need that log for the fire. They cut trees to get wood)

el manto	a cloak; a geological layer
la manta	a blanket; *la frazada* (in Latin America)

Necesito un manto para la obra de teatro. Tengo frío, ¿tienes otra manta?

(I need a cloak for the play. I am cold; do you have another blanket?)

| el mareo | seasickness; travel sickness; dizziness |
| la marea | tide |

¡Qué mareo! Creo que voy a vomitar. Está subiendo la marea.
(I'm feeling sick. I think I'm going to vomit. The tide is coming in)

| el medio | the middle; the center; a means, by means of (*por medio de*); the environment (*el medio ambiente*) |
| la media | the average; stocking, tights; a sock (Latin America) (*el calcetín*, in Spain) |

Nadó hasta el medio del lago y se quitó una media.
(He swam to the middle of the lake and took off a sock)

| el modo | the way; the manner; the mood (in grammar) (*el modo subjuntivo*) |
| la moda | fashion |

Ese modo de hablar que tiene es encantador y siempre se viste a la moda.
(Her way of talking is charming, and she is always in fashion)

| el moro | Moor (note that this word may nowadays have a pejorative connotation) |
| la mora | a blackberry; a mulberry |

El moro Otelo mató a Desdémona y se puso a comer moras.
(Othello the Moor killed Desdemona and began to eat blackberries)

| el muñeco | a puppet (*una marioneta*); a male doll; a cuddly or soft toy (*un peluche*); a snowman (*muñeco de nieve*) |
| la muñeca | wrist; a female doll |

Está nevando, vamos a hacer un muñeco de nieve. Me duele la muñeca.
(It's snowing! Let's make a snowman. My wrist hurts)

| el navajo | Navajo |
| la navaja | a penknife, a flick knife (*la navaja automática*) |

El indio navajo vive en el estado de Utah y siempre lleva una navaja.
(The Navajo Indian lives in Utah and always carries a pocketknife)

| el nevero | a snowfield, an ice field; a place of perpetual snow |
| la nevera | a fridge |

La Antártida es un nevero. Y mi nevera está llena de frutas y vegetales.
(Antarctica is a field of ice. And my fridge is full of fruit and vegetables)

el palo	a stick; a mast; a suit (of cards)
la pala	a spade; a shovel

Usó un palo para ahuyentar al león. Necesitamos una pala para cavar en el jardín.

(He used a stick to scare the lion away. We need a shovel to dig in the garden)

el partido	a (football) match (*un partido de fútbol*); a political party
la partida	a game of chess (*una partida de ajedrez*); a departure; a certificate or official document; a consignment or a batch of goods

Barack Obama representa al Partido Demócrata. Tengo mi partida de nacimiento.

(Barack Obama represents the Democratic Party. I have my birth certificate)

el pasto	pasture; fodder; lawn or grass
la pasta	pasta; a paste; a cookie; money (colloq. in Spain)

Las ovejas estaban en el pasto. Te llevaré una caja de pastas de té.

(The sheep were in the pasture. I'll bring you a box of tea cookies)

el pato	a duck
la pata	a leg of an animal or piece of furniture; a female duck

El pato no podía caminar porque tenía la pata rota.

(The duck could not walk because of a broken leg)

el pimiento	pepper (vegetable) (*el chile* in Mexico and Central America)
la pimienta	white/black pepper

En México y en Centroamérica el pimiento se llama chile. Yo le pongo sal y pimienta a la carne.

(In Mexico and Central America peppers are called chillies. I put salt and pepper on the meat)

el plazo	a period of time; installment; in the long run (term) (*a largo plazo*)
la plaza	a square; a seat; a vacancy (*una plaza vacante*); a bull-ring (*la plaza de toros*)

Tendremos que pagar el coche a plazos. El vehículo tiene dos plazas.

(We'll have to pay for the car in installments. It's a two-seater vehicle)

el preso	a prisoner; a convict (generally for having committed a crime; different from *el prisionero/la prisionera*, someone imprisoned against his/her will)
la presa	a prey; a water dam; a female prisoner or convict

El preso se presentó ante el juez. El perro del cazador encontró la presa.
(The convict went before the judge. The hunter's dog found the prey)

el poleo	a type of mint tea
la polea	a pulley

El poleo menta se bebe mucho para calmar los nervios. Subimos el piano con una polea.
(Mint tea is drunk a lot to calm nervousness. We got the piano up with a pulley)

el puerto	a port (sea, computer); a pass (mountain)
la puerta	a door; a gate; a gateway

La mercancía llegó al puerto. ¿Donde está la puerta de salida?
(The merchandise got to the port. Where is the exit door?)

el punto	spot; a dot; a full stop; semicolon (*punto y coma*); colon (*dos puntos*); neutral gear (*punto muerto*)
la punta	the point of a pencil or knife; rush hour (*la hora punta*); the point of one's foot (*la punta del pie*); the tip (tongue, nose, fingers)

Se pone un punto al terminar una oración. Me atacó con la punta del cuchillo.
(One puts a period at the end of a sentence. He attacked me at knifepoint)

el ramo	a bunch; a bouquet
la rama	a tree branch

Me trajo un ramo de flores por mi cumpleaños. Hay un pájaro muy raro en esa rama.
(He brought me a bouquet for my birthday. There is a very strange bird on that branch)

el rato	a while
la rata	a rat; a stingy person (figurative)

La rata estuvo aquí un rato, pero no me moví de encima de la mesa.
(The rat was here for a while, but I didn't move from the top of the table)

el rodillo   a paint roller; a rolling pin for baking
la rodilla   a knee

El niño se pintó las rodillas con un rodillo de pintura.
(The little boy painted his knees with a paint roller)

el ruedo   a bullfighting ring
la rueda   a wheel

Como si de un misterio se tratara, había una rueda en el centro del ruedo.
(Mysteriously, there was a wheel in the center of the bullfighting ring)

el secador   a hairdryer
la secadora   a tumble-dryer; a hairdryer (in Mexico)

Necesito el secador para secarme el pelo. Pondré la ropa en la secadora.
(I need a hairdryer to dry my hair. I'll put the clothes in the dryer)

el suelo   floor; ground; soil; surface
la suela   the sole of a shoe

Se desmayó y se cayó al suelo. Tenía las suelas tan desgastadas que me resbalé.
(He fainted and fell to the ground. My soles were so smooth that I slid)

el tallo   stem (of a plant); a sprout, shoot
la talla   a size; a wood carving

El tallo de la planta crecerá en primavera. ¿Qué talla usas?
(The stem will grow in spring. What's your size?)

el ternero   a calf
la ternera   female calf; veal

Los terneros están en el pasto. Me gustan las costillas de ternera.
(The calves are in the pasture. I like veal chops)

el torero   the bullfighter
la torera   female bullfighter; a bolero jacket

El torero llevaba un elegante traje y su novia una bonita torera.
(The bullfighter was wearing an elegant suit and his girlfriend a beautiful bolero jacket)

el tubo   a tube: a pipe; a tract (anatomy); hair roller, curler (for hair) (in Chile), (*los rulos*, in Spain)
la tuba   a tuba (musical instrument)

Necesitaremos un tubo para canalizar el agua. No sé si estudiar trompeta o tuba.
(A pipe will be needed to channel the water. I am not sure whether to study trumpet or tuba)

| **el velo** | a veil |
| **la vela** | a sail; sailing; a candle |

Algunas mujeres musulmanas llevan velo, otras no. Hicimos un curso de vela en Lanzarote.

(Some Muslim women wear a veil, others don't. We took a sailing course in Lanzarote)

Same word – different gender – different meaning

These words are identical in form and pronunciation but change their gender according to the context.

> **Mnemonic device**
> Think of the phrase: **No es lo mismo el capital que la capital**. It will help you remember the different meanings of these identical words with different genders.

| **el batería** | a drummer |
| **la batería** | a battery; a set of cookware; a set of drums; a female drummer |

El batería tocaba la batería.
(The drummer was playing the drums)

| **el capital** | capital (money) |
| **la capital** | a capital city |

No podemos pagar el coche con nuestro capital. Nueva York no es la capital del estado de NY.

(We cannot use our capital to pay for the car. New York is not the capital of NY State)

| **el cólera** | cholera (illness) |
| **la cólera** | anger; rage |

Hubo una epidemia de cólera en ese pueblo. Eso me hizo entrar en cólera.
(There was a cholera outbreak in that town. That made me very angry)

| **el coma** | a coma (medicine) |
| **la coma** | a comma |

El herido todavía está en coma. Tienes que poner una coma aquí.
(The wounded man is still in a coma. You have to put a comma here)

el cometa	a comet
la cometa	a kite

El cometa Halley se ve cada 76 años. El niño juega con su cometa.

(You can see Halley's comet every 76 years. The boy plays with his kite)

el corte	a cut (injury); the cut of a suit
la corte	a court of law in Latin America; (*los juzgados* in Spain); the royal court of a monarch; to court someone (*hacer la corte*)

Ese traje tiene buen corte. Este asunto se resolverá en la corte.

(That suit has a good cut. This matter will be resolved in court)

el cura	a priest
la cura	the cure

El cura entró en la iglesia. Todavía no hay cura para el SIDA.

(The priest walked into the church. There is no cure for AIDS yet)

el disco	a record; a disk (computer; anatomy)
la disco	a discotheque (short form for *la discoteca*); *el antro* (in Mexico and Venezuela); *el boliche* (in Argentina and Uruguay)

No me lo repitas más; eres como un disco rayado. Bailemos esta noche en la disco.

(Don't say it again; you're like a broken record. Let's dance in the discotheque tonight)

el editorial	the editorial (leading article)
la editorial	the publishing house

El editorial fue muy crítico con el gobierno. Routledge es una de las mejores editoriales.

(The editorial was very critical of the government. Routledge is one the best publishing companies)

el final	the end
la final	the sports final; the playoffs

Éste es el final feliz del cuento. Rafael Nadal jugó la final de Wimbledon.

(This is the happy end to the story. Rafael Nadal played in the final at Wimbledon)

el frente	the front (military)
la frente	the forehead

Los soldados se marcharon ayer al frente. Ella tiene la frente grande.

(Yesterday, the soldiers left for the front. She has a high forehead)

el guardia   a policeman; a watchman; *estar de guardia* (to be on duty)
la guardia   a policewoman; guard (a body of soldiers)
Ese guardia se quedó dormido mientras estaba de guardia.
(That watchman fell asleep while on duty)

el guía   a male guide
la guía   a guide book; a female guide; telephone book
Tuvimos un buen guía en la excursión. Lo encontramos en la guía telefónica.
(We had a good guide for the excursion. We found him in the telephone book)

el mañana   the future
la mañana   the morning
Deseamos un mañana de paz. Esta mañana nos levantamos temprano para ir al trabajo.
(We desire a future of peace. This morning we got up early to go to work)

el margen   the margin
la margen   a riverbank
El maestro escribió su comentario en el margen. Luego se sentó en la margen del río.
(The teacher wrote his comment in the margin. Then he sat down on the riverbank)

el moral   blackberry bush
la moral   morality (the moral of a story: *la moraleja*)
Se sentó a la sombra del moral y empezó a hablarnos de moral.
(He sat down in the shadow of the blackberry bush and began to talk to us about morality)

el orden   order
la orden   a command; a restaurant order
Es importante que haya orden en este cuarto. El capitán dio la orden de disparar.
(It is important that there be order in this room. The captain gave the order to shoot)

el ordenanza   an office boy; a porter
la ordenanza   the regulation; by-laws; a female porter
El ordenanza vino y nos dio la noticia. El presidente emitió la ordenanza.
(The orderly came and gave us the news. The president issued the regulation)

el Papa	the Pope
la papa	a potato (in Latin America and the Canary Islands) (*la patata*, in Spain)

El Papa vive en el Vaticano y la papa está en el horno.

(The Pope lives in the Vatican, and the potato is in the oven)

el parte	medical or weather report; a communiqué
la parte	a part, a portion

El meteorólogo nos dio el parte meteorológico. Es parte del programa diario de noticias.

(The weatherman gave his weather report. It is part of the daily program of news)

el pendiente	an earring (in Spain) (*el arete*, in Latin America)
la pendiente	an incline; a slope

Ella llevaba pendientes, collares y anillos. La vimos bajar por la pendiente.

(She wore dangle earrings, necklaces and rings. We saw her coming down the slope)

el pez	a fish (animal); blue/white fish (*pescado azul/blanco*)
la pez	pitch; tar (substance)

Vimos un pez dorado en el agua. La pez es negra y pegajosa.

(We saw a golden fish in the water. Tar is black and sticky)

el policía	a policeman
la policía	the police force; a policewoman

El policía vino ayer, después de que llamara a la policía.

(The policeman came after I called the police station)

el terminal	terminal (computer)
la terminal	airport or bus terminal

¿Dónde está el terminal de la computadora? Estaba esperándola en la nueva terminal aérea de la Ciudad de México.

(Where is the computer's terminal? He was waiting for her at the new airport terminal in Mexico City)

el trompeta	a male trumpeter (also *el trompetista*)
la trompeta	a trumpet; a female trumpeter (also *la trompetista*)

Se necesita un nuevo trompeta para la orquesta. Me encanta el sonido de la trompeta.

(We need a new trumpeter in this orchestra. I love the sound of the trumpet)

el vocal	a male committee member
la vocal	a vowel, or female committee member

Los vocales votaron durante la sesión del comité. La A, la E y la O son vocales fuertes.

(The members voted during the committee meeting. A, E, O are strong vowels)

Exercises

EXERCISE 5. In the following stories choose the word that best completes the sentence, paying attention to its gender, meaning and context.

5.1."Un día de compras"

Ayer por _____ (el mañana / la mañana) salí por _____ (el puerto / la puerta) principal de mi casa y caminé _____ (un rato / una rata) hasta _____ (el cuadro / la cuadra) del mercado que está cerca _____ (del puerto / de la puerta). Lo primero que vi en _____ (medio / media) _____ (del plazo / de la plaza) fue un magnífico puesto lleno de _____ (olivos / olivas) y _____ (pimientos / pimientas) de muchos colores. En otro puesto había _____ (manzanos / manzanas) de diferentes variedades. Después fui al puesto de _____ (fruto / fruta) donde compré 5 cajitas de _____ (cerezos / cerezas) y de _____ (moros / moras) campestres; ¡mis favoritas! Por último fui a ver al carnicero, que me vendió tres _____ (libros / libras) de salchichas caseras, y con _____ (un poleo / una polea) pesó la carne de _____ (ternero / ternera) para la cena de esa noche, y me lo puso todo en _____ (un bolso / una bolsa) de papel. Al llegar a casa con tanta comida me di cuenta de que no cabía en _____ (el nevero / la nevera). Así que decidí darle _____ (un parte / una parte) de todo lo que había comprado a mi vecina Nora.

5.2. "Valeria y sus amigos"

Se llamaba Valeria, era rusa y vivía con _____ (un trompeta / una trompeta) y _____ (un batería / una batería) de la tribu _____ (navajo / navaja). Valeria iba muy bonita, muy _____ (al modo / a la moda), siempre vestida con _____ (un torero / una torera) y con una cinta roja en _____ (el frente / la frente). Contenta me contó que uno de sus compañeros de piso había ido a jugar _____ (un partido / una partida) de ajedrez en un campeonato internacional, y que había hecho _____ (un apuesto / una apuesta) de que su amigo llegaría _____ (al final / a la final). También estaba contenta porque el hijo de su amigo Pepe quería ser _____ (torero / torera). Era _____ (un buen partido / una buena partida) pues era simpático, atractivo, muy inteligente y tenía a todas las chicas enamoradas de él. De repente llegó el otro compañero de piso de Valeria, _____ (un ordenanza / una ordenanza) municipal que les dijo que _____ (un guardia / una guardia) con bigote se había llevado al hijo de Pepe _____ (al corte / a la corte) por robar en _____ (un banco / una banca), en _____ (un disco / una disco) y en _____ (un bolero / una bolera). Afortunadamente todo había sido un malentendido. Valeria habló con un comisario que era _____ (el vocal / la vocal) de _____ (el policía / la policía), quien condujo a Pepe de inmediato hasta su casa sobre _____ (el margen / la margen) del río cerca del centro _____ (del capital / de la capital).

5.3. "El novio de Laura"

La famosa pintora, Laura de Montebello, no podía controlar _____ (el cólera / la cólera) que sentía, y decidió sentarse a comer bajo _____ (el ramo / la rama) de _____ (un cerezo / una cereza) antes de ir a visitar _____ (al preso / a la presa). Su novio, un conocido activista político, estaba en la cárcel por tirarle _____ (un pimiento / una pimienta) al presidente en _____ (el terminal / la terminal) del aeropuerto. Pensando en lo que había sucedido, Laura sacó _____ (un navajo / una navaja) y se metió _____ (medio naranjo / media naranja) en la boca con _____ (el punto / la punta) _____ (del cuchillo / de la cuchilla). Con la otra mano comenzó a buscar algo en _____ (el guía / la guía) de teléfonos, y a redactar _____ (el editorial / la editorial) para el periódico en el que trabajaba. La vi escribir unas palabras, luego _____ (un coma / una coma) y unas palabras más, para terminar con _____ (un punto / una punta) final. Se levantó y corrió hacia _____ (el fondo / la fonda) 'El periquito alegre', donde había conocido a su novio una tarde de verano. Allí recogió un _____ (un cuadro / una cuadra) con el marco de _____ (madero / madera) que ella misma había pintado, y conteniendo _____ (el llanto / la llanta) fue con él por el camino hacia _____ (el corte / la corte). Evidentemente, ése era _____ (el capital / la capital) que tenía, y lo iba a utilizar para sacar a su novio del lío en que se había metido.

EXERCISE 6. Choose the most logical synonym.

1	la papa (Lat. Am.)	a	la disco
2	la historia	b	el suelo
3	la ciudad principal	c	el pendiente
4	el refrigerador	d	un rato
5	el juzgado	e	el fallo
6	el dinero	f	el preso
7	la manzana (Spain)	g	la capital
8	la sala de baile	h	la orden
9	el piso (Lat. Am.)	i	el pez
10	el arete (Lat. Am.)	j	el derecho
11	un momento	k	el barro
12	la tubería	l	la terminal
13	el error	m	la media
14	el retrato	n	el capital
15	el prisionero	o	un muñeco
16	la colina	p	la corte
17	el mandato	q	el conducto
18	el pescado	r	el cuadro
19	la ley	s	el cuento
20	el calcetín (Spain)	t	la manta
21	la estación de autobuses	u	la loma
22	una marioneta	v	la patata
23	la frazada (Lat. Am.)	w	la nevera
24	la arcilla	x	la cuadra

 Notes

Number

Formation of the plural

1   To form the plural in Spanish simply add **–s** to nouns that end in an **unstressed vowel** and **–es** to nouns that end in a **consonant different from s or x:**

la casa	las casa-**s**
el perro	los perro-**s**
la pared	las pared-**es**
el examen	los exámen-**es**
la universidad	las universidad-**es**

Note the change from **z** to **c** in words that end in **z:**

el pez	los pec-**es**
la luz	las luc-**es**

The plural of nouns ending in stressed **–á**, **–é** or **–ó** is formed by adding **–s** to the singular form:

el sofá	los sofa-**s**
el café	los café-**s**
el dominó	los dominó-**s**

The plural of nouns ending in stressed **–í** is normally formed by adding **–es** to the singular:

el jabalí	los jabalí-**es**
el/la israelí	los/las israelí-**es**
el rubí	los rubí-**es**
el maniquí	los maniquí-**es**

However, for some nouns ending in **–í**, the plural form with **–s** is more common:

el esquí	los esquí-**s**
el bisturí	los bisturí-**s**

Nouns ending in **–ú** can form their plural by adding either **–es** or **–s**. However, some nouns can only add **–s** to form their plural, while others admit both endings:

el/la hindú	los/las hindú-**es**/los/las hindú-**s**
el iglú	los iglú-**es**/los iglú-**s**
el tabú	los tabú-**es**/los tabú-**s**
el champú	los champú-**s**
el menú	los menú-**s**

Nouns ending in **–s** or **–x** form their plural with **–es** if the accent falls on the last syllable, **or remain the same**, if the accent falls on the penultimate or antepenultimate syllable. In this case the plural is evidenced only by the article.

el autobús	los autobus-**es**
la tesis	**las** tesis
el fax	los fax-**es**
el tórax	**los** tórax

Nouns ending in **–y** form their plural with **–es**:

el rey	los rey-**es**
la ley	las ley-**es**
el buey	los buey-**es**

But some words of foreign origin form their plural with **–s**:

el jersey	los jerséi-**s**

2   **Special cases:**

- **Vowels** form their plural by adding **–es**: la a/las aes; la e/las es, la i/las íes.
- **Consonants** normally form their plural by adding **–s**: una be/dos bes; una pe/dos pes.
- To form the plural of the words **yo, no** and **sí**, add **–es**: el yo/los yoes; el no/los noes; el sí/los síes.
- **Musical notes** form their plural as follows: el do/los dos, el re/los res, el mi/los mis.

3   Note that some nouns **change their stressed syllable** to become plural, thereby affecting the position of the written accent:

el **ré**-gi-men	los re-**gí**-me-nes
el es-**pé**-ci-men	los es-pe-**cí**-me-nes

4   **Collective nouns** are usually singular:

La **familia llegó** a tiempo.
El **equipo ganará** el partido.
El **grupo vino** a la misma hora.
La **gente va** a comprar en rebajas. ⊗ Never: la gente ~~van, son, están~~, etc.
Todo **el mundo está** aquí.
La **muchedumbre llenaba** la plaza.
El **público aplaudió** con fervor.

5   Some nouns are only used in their **singular form**:

la arquitectura, el caos, el cosmos, la física, la salud, la sed, la tez; proper names such as the name of continents: África, América, Asia, Europa, Oceanía; (but: las Américas)

6 Other nouns **only have plural forms** or are normally used in the plural:

las afueras (outskirts), los alicates (pliers), los alrededores (surrounding area; outskirts), los anteojos (glasses, in Latin America; *las gafas*, in Spain), los añicos; (*hacer añicos*: to smash into tiny pieces), las arras (coins given by the bridegroom to the bride), los bártulos (things, bits and pieces; stuff), los celos (jealousy), los comicios (elections), los enseres (fixtures and fittings; tools), las esposas (handcuffs), los esquís (skis), las exequias (funeral rites), las gafas (glasses), los modales (manners), las nupcias (nuptials), los pertrechos (military supplies and ammunition; equipment gear), los prismáticos (binoculars), las trizas; (*hacer trizas*: to smash into tiny pieces), las urnas (ballot box), las vacaciones (holidays), las vísperas (evensong, vespers), los víveres (supplies; food), etc.

7 Some **adverbial expressions** are always used in the plural:

a sabiendas de que (knowing full well that), a solas (alone), a expensas de (to live by favor, at the cost of another), a marchas forzadas (against the clock), a duras penas (with difficulty and labor), de veras (really, seriously), de buenas a primeras (all at once, without reflection, unexpectedly), de rodillas (on one's knees), de puntillas (on tiptoe), en brazos (in one's arms), en cuclillas (to squat, to sit cowering, to sit close to the ground), de espaldas (with one's back turned on somebody), por las buenas or por las malas (whether you like it or not, willingly or unwillingly), a oscuras (in the dark), a gatas (on all fours), a secas (pure and simple, simply), a escondidas (furtively, in a secret manner, without being seen), a hurtadillas (stealthily, artfully, in a hidden manner), a trancas y barrancas (with great difficulty), en volandas (rapidly, in an instant), etc.

8 Some nouns **both in the singular and the plural** have the same meaning:

barba/barbas, espalda/espaldas, nariz/narices, tripa/tripas, pantalón/pantalones, calzoncillo/calzoncillos, braga/bragas, pinza/pinzas, tenaza/tenazas, tijera/tijeras, etc.

9 Other nouns ending in **–s** are invariable with either singular or plural articles and adjectives:

el cumpleaños — ¡Feliz cumpleaños!
los cumpleaños — El fin de semana que viene tengo dos cumpleaños.

There are many others:

el abrebotellas (bottle opener), el abrelatas (can opener), el abrecartas (letter opener), el/la aguafiestas (party pooper), el/la cantamañanas (an unreliable person), el cascanueces (nutcracker), el cascarrabias (grumpy old man), el / la cazatalentos (headhunter), el ciempiés (centipede), el cortaúñas (nail clippers), el cortapuros (cigar cutter), el espantapájaros (scarecrow), el guardabarros (fender, mudguard), el/la guardabosques (also possible: el/la guardabosque) (forest ranger), el/la guardacostas (coastguard), el/la guardaespaldas (bodyguard), el lanzallamas (flamethrower), el lavavajillas (dishwasher), el limpiaparabrisas (windshield wiper), el matamoscas (flyswatter; fly spray), el matarratas (rat poison; rotgut), el matasuegras (party blower), el montacargas (freight elevator), el paraguas (umbrella), el parabrisas (windshield), el paracaídas (parachute), el parachoques (bumper), el pararrayos (lightning conductor), el pasamontañas (balaclava), el/la pelagatos (a nobody), el pisapapeles (paperweight), el portaviones (aircraft carrier), el quitamanchas (stain remover), el quitanieves (snowplough), el quitapelusillas (lint remover), el rascacielos (skyscraper), el rompecabezas (jigsaw), el rompeolas (breakwater), el sacacorchos (corkscrew), el sacapuntas (pencil sharpener), el saltamontes (grasshopper), el (chaleco) salvavidas (lifejacket), el trabalenguas (tongue-twister), la (máquina) tragaperras (slot machine), etc.

Note that most of these nouns are masculine.

Weekdays are also invariable:

el lunes, el martes, el miércoles, el jueves y el viernes. But: el/los sábado/s, el/los domingo/s

10 **Plural of foreign words.** There are no set rules for the plural of foreign words, but we do have the following recommendations:

Foreign words **ending in a vowel** usually follow the general rules.

la boutique	las boutiques
el café	los cafés
el chalé	los chalés
el menú	los menús

Foreign words **ending in the following consonants: -l, -n, -d, -z, -r, -s, -x** (-s and -x in words whose stress falls on the last syllable) normally adopt the plural in **–es**:

el cóctel	los cócteles
el eslogan	los eslóganes
el esmoquin	los esmóquines
el fax	los faxes

Foreign words **ending in a consonant different from the ones mentioned above** take an **–s**:

el debut	los debut**s**
el entrecot	los entrecot**s**
el pub	los pub**s**
el anorak	los anorak**s**
el ballet	los ballet**s**
el bistec	los bistec**s**

However, the RAE (Real Academia Española) recommends 'clubes' for the plural of 'club.' Also, 'sándwiches' is widely used for the plural of 'sándwich.'

Latin words that have kept their original form do not change in the plural:

el/los currículum
el/los memorándum

However **Latin words that have adopted a Spanish form** follow the general rules for the formation of plurals:

el currículo	los currículos
el memorando	los memorandos

Exercises

EXERCISE 7. Write the plural of the following nouns.

1   la libertad   _____
2   el camión   _____
3   la avestruz   _____
4   el hindú   _____
5   la ley   _____
6   el carácter   _____
7   el césped   _____
8   el esquí   _____
9   el lunes   _____
10 el pantalón   _____
11 el holandés   _____
12 el paraguas   _____
13 el ultimátum   _____
14 el fax   _____
15 la hipótesis   _____

EXERCISE 8. Insert the correct adverbial expression from the box below that best corresponds to each sentence. Remember that these expressions are always used in the plural.

> a trancas y barrancas • a oscuras • a gatas • a sabiendas • de espaldas •
> a hurtadillas • a marchas forzadas • de rodillas • en cuclillas • de puntillas •
> por las buenas o por las malas • a secas • de buenas a primeras • a solas •
> en brazos

1   Déjanos un momento _____ que tenemos que hablar de algo en secreto.
2   En cuanto llegó a la catedral, se puso _____ ante el altar.
3   _____ de que la economía iba mal, invirtió todo su dinero en la bolsa.
4   Me puedes llamar Pedro _____; no hace falta que me digas Señor Pedro.
5   Tendremos que ir _____ o si no, no llegaremos.
6   No sé si era él, porque estaba _____ y no le vi la cara.
7   Lo más doloroso para una bailarina es aprender a ponerse _____.
8   El bebé iba _____ hasta que se puso a llorar.
9   _____ le dijo a todo el mundo que estaba muy enfadado.
10 Lo hizo en el último momento y _____, pero consiguió hacerlo.
11 No aguantaba más de pie y como no quedaban sillas libres se puso _____.
12 Siempre que cojo a su hijo _____ empieza a llorar. ¿Será que le caigo mal?
13 Como siga esta tormenta, igual se va la luz y nos quedamos _____.
14 Entró _____ para que nadie se diera cuenta de que había llegado muy tarde.
15 No te hagas el enfermo. Irás al colegio _____.

EXERCISE 9. Identify 11 errors in the formation and/or usage of the plural in the following text and correct them.

En las escuelas de Seattle hay varias asociaciones estudiantiles, como la asociación de esquís. Los chicos se ponen los suéters y salen en autobúses hacia la afuera de la ciudad todos los sábadoes por la mañana. Es increíble que haya tanta afición por los deportes de inv iernos. En el mismo centro hay una pequeña pista en un rascacielo. También durante la vacación de veranos los chicos cargados de equipamiento y víveres se van a hacer campings. A veces se pierden, y es el guardabosques el que hace sonar la alerta, y la familia van a recuperar al chico perdido.

2 Mastering false friends: verbs

PERDONE QUE LE MOLESTE...

MOLESTAR = TO BOTHER

Although pronounced and spelled much like English, Spanish false friends have very different meanings. Below you will find verbs that tend to present difficulties to students of Spanish. While some of them have various connotations, we have given priority to the most frequently used meanings. Once you understand them in context, you are not likely to forget or confuse them again.

1   Aplicar

Aplicar does not mean 'to apply to a university or for a job.' Rather, it means physically putting one thing onto another, i.e., 'to apply an ointment or a cream.'

> Si no quieres tener granos, **aplícate** esta crema.
> (If you don't want to have pimples, *apply* this cream)

You can also use this verb for abstract concepts, e.g., **aplicar una regla** (*to apply a rule*).

▶ However, if you want to say:

> *to apply to an institution* ⇨ **solicitar plaza en, postular a**

> Quiero **solicitar plaza en** Harvard.
> (I want to *apply* to Harvard)

*Learn the expression: **iy aplícate eso tú también!** (… and that goes for you as well!)

2   Apuntar

Apuntar does not mean 'to appoint.' It means 'to write down' or 'to aim.'

> Tengo que **apuntar** tus señas.
> (I have to *write down* your address)

> El cazador **apuntó** y disparó.
> (The hunter *aimed* and shot)

▶ However, if you want to say:

> *to appoint* ⇨ **nombrar**

> El presidente **nombra** a los jueces de la Corte Suprema.
> (The president *appoints* the judges of the Supreme Court)

*Learn the expression: **apuntar a alguien** (to write someone's name on a list, to sign somebody up)

3   Asistir

Asistir does not mean 'to help.' It means 'to attend' an event such as a lecture, a concert, a party, a conference, etc.

> Nadie **asistió** a la reunión de ayer.
> (Nobody *attended* the meeting yesterday)

▶ However, if you want to say:

> *to assist someone* ⇨ **ayudar, atender**

> Quiero que me **ayudes** con este proyecto.
> (I want you to *assist* me with this project)

Voy a **atender** al cliente.
(I'm going to *help* the client)

4   Atender

Atender means 'to serve,' 'to take care,' or 'to look after.'

Tengo que **atender** a este paciente.
(I have to *take care of* this patient)

▶ However, if you want to say:

to attend (an event) ⇨ **asistir a**

Quiero **asistir a** la conferencia.
(I want to *attend* the lecture)

*Learn the expression: **estar atento/a** (to pay attention)

5   Avisar

Avisar does not mean 'to advise.' It means 'to inform,' 'to let someone know,' 'to call to one's attention' or 'to warn beforehand,' especially of some danger.

Avísame si no puedes venir.
(*Let me know* if you cannot come)

▶ However, if you want to say:

to advise ⇨ **aconsejar**

Te **aconsejo** que estudies para el examen.
(I *advise* you to study for the exam)

*Learn the word: **el aviso** (the warning, the notice)

6   Blindar

Blindar has nothing to do with 'blind.' It means 'to armor-plate' or 'to shield.'

Van a **blindar** el coche del presidente para protegerlo contra atentados.
(The president's car will be *armor-plated* to protect it against assassination attempts)

▶ However, if you want to say:

to blind ⇨ **cegar, dejar ciego, deslumbrar**

Cuando salimos de la caverna nos **deslumbraron** las luces.
(On leaving the cavern we were *blinded* by the lights)

*Learn the expression: **el chaleco antibalas** (a bulletproof vest)

7   Comprometer(se)

Comprometer is not used in the sense of 'to adjust or settle by mutual consent.' It means 'to compromise' in the sense of 'to jeopardize' or 'to put someone in a predicament.' On the other hand, the reflexive form **comprometerse** has various meanings: 'to commit oneself to something, i.e., politics, etc.,' or 'to get engaged.'

Su firma le **compromete** a pagar la factura.
(Your signature *obliges* you to pay the invoice)

María y Eliseo **se comprometieron** en Las Vegas.
(María y Eliseo got *engaged* in Las Vegas)

▶ However, if you want to say:

to compromise ⇨ **llegar a un acuerdo mutuo, llegar a un compromiso**

Llegamos a un acuerdo para compartir los gastos del viaje.
(We *agreed to* share the expenses of the trip)

8   Contestar

Contestar means 'to answer' or 'to reply' to a question or a letter.

La actriz no **contestó** a las preguntas.
(The actress did not *answer* the questions)

▶ However, if you want to say:

to contest ⇨ **impugnar** (una decisión)

Los abogados **impugnaron** la decisión del juez.
(The lawyers *contested* the judge's decision)

*Learn the expression: **contestar el teléfono** (to answer the phone)

9   Chocar

Chocar is the most common verb used in Spanish to mean 'to crash' or 'to collide.'

Como el conductor iba borracho, el autobús **chocó** contra un árbol.
(The driver was drunk, so the bus *collided* with a tree)

▶ However, if you want to say:

to choke ⇨ **ahogarse, asfixiarse,** (~ on something) **atragantarse**

Ana casi **se atragantó** con una espina de pescado.
(Ana almost *choked* on a fish-bone)

*Learn the expression: **¡choca esos cinco!** (give me five!)

10   Demandar

Demandar does not mean 'to demand.' It means 'to sue' in a court of law.

Demandó a la compañía de seguros por fraude.
(He *sued* the insurance company for fraud)

▶ However, if you want to say:

to demand ⇨ **pedir, exigir, reclamar, reivindicar**

Exigió una compensación a la compañía.
(He *demanded* compensation from the company)

11 Discutir

Discutir is mainly used to mean 'to contend or disagree.' Although **discutir** is starting to be used in the sense of 'to discuss,' 'to debate' or 'to consider or debate the pros and cons of something,' its meaning in Spanish is still closer to the verb 'to argue.'

Se pusieron a **discutir** en público.
(They started *to argue* in public)

▶ However, if you want to say:

to discuss ⇨ **hablar de**

Vamos a **hablar del** asunto en la reunión.
(Let's *discuss* the matter at the meeting)

12 Disgustar

Disgustar means 'to upset, to trouble someone mentally or emotionally,' or 'to be displeased.'

Me **disgustó** mucho tu comportamiento.
(I was very *displeased* by your behavior)

▶ However, if you want to say:

to disgust ⇨ **dar asco, repugnar**

Las ancas de rana me **dan asco**.
(Frog legs *disgust* me)

*Learn the expression: **tener un disgusto** (to be really upset)

13 Divertirse

Divertirse means 'to enjoy oneself,' 'to have fun,' or 'to have a good time.'

Siempre *me divierto* en la clase de español.
(I always **have fun** in Spanish class)

▶ However, if you want to say:

to divert ⇨ **desviar**

Tuvimos que **desviar** el río para regar el campo.
(We had *to divert* the course of the river to irrigate the field)

*Learn the expression: **¡que te diviertas / os divirtáis / se diviertan!** (have a nice time!, enjoy yourself / yourselves!)

14 Dragar

Dragar does not mean 'to drag,' but 'to dredge.'

Hay que **dragar** el lago detrás de la casa.
(We have *to dredge* the lake behind the house)

▶ However, if you want to say:

to drag ⇨ **arrastrar**

El chico se bajó del tren y **arrastró** su pesada valija por el andén.
(The boy got off the train and *dragged* his heavy suitcase on the platform)

15 Envolver

Envolver does not mean 'to involve.' It means 'to wrap' or 'to envelop.'

Envolví el regalo y se lo di a mi mamá.
(I *wrapped* the gift and gave it to my mother)

▶ However, if you want to say:

to involve ⇨ **implicar, involucrar**

No quiero **involucrarte** en mi problema.
(I don't want to *involve* you in my problem)

*Learn the expression: **envolverse en** (to wrap oneself in something)

16 Estrechar(se)

Estrechar(se) does not mean 'to stretch.' It means precisely quite the opposite: 'to make narrower,' 'to tighten.'

Mi vestido de lana **se estrechó** después de lavarlo.
(My wool dress *shrank* after washing it)

▶ However, if you want to say:

to stretch ⇨ **estirar**

Antes de salir a correr hago ejercicios para **estirar** los músculos.
(Before going out running I do *stretching* exercises)

*Learn the expressions: **estrechar la mano** (to shake hands); **estirarse** (to stretch one's muscles)

17   **Excitar**

In Spanish **excitar** means 'to arouse sexually,' or 'to get overexcited or nervous,' e.g., from caffeine.

> El café **me excita** pero el té no.
> (Coffee *makes me jumpy* but tea doesn't)

▶ However, if you want to say:

> *to get excited or enthusiastic* ⇨ **entusiasmar, entusiasmarse por / con**

> Estaba tan **entusiasmada** que no paraba de hablar de la representación.
> (She was so *excited* she couldn't stop talking about the performance)

*Learn the expression: **tener ganas de** (to be excited about something that's coming up, to feel like doing something)

18   **Fabricar**

Fabricar does not mean 'to fabricate,' 'to deceive' or 'to invent.' Rather, it means 'to manufacture,' 'to make' or 'to produce.'

> Esa compañía **fabrica** piezas de repuesto para carros.
> (That company *manufactures* spare parts for cars)

▶ However, if you want to say:

> *to fabricate* ⇨ **inventar, mentir**

> El acusado se **inventó** una defensa verosímil.
> (The defendant *fabricated* a believable defense)

*Learn the expression: **fabricado en Chile** (made in Chile)

19   **Grabar**

Grabar simply means 'to record, to tape,' or 'to engrave' on a surface.

> Voy a **grabar** la ceremonia de apertura de los Juegos Olímpicos.
> (I am going to record the opening ceremony of the Olympic Games)

▶ However, if you want to say:

> *to grab, to take* ⇨ **coger** (mainly Spain), **agarrar** (mainly Latin America)

> **Cogí / agarré** el metro para llegar a tiempo a la reunión.
> (I *took* the subway to arrive on time for the meeting)

Note that whereas **coger** in Spain is the most commonly used verb for 'to take,' in Latin America, however, it may have a sexual connotation. Make sure you use the right form in the right context in order to avoid embarrassment.

*Learn the word: **un grabado** (an engraving); for example: un grabado de Goya.

20 Intentar

Intentar does not mean 'to intend.' It means 'to try.'

El anciano **intentó** levantarse de la silla.
(The old man *tried* to get up from his chair)

▶ However, if you want to say:

to intend ⇨ **tener la intención de (hacer algo), pensar (hacer algo)**

Pensamos viajar a China este verano.
(We *intend* to travel to China this summer)

*Learn the expressions: **¡inténtalo!** (give it a try!); **¡ni lo intentes!** (don't even try it!)

21 Introducir

Introducir is not used when making someone's acquaintance or introducing someone. Its meaning is purely physical, that is, 'to insert' or 'to put in.'

Introduce una moneda de 25 centavos en la máquina.
(*Insert* a quarter in the vending machine)

▶ However, if you want to say:

to introduce one person to another ⇨ **presentar a alguien**

Te quiero **presentar** a mi prima la guitarrista.
(I want to *introduce* you to my cousin the guitar player)

22 Manejar

Manejar does not mean 'to manage.' It means 'to handle,' 'to use' or 'to operate' (a machine). In Latin America it means 'to drive' (*conducir* is used in Spain).

Tenemos que aprender a **manejar** la nueva tecnología.
(We have to learn *to operate* new technology)

▶ However, if you want to say:

to manage ⇨ **lograr, conseguir, dirigir** (una compañía, un proyecto)

Ese joven **logró** ganar las elecciones. Ahora **dirige** el proyecto.
(That young man *managed* to win the election. Now he *manages* the project)

23 Molestar

Molestar does not mean 'to molest.' In Spanish it has no sexual connotation; it simply means 'to bother.'

Me **molesta** el ruido de la carretera.
(The noise of the road *bothers* me)

► However, if you want to say:

> *to molest* ⇨ **abusar**

> El criminal fue a prisión por **abusar** de menores.
> (The criminal went to jail for *molesting* minors)

*Learn the expression: **No molestar** (do not disturb)

24   Mover

Mover does not mean 'to change one's residence or location,' or 'to move from one place to another.' It simply means 'to move something' in a physical sense, 'to change position.'

> Me duele la espalda y no puedo **mover** las piernas.
> (My back hurts, and I can't *move* my legs)

► However, if you want to say:

> *to move one's residence* ⇨ **mudarse**
> *to move emotionally* ⇨ **conmover**

> Ellos **se mudaron** a una nueva casa en la costa.
> (They *moved* to a new house on the coast)

> El concierto de guitarra nos **conmovió** profundamente.
> (The guitar concert *moved* us deeply)

*Learn the word: **la mudanza** (the move)

25   Patrocinar

In Spanish, **patrocinar** does not mean 'to patronize.' It means 'to sponsor.'

> Goldman Sachs **patrocina** la exhibición de arte.
> (Goldman Sachs is *sponsoring* the art exhibit)

► However, if you want to say:

> *to patronize* (a shop or a restaurant) ⇨ **frecuentar, ser cliente de**
> *to patronize* (treat condescendingly) ⇨ **tratar con condescendencia o paternalismo**

> A nadie le gusta que lo **traten con condescendencia**.
> (No one likes *to be patronized*)

> No **somos clientes de** una tienda que trata mal a sus empleados.
> (We will not *patronize* a store that treats its employees badly)

*Learn the expression: **patrocinado por …** (under the auspices of …)

26   Plantear

Plantear means 'to present an idea or situation' for attention or consideration. It also means 'to pose a problem' (**plantear un problema**), 'to raise a question' (**plantear una pregunta**), or 'to suggest something' (**plantear una sugerencia**).

> El abogado le **planteó** el problema al jurado.
> (The lawyer *posed* the problem to the jury)

▶ However, if you want to say:

> *to plant* ⇨ **plantar**

> Las cebollas se **plantan** en primavera.
> (Onions are *planted* in the spring)

*Learn the expression: **dejar plantado a alguien** (to stand someone up)

27   Presumir

Presumir means 'to brag, show off, boast,' or 'to be conceited.'

> No para de **presumir** de su nuevo BMW descapotable.
> (He can't stop *boasting* about his new BMW convertible)

▶ However, if you want to say:

> *to presume* ⇨ **suponer**

> Aunque no conozco a mucha gente, **supongo** que iré a la fiesta.
> (Even though I know few people, I *presume* I'll go to the party)

28   Pretender

Pretender does not mean 'to pretend or fake something.' It means 'to aspire,' 'to expect' or 'to attempt to do something.'

> Este año Juan **pretende** ganar el maratón de Nueva York.
> (This year Juan *aspires* to win the New York marathon)

▶ However, if you want to say:

> *to pretend* ⇨ **fingir, aparentar**

> Le gusta **fingir** que habla japonés, pero sólo sabe unas palabras.
> (He likes to *pretend* that he speaks Japanese, but he only knows a few words)

*Learn the expression: **pretender que alguien haga algo** (to want somebody to do something)

29   Probar

Probar does not mean 'to probe.' It means 'to try' or 'to taste.'

> Tienes que **probar** mi sopa de espárragos.
> (You have *to taste* my asparagus soup)

¿Te **probaste** el vestido que te compré?
(Did you *try* on the dress I bought you?)

▶ However, if you want to say:

to probe ⇨ **investigar, sondar** (medicine)

Esta cuestión requiere mucha **investigación**.
(This matter needs much *probing*)

*Learn the expression: **escarbar en** (to probe into)

30 **Procurar**

Procurar means 'to manage,' 'to try to do something,' or 'to make sure.'

¡**Procura** llegar a tiempo para tu propia boda!
(*Try / Make sure to* arrive on time for your own wedding!)

▶ However, if you want to say:

to procure ⇨ **obtener, conseguir**

El gobierno quiere **conseguir** más tropas.
(The government wants to *procure* more troops)

31 **Quitar**

Quitar does not mean 'to quit.' It means 'to remove,' or 'to get out' (a stain), or 'to take something away from someone else.'

Le **quitaron** su teléfono móvil el primer día de clase.
(They *took away* his cell phone on the first day of class)

▶ However, if you want to say:

to quit ⇨ **dejar** (a job), **dejar de, abandonar, irse, marcharse, salir de**

Dejó su trabajo porque no le pagaban lo suficiente.
(She *quit* her job because she wasn't being paid enough)

Pedro **dejó de** fumar cuando tenía 30 años.
(Pedro *quit* smoking when he was 30)

*Learn the expressions: **quitar la mesa** (to clear the table); **de quita y pon** (removable; detachable)

32 **Realizar**

Realizar in Spanish does not mean 'to become aware.' It means 'to realize' in the sense of making real, 'to fulfill.'

Él **realizó** su sueño de llegar a ser médico.
(He *realized* his dream of becoming a doctor)

▶ However, if you want to say:

> *to realize* (in the sense of becoming aware) ⇨ **darse cuenta de**

Él **se dio cuenta de** que había cometido un error.
(He *realized* that he had made a mistake)

33   Recordar

Recordar does not mean 'to record;' it means 'to remember,' 'to recall' or 'to remind someone.'

No **recuerdo** el nombre de tu calle.
(I don't *remember* the name of your street)

▶ However, if you want to say:

> *to record* ⇨ **grabar**

¿Puedes **grabar** unos discos para la fiesta?
(Can you *record* some CDs for the party?)

*Learn the expression: **recordarle algo a alguien** (to remind somebody of something)

34   Relatar

Relatar has nothing to do with 'relationship,' or with relating one thing with another. It simply means 'to tell a story.'

Te voy a **relatar** un cuento.
(I am going *to tell* you a story)

▶ However, if you want to say:

> *to relate* ⇨ **relacionar**

No quiero **relacionar** una cosa con la otra. Son dos cosas diferentes.
(I don't want *to relate* one thing with another. They are separate)

35   Remover

Remover has nothing to do with removing anything from anywhere. It means 'to stir' or 'to turn something.'

Tengo que **remover** el arroz.
(I have *to stir* the rice)

▶ However, if you want to say:

> *to remove* ⇨ **sacar, quitar**

Este detergente es caro, pero **saca** / **quita** las manchas.
(This detergent is expensive, but it does *remove* stains)

*Learn the expressions: **el quitamanchas** (stain remover); **remover Roma con Santiago** (to move heaven and earth)

36 Restar

Restar has nothing to do with 'to rest.' It simply means 'to subtract' or 'to take away.'

> Tienes que **restar** los impuestos para saber cuánto ganas.
> (You have to *subtract* the taxes to know how much you are earning)

▶ However, if you want to say:

to rest ⇨ **descansar**

> Este fin de semana no voy a salir, voy a **descansar**.
> (This weekend I am not going to go out, I'm *resting*)

*Learn the expression: **restarle importancia a algo** (to minimize or to play down the importance of something)

37 Resumir

Resumir does not mean 'to resume.' It means 'to summarize.'

> El conferenciante **resumió** los eventos de ayer.
> (The lecturer *summarized* yesterday's events)

▶ However, if you want to say:

to resume ⇨ **continuar, empezar de nuevo, reanudar**

> Después de los aplausos, el violinista **continuó** su concierto.
> (After the applause, the violinist *resumed* playing)

*Learn the expression: **tomar el hilo de un discurso** (to resume a speech)

38 Retirar

Retirar does not mean 'to retire.' It means 'to remove,' 'to take away,' 'to withdraw,' or 'to pull out' from a competition.

> **Retiraron** la vieja bandera y pusieron una nueva.
> (They *removed* the old flag and put a new one in its place)

> El entrenador **retiró** al jugador a los cinco minutos del comienzo del partido.
> (The trainer *withdrew* the player five minutes after the match began)

▶ However, if you want to say:

to retire from a job ⇨ **jubilarse**

> Pepe **se jubiló** de su trabajo a los 65 años.
> (Pepe *retired* from his job at the age of 65)

39   Revolver

Revolver means 'to stir' or 'to rummage through.'

> **Revolvió** en mis cosas sin mi permiso.
> (He *rummaged through* my things without my consent)

▶ However, if you want to say:

> to revolve ⇨ **rotar, girar**

> Es tan engreído que cree que el mundo **gira** a su alrededor.
> (He is so conceited that he thinks the world *revolves* around him)

*Learn the expression: **me revuelve el estómago** (it turns my stomach)

40   Soportar

Soportar does not mean 'to support a family, a claim or an idea.' It means 'to stand,' 'to bear' or 'to endure.'

> ¡No **soporto** este calor!
> (I can't *stand* this heat!)

▶ However, if you want to say:

> to support (i.e., supporting someone in an economic sense) ⇨ **mantener**

> Necesito hacer horas extra para **mantener** a mi familia.
> (I need to work overtime to *support* my family)

> to support (an idea or someone) ⇨ **apoyar, respaldar**

> Yo te **apoyo** en cualquier cosa que hagas.
> (I *support* you in whatever you do)

> **Respaldo** tu idea.
> (I *support* your idea)

> to support (a physical structure) ⇨ **sostener**

> Cuatro columnas dóricas **sostienen** el techo de este templo antiguo.
> (Four Doric columns *support* the roof of this ancient temple)

*Learn the expression: **¡no lo soporto!** (I can't stand him / it)

41   Suceder

Although **suceder** can be used in Spanish to mean 'to follow in sequence,' its primary meaning is 'to happen.'

> Parece bastante preocupado. ¿Le ha **sucedido** algo?
> (He looks quite sad. Has something *happened* to him?)

▶ However, if you want to say:

> to succeed ⇨ **tener éxito, lograr, triunfar**

Compró el libro *Speed Up Your Spanish* y **logró** aprobar el examen de español.
(He bought the book *Speed Up Your Spanish* and *succeeded* in passing his Spanish exam)

*Learn the expression: **suceda lo que suceda** (whatever happens)

42   Suspender

Suspender is used in Spanish to speak about failing an exam. It can be used in the sense of 'to cancel, postpone or call off an event.'

No estudió mucho para el examen y lo **suspendió**.
(He did not study much for the exam and he *failed* it)

Suspendieron el concierto por falta de público.
(They *cancelled* the concert because of low attendance)

▶ However, if you want to say:

to suspend ⇨ **colgar**

Colgaron la araña de luces en el techo del salón de baile.
(They *hung* the chandelier from the ballroom ceiling)

*Learn the word: **los tirantes** (suspenders)

43   Tratar

Tratar in Spanish has various uses. It can mean 'to treat a disease,' or 'to treat someone' well or badly.

Ese doctor me **trató** muy bien.
(That doctor *treated* me very well)

▶ However, in many instances the use of **tratar** is different from the English verb 'to treat':

tratar de + infinitive = 'to try to do something' (synonym of **procurar hacer algo**)

Trato de (procuro) adelgazar, pero ¡es tan difícil!
(I *try to* lose weight, but it's so hard!)

tratar de + noun = 'to be about'

¿**De** qué **trata** ese libro? **Trata de** la globalización.
(What *is* that book *about*? *It is about* globalization)

tratar con = 'to deal with someone'

En mi trabajo **trato** con gente de todo tipo.
(In my job I *deal with* all kinds of people)

*Learn the expression: **tratar a alguien de usted / tú** (to address somebody as 'usted' or 'tú')

Mnemonic device[1]

How to remember the meaning of a verb?

Although this mnemonic device comes from an elementary Spanish class, it shows how students are able to look for ways to remember the meaning of verbs in a useful and practical way.

Easy ways to remember Spanish verbs

Bailar – If someone pays **bail** for you it's a good reason *to dance*

Buscar – If you have a **bus** and a **car** you probably are *looking for* something

Cantar – A **cantor** *sings* in a synagogue

Comprar – On a **comp**uter you can *buy* **Pra**da

Contestar – If you are a **contestant** on a game show you *answer* questions

Descansar – When you put something down to **scan** it you *rest* it on the scanner

Esperar – The young woman d**espera**tely *waits* for her love to arrive

Llegar – Your lllllllegs help you *arrive* at a place

Mirar – You *look at* yourself in the **mirror**

Tomar – Tom *takes* two **toma**toes

Trabajar – *Working* on a train is a **B**ad **J**ob

Terminar – What do ex**terminat**ors do? *End* bugs' lives

In the process of associating each verb with English words that humorously convey the meaning of the Spanish verb, it becomes easier to recall their meaning. Similarly, you can think of strategies to differentiate the meaning of verbs that have been presented here, for instance paying attention to the meaning of the different prefixes, expressions that you can recall easily or other strategies that you may find useful.

---

1   This mnemonic device was created by Anna Strasser, a former student at the Trinity School in New York.

 **Exercises**

EXERCISE 1. Choose the option that best completes the sentence by crossing out the wrong one.

Example: Este verano (nos mudamos / ~~nos movemos~~) a Londres.

1   Juan (presuponía / presumía) de que había cenado con Salma Hayek.
2   Si no quieres (chocar / colgar) contra un árbol, tendrás que conducir con más atención.
3   En las noticias dicen que han (suspendido / sostenido) los vuelos por el mal tiempo.
4   ¿Cuándo me vas a (introducir / presentar) a tu primo el cineasta?
5   Es muy difícil (sacar / remover) las manchas de vino de la ropa.
6   Creo que vamos a (desviarnos / divertirnos) esta noche.
7   ¿Podría Ud. (avisar / aconsejar) al médico? El paciente está grave.
8   Me (disgustó / desplazó) que Andrés no viniera a la fiesta.
9   Este semestre voy a (ayudar / asistir) a un curso de nutrición.
10 ¿Ya has pensado lo que vas a decir antes de (avisar / contestar) al teléfono?
11 Me voy a (apuntar / aplicar) a clases de salsa los sábados por la mañana.
12 Durante la cena, el presidente (se chocó / se atragantó) con una galleta de la suerte.
13 Si no quieres tener problemas de salud, tendrás que (quitar / dejar) de fumar.
14 Tienes razón. Voy a (apoyar / soportar) tu idea para el proyecto.
15 Para solucionar el problema tenemos que (relatar / relacionar) el elemento A con el B.
16 Heidi (se entusiasmó / se excitó) cuando supo que irían al monte a ver las ovejas.
17 ¡Acuérdate de (recordar / grabar) el partido de la final de fútbol!
18 Antes de pintar el resto de la casa, voy a (restar / descansar) un rato.
19 Como tenía suficiente dinero mi padre (se jubiló / se retiró) a los 55 años.
20 Dicen por la radio que van a (divertir / desviar) la carretera por obras.
21 La serpiente (se arrastraba / se dragaba) lentamente hacia su presa.
22 Si quieres (suceder / triunfar) en la vida, tienes que estar alerta a las oportunidades que se te presenten.

EXERCISE 2. Fill in the blanks with the most appropriate word.

1 Para _____ la lámpara de cristal en el techo necesitamos una escalera.
   a) soportar   b) respaldar   c) colgar   d) colmar
2 ¿Me puedes _____ a hacer la mudanza? Tengo demasiadas cosas y sólo dos manos.
   a) ayunar   b) asistir   c) alegrar   d) ayudar
3 He lavado muchas veces esta camisa, pero es imposible _____ esta mancha.
   a) retocar   b) remover   c) quitar   d) tomar
4 Todavía no sé en qué universidad voy a _____ plaza el año que viene.
   a) solucionar   b) solicitar   c) licitar   d) aplicar
5 Hay que _____ a la policía. Hay alguien robando en la tienda.
   a) animar   b) alisar   c) aliviar   d) avisar
6 A Pedro le gusta _____ de que tiene 5 apartamentos en la Costa Brava.
   a) presuponer   b) presumir   c) presidir   d) prescindir
7 No puedes _____ que hablas chino si no sabes decir ni una palabra.
   a) fingir   b) suponer   c) fundir   d) relatar
8 Te aconsejo no _____ con el jefe porque es muy irascible.
   a) disfrutar   b) disponer   c) discutir   d) discernir
9 No es bueno _____ en exceso del chocolate.
   a) abrumar   b) abuchear   c) adular   d) abusar
10 Los no fumadores van a _____ a la compañía tabacalera.
   a) destapar   b) demandar   c) derramar   d) degradar
11 Se casaron ayer, pero Yolanda y José se _____ durante su viaje por Galicia.
   a) correspondieron   b) decidieron   c) comprometieron   d) derritieron
12 Cuando vio que le había tocado la lotería, _____ el primer avión y se fue a una isla desierta.
   a) recogió   b) cogió   c) grabó   d) escogió
13 Antes de echar la salsa en el plato hay que _____ 5 minutos la mezcla.
   a) reponer   b) remover   c) promover   d) remoler
14 Antes de un examen siempre _____ de relajarme.
   a) espero   b) intento   c) entiendo   d) trato
15 Voy a _____ salir cuanto antes del trabajo para poder irme a casa.
   a) promulgar   b) proponer   c) postergar   d) procurar
16 Nos vamos a _____ a un chalet con piscina en cuanto llegue el verano.
   a) llevar   b) llegar   c) mudar   d) mover
17 Esta primavera queremos _____ tulipanes en la finca Ramio.
   a) plantear   b) plantar   c) planear   d) platicar
18 Al final, la editorial va a _____ nuestra propuesta para editar el libro de gramática.

a) restaurar   b) respetar   c) respaldar   d) rescatar

19 ¿Cuánta gente _____ al concierto de música clásica?

a) atendió   b) aplaudió   c) asestó   d) asistió

20 No sé a qué hora van a llegar, pero _____ que llamarán por teléfono antes.

a) presumo   b) sostengo   c) supongo   d) pretendo

21 Hasta que no _____ los caracoles, no sabrás si te gustan o no.

a) intentes   b) trates   c) promulgues   d) pruebes

22 El presidente de EE.UU y de Rusia se _____ la mano al final de la conferencia.

a) estrecharon   b) estiraron   c) espesaron   d) tocaron

EXERCISE 3. Choose the most logical phrase for each verb.

Example: Aplicarse … *una crema en la cara para los granos*.

1	Atender …	a. *una tomatera en el jardín para que salgan tomates.*
2	Asistir …	b. *muy bien a unos invitados y ser un buen anfitrión.*
3	Contestar …	c. *un coche a prueba de balas.*
4	Quitar …	d. *las camisetas de un equipo de fútbol con el logotipo de una empresa.*
5	Plantar …	
6	Grabar …	e. *a alguien intencionadamente para ponerlo/la nervioso/a.*
7	Molestar …	f. *sobre una hamaca al aire libre.*
8	Suspender …	g. *un examen extremadamente fácil.*
9	Mudarse …	h. *la sartén por el mango.*
10	Hablar de …	i. *a una reunión muy importante.*
11	Sacar …	j. *qué vas a hacer el fin de semana o del sexo de los ángeles.*
12	Coger …	
13	Descansar …	k. *el capítulo de un libro o el argumento de una novela.*
14	Jubilarse …	l. *a otro país para vivir y trabajar allí.*
15	Envolver …	m. *la mesa después de cenar para fregar los platos.*
16	Tratar …	n. *a un paciente con una urgencia médica.*
17	Blindar …	o. *con el vecino una y otra vez para que baje el volumen de la televisión.*
18	Discutir …	
19	Patrocinar …	p. *al teléfono o a una pregunta.*
20	Resumir …	q. *la basura a la calle por la noche para que no huela.*
		r. *un bocadillo con papel de aluminio para que esté caliente.*
		s. *al cumplir 65 años y empezar a vivir la vida.*
		t. *con el vídeo la final de baloncesto.*

EXERCISE 4. In the following letter, fill in the blanks with the appropriate verbs.

Querida mamá:

Ayer conocí a un chico muy raro en una fiesta universitaria. Además de ser feo, (1)_____ (pretended) saberlo todo y tener mucho éxito con las chicas, no paraba de (2)_____ (brag). Me dijo que estaba (3)_____ (engaged) con una princesa real y que (4)_____ (frequented) las casas de las familias más renombradas de Europa. Se (5)_____ (invented) todo un cuento lleno de mentiras. Según él, su padre (6)_____ (drives) un Rolls-Royce y (7)_____ (sponsors) exhibiciones de arte en Praga, Kiev y Budapest. También dijo que su padre está (8)_____ (involved) en grandes negocios petroleros, y que lo acaban de (9)_____ (appoint) a un cargo altísimo para (10)_____ (advise) a los presidentes de los países de la Unión Europea.

Pues imagínate, yo (11)_____ (upset), no sabía cómo deshacerme de él. Así que le dije que mi padre acababa de ser acusado de ladrón y de asesino, y que tuvieron que (12)_____ (armor-plate) el coche de policía para llevarlo a la cárcel, pero que yo iba a (13)_____ (contest) la acusación. Lo cierto es que al oír esto, el chico se puso rojo como un tomate, (14)_____ (choked) con la galletita que tenía en la boca, y se fue corriendo al baño.

Mañana te cuento más novedades de mi vida universitaria, que como ves está de lo más interesante.

Un abrazo muy fuerte de tu hija,
Mariana

 Notes

3 Mastering false friends: nouns

The Spanish nouns in this chapter are easy to confuse with similar English words. But once you know how they are used in context, you are not likely to forget their meaning. Learn them, and you will see how much more accurate your Spanish sentences will be.

Mastering false friends: nouns (Part 1)

1   La advertencia

Una advertencia is not an advertisement. It is a warning or a notice about a danger looming ahead. It can also be given to let people know that they have to abide by the rules.

> El policía le dio al chico una última **advertencia**.
> (The policeman gave the kid a last *warning*)

▶ However, if you want to say:

> *advertisement* ⇨ **el anuncio**

> El **anuncio** en el periódico dice que necesitan camareros.
> (The *advertisement* in the paper says they need waiters)

2   El alumno / la alumna

Un alumno is a student in primary or secondary school or at a university.

> En mi escuela hay quinientos **alumnos** en el bachillerato.
> (At my school there are five hundred high school *students*)

▶ However, if you want to say:

> *alumnus / alumna* ⇨ **el ex alumno / la ex alumna**

> Mi amiga Marianne es una **ex alumna** de la Universidad de Yale.
> (My friend Marianne is an *alumna* of Yale University)

3   La apología

Una apología is a high praise or defense of someone or something. It is not an apology.

> Fue a la cárcel por hacer **apología** del terrorismo.
> (He went to jail for *defending* terrorism)

▶ However, if you want to say:

> *apology* ⇨ **la disculpa**

> Usted me debe una **disculpa** por su comportamiento.
> (You owe me an *apology* for your behavior)

4   La arena

Arena is commonly used in Spanish for 'sand.'

> La **arena** de la playa de La Pineda es fina y dorada.
> (The *sand* on La Pineda beach is fine and golden)

▶ However, if you want to say:

arena ⇨ **el estadio**

El gladiador entra en el **estadio** con una espada.
(The gladiator enters the *arena* with a sword)

5 El argumento

Un argumento is neither an argument nor a discussion. It is the plot of a novel, story, play, film, etc.

La película tiene un **argumento** interesante.
(The movie has an interesting *plot*)

▶ However, if you want to say:

argument ⇨ **la discusión**

Tuve una tremenda **discusión** con mi jefe.
(I had a huge *argument* with my boss)

6 El arma (las armas)

Arma does mean 'arm,' but only in the sense of a weapon. It does not refer to a part of the body.

Los policías normalmente llevan **armas**.
(Policemen usually carry *arms*)

▶ However, if you want to say:

arm (the body part) ⇨ **el brazo**

Tengo los **brazos** fuertes de levantar pesas.
(My *arms* are strong from lifting weights)

Note that just like other nouns that start with a stressed **a** or **–ha**, (e.g., **un** / **el** agua clara – **unas** / **las** aguas claras – **un** / **el** hada madrina – **unas** / **las** hadas madrinas), this noun takes a masculine article in the singular even though for agreement purposes the noun is feminine in both the singular & plural: **un** / **el** arma bélica – **unas** / **las** armas bélicas.

(See Chapter 1 for more information)

7 La asignatura

Una asignatura is a subject or area of study taught at an educational institution. It is not an assignment or task, nor is it a signature.

Este año mis **asignaturas** favoritas son las matemáticas y el árabe.
(This year my favorite *subjects* are mathematics and Arabic)

▶ However, if you want to say:

> *signature* ⇨ **la firma**
> *assignment* ⇨ **la tarea**

Necesitamos su **firma** para sacar dinero del banco.
(We need your *signature* to withdraw money from the bank)

8 La asistencia

La asistencia can mean 'assistance' in some contexts, e.g., *asistencia técnica* (technical assistance), but it is more frequently used to mean 'attendance at an event.'

El profesor tomó nota de la **asistencia** de los alumnos.
(The teacher took the students' *attendance*)

▶ However, if you want to say:

> *assistance* ⇨ **la ayuda, el auxilio** (more dramatic)

Voy a necesitar tu **ayuda** para pintar la casa.
(I will need your *assistance* in painting the house)

*Learn the expression: **primeros auxilios** (first aid)

9 El bachillerato

El bachillerato is the equivalent of a high school diploma in the US, or the A-levels in the UK.

El **bachillerato** sirve de preparación para la universidad.
(A *high school diploma* is preparation for college)

▶ However, if you want to say:

> *bachelor* ⇨ **el soltero / la soltera** (bachelorette)

Ese hombre siempre estará **soltero**.
(He is a confirmed bachelor)

*Learn the expression: **una licenciatura** (a bachelor's degree)

10 El balón

Balón does not mean 'balloon.' It means 'a soccer ball.'

El jugador tiró el **balón** muy alto.
(The player threw the *ball* very high)

▶ However, if you want to say:

> *balloon* ⇨ **el globo** (Spain), **la bomba** (Colombia), **la chimbomba** (Central America)

En el parque siempre hay un vendedor de **globos**.
(In the park there's always a *balloon* salesman)

11 El bufete

Un bufete is a law firm, a lawyer's office or a legal practice.

> Al terminar sus estudios de derecho, ella abrió su propio **bufete**.
> (Upon finishing law school, she began her own *law practice*)

▶ However, if you want to say:

buffet ⇨ **el bufet** or **bufé libre**

Hay un **bufé** de comida cubana en la cafetería.
(The cafeteria has a Cuban *buffet*)

12 El campo

Un campo refers to a field, the countryside, or an open land used for cultivation or pasture. It also refers to a field in a figurative sense, such as a domain or area of knowledge.

> En ese **campo** hay vacas y toros.
> (There are cows and bulls in that *field*)

> La psicología infantil no es mi **campo** de especialización.
> (Child psychology is not my *field* of specialization)

▶ However, if you want to say:

camp ⇨ **el campamento**

Este año voy a ir a un nuevo **campamento** de verano.
(This year I'm going to a new *summer camp*)

*Learn the verb: **acampar** (to camp)

13 El carácter

This word refers not to a person, but to the type of personality.

> Esta chica tiene buen **carácter**.
> (This girl has good *character*)

▶ However, if you want to say:

character (in a play or film) ⇨ **el personaje**

Don Quijote es un **personaje** insólito.
(Don Quixote is a very unusual *character*)

*Learn the expression: **tener buen** / **mal carácter** (to be good-natured / bad-tempered)

14   El carbón

This word does not refer to 'carbon,' the chemical element. Instead, it means 'coal.'

En Pensilvania hay minas de **carbón**.
(In Pennsylvania there are *coal* mines)

▶ However, if you want to say:

carbon (dioxide or monoxide) ⇨ **(el dióxido o monóxido) de carbono**

Las plantas producen **dióxido de carbono**.
(Plants produce *carbon dioxide*)

15   El cargo

Un cargo is a job (post, position), as well as a charge or accusation.

El **cargo** de presidente requiere mucha capacidad.
(The *job* of president is very demanding)

Inculparon al joven con el **cargo** de espionaje.
(The young man *was charged* with espionage)

▶ However, if you want to say:

cargo, freight, load ⇨ **el cargamento, la carga**

El **cargamento** de trigo llegará en barco.
(The wheat *cargo* will arrive by ship)

*Learn the expressions: **hacerse cargo de** (to take charge)**, retirar los cargos contra** (to drop the charges against)

16   La carpeta

Una carpeta is not a rug; it is a folder for filing papers or documents.

Necesito una **carpeta** para archivar estas hojas.
(I need a *folder* in which to file these papers)

▶ However, if you want to say:

carpet ⇨ **la alfombra**

Necesitamos una **alfombra** roja para la ceremonia.
(We need a red *carpet* for the ceremony)

17 La carta

Una carta is simply a letter. But it also means 'a menu' (**la carta**) or 'wine list' (**la carta de vinos**), as well as 'a set of cards to play' (**las cartas o los naipes**).

¿Cuántos sellos necesito para una **carta** vía aérea a Europa?
(How many stamps do I need for an air mail *letter* to Europe?)

Vamos a jugar a las **cartas**.
(Let's play *cards*)

▶ However, if you want to say:

card ⇨ **la tarjeta (de débito, crédito)**
cart ⇨ **el carro, la carreta**

¿Aceptan la **tarjeta** Amex en este restaurante? No, sólo Visa o Mastercard.
(Do you take Amex *card*? No, only Visa or Mastercard)

En el supermercado hay **carros** para los clientes.
(At the supermarket there are *carts* for the clients)

*Learn the expressions: **poner las cartas sobre la mesa** (to put one's cards on the table); **una carta de recomendación** (a reference letter)

18 El cartón

Cartón does not mean 'cartoon,' it means 'cardboard.'

Todo estaba empaquetado en cajas de **cartón**.
(Everything was packed in *cardboard* boxes)

▶ However, if you want to say:

cartoon ⇨ **los dibujos animados, la viñeta**

A los niños les encanta ver **los dibujos animados** en la tele.
(Children love to watch *cartoons* on TV)

19 La casualidad

When events happen by chance, yet seem to be connected, we have **una casualidad**.

Me encontré con Alejandro por **casualidad**.
(I ran into Alejandro *by accident*)

▶ However, if you want to say:

casualty ⇨ **la víctima**

Hubo muchas **víctimas** en la Primera Guerra Mundial.
(There were many *casualties* in World War I)

*Learn the expression: **¡qué casualidad!** (what a coincidence!)

20 El colegio

Un colegio is not a college, but a primary or secondary school.

> Despúes del **colegio** voy a estudiar en la universidad.
> (After *high school*, I am going to study at a university)

▶ However, if you want to say:

> college ⇨ **la universidad**

> Mi amiga Ilena va a la **universidad** de Vassar.
> (My friend Ilena goes to Vassar *College*)

21 El collar

Un collar is a necklace or ornament worn around the neck.

> Me he comprado un **collar** de perlas.
> (I have bought myself a pearl *necklace*)

▶ However, if you want to say:

> collar ⇨ **el cuello de la camisa**

> Él siempre se pone camisas con el **cuello** abotonado.
> (He always wears shirts with buttoned down *collars*)

*To refer to a pet collar you would use: **un collar (de perro)**

22 El compromiso

Un compromiso refers to a commitment, an obligation, or an engagement.

> María y Pablo anunciaron su **compromiso**.
> (María and Pablo announced their *engagement*)

▶ However, if you want to say:

> compromise ⇨ **un acuerdo mutuo, un arreglo**

> Los abogados llegaron a un **acuerdo mutuo** sobre la herencia.
> (The lawyers reached a *compromise* on the inheritance)

23 El/la conductor/a

This word is used to refer to someone who operates a motor vehicle.

> En Dublín los pasajeros siempre le dan las gracias al **conductor** del autobús.
> (In Dublin passengers always thank the bus *driver*)

▶ However, if you want to say:

conductor ⇨ **el/la director/a (de orquesta)**

Daniel Barenboim es un famoso **director** de orquesta.
(Daniel Barenboim is a famous *conductor*)

24 La conferencia

Una conferencia refers to a talk, speech or lecture given before an audience.

La **conferencia** fue sobre el cambio climático.
(The *lecture* was on global warming)

▶ However, if you want to say:

conference (as a group of lectures) ⇨ **el congreso**

En el **congreso** de Madrid hubo muchas conferencias interesantes.
(At the Madrid *conference* there were many interesting lectures)

25 La confidencia

Una confidencia is a less commonly used word for 'secret' (**secreto**).

Mi hermana me hizo una **confidencia**: tiene novio.
(My sister told me a *secret*: she has a boyfriend)

▶ However, if you want to say:

confidence ⇨ **la confianza**

Tengo mucha **confianza** en mi hijo.
(I have a lot of *confidence* in my son)

*Learn the expression: **gente de confianza** (people who can be trusted)

26 La copa

Una copa is used in Spanish to refer to a wine glass, a trophy or an alcoholic drink.

España ganó la **copa** del mundo de fútbol contra Brasil.
(Spain won the football World *Cup* against Brazil)

Vamos a tomar una **copa**. No gracias, tengo que conducir.
(Let's have *a drink*. No thanks, I am driving)

▶ However, if you want to say:

cup ⇨ **un vaso** (glass), **una taza** (a mug), **un vaso de papel** (paper cup)

Le quitamos el biberón y ya bebe con el **vaso**.
(We took the bottle away, and now he drinks from the *glass*)

27   El crimen

Un crimen in Spanish refers only to a serious crime, one that usually involves a bloody event.

¿Has visto la película *Los crímenes de Oxford*?
(Have you seen the movie *The Oxford Murders*?)

▶ However, if you want to say:

crime ⇨ **la delincuencia**

Hoy en día hay mucha **delincuencia** en la ciudad de México.
(There is a lot of *crime* these days in Mexico City)

28   La cuestión

Una cuestión is not a question, but rather an issue or a matter.

La enseñanza es una **cuestión** de vocación más que de dinero.
(Teaching is a *matter* of vocation, not money)

▶ However, if you want to say:

question ⇨ **la pregunta**

Los periodistas le hicieron muchas **preguntas** a la actriz.
(The journalists asked the actress many *questions*)

*Learn the expression: **poner algo en cuestión** (to doubt something)

29   La decepción

Una decepción is the result of a failed expectation.

Fue una **decepción** no verte el domingo.
(Not to see you on Sunday was a *disappointment*)

▶ However, if you want to say:

deception or betrayal ⇨ **el engaño**

Cuando vi a mi novio con otra mujer me di cuenta de su **engaño**.
(When I saw my boyfriend with another woman, I felt *betrayed*)

30   El delito

Un delito is a crime, an offence or a felony.

Su **delito** fue no decírselo a la policía.
(His *crime* was not telling the police)

▶ However, if you want to say:

> *delight* ⇨ **el deleite, el placer, el encanto**

> El concierto de piano y guitarra fue un verdadero **deleite**.
> (The piano and guitar performance was a true *delight*)

*Learn the expression: **estar encantado de** (to be delighted)

31 La demostración

Unlike in English, this word is not used in Spanish in a political sense, i.e., the public display of collective opinion about a person or cause. It is more like a show or a display.

> La **demostración** del nuevo producto fue un éxito.
> (The *demonstration* of the new product was a success)

▶ However, if you want to say:

> *demonstration* ⇨ **la manifestación**

> Ayer hubo una **manifestación** en contra del nuevo gobierno.
> (Yesterday there was a *demonstration* against the new government)

32 El/la dependiente/a

Besides meaning 'a dependent,' this word is more commonly used to refer to a salesperson.

> Esa chica es una **dependienta** de El Corte Inglés.
> (She is a *salesperson* working at El Corte Inglés)

▶ However, if you want to say:

> *depending on* ⇨ **dependiendo de**

> **Dependiendo del** tiempo, iremos a la playa mañana.
> (*Depending on* the weather, we will go to the beach tomorrow)

33 La desgracia

Una desgracia is not something embarrassing or disgraceful; it is a misfortune, a tragedy.

> El 11 de septiembre fue una **desgracia** nacional.
> (September 11th was a national *tragedy*)

▶ However, if you want to say:

> *disgrace* ⇨ **la vergüenza**

> Es la **vergüenza** de la familia, porque todos tocan el piano menos él.
> (He is the *disgrace* of the family, since they all play the piano except him)

*Learn the expressions: **por desgracia** (unfortunately) / **las desgracias nunca vienen solas** (when it rains it pours)

34   La discusión

Although **una discusión** can mean 'a discussion,' it usually refers to a dispute or argument.

> Empezaron una **discusión** por una tontería.
> (They had an *argument* about something silly)

▶ However, if you want to say:

> discussion ⇨ **el debate, la charla** (informal)

> Tuvimos un **debate** sobre cómo mejorar la economía.
> (We had a *discussion* on ways to improve the economy)

35   La educación

The word **educación** has a broad meaning that includes 'school education' as well as 'upbringing' at home.

> Con un padre dictatorial tuvo una **educación** muy estricta.
> (With a domineering father, she had a very strict *upbringing*)

▶ However, if you want to say:

> education ⇨ **la formación**

> Según su currículum, ha tenido una excelente **formación**.
> (According to her CV, she has had an excellent *education*)

36   El ejército

Un ejército is an organized military force.

> Costa Rica no tiene **ejército** porque depende de EE.UU.
> (Costa Rica has no *army* since it depends on the U.S.)

▶ However, if you want to say:

> exercise ⇨ **el ejercicio**

> Como tarea hagan el **ejercicio** número dos.
> (For homework do *exercise* number two)

37   La etiqueta

Una etiqueta is a label or tag for purposes of identification or description. This word can also be used in Spanish with the meaning of 'etiquette.'

> La maleta tardó en llegar porque no tenía **etiqueta**.
> (The suitcase arrived late because it didn't have any *tag*)

▶ However, if you want to say:

etiquette ⇨ **el protocolo, la etiqueta**

En la fiesta tienes que seguir el **protocolo**.
(At the party you have to observe the rules of *etiquette*)

*Learn the expression: **un traje de etiqueta** (a dinner jacket)

38   El éxito

It is the result or a desired outcome, or the attainment of wealth, favor or glory.

Las películas de Pedro Almodóvar tienen mucho **éxito** en EE.UU.
(Almodovar's films are a *success* in the U.S.)

▶ However, if you want to say:

exit ⇨ **la salida**

¿Dónde está la **salida** de emergencia?
(Where is the emergency *exit*?)

*Learn the expression: **con éxito** (successfully)

39   La fábrica

Una **fábrica** in Spanish is a place of production or manufacture, i.e., a factory.

Muchas compañías están trasladando sus **fábricas** a China.
(Many companies are moving their *factories* to China)

▶ However, if you want to say:

fabric ⇨ **la tela**

Necesito comprar **tela** para hacerme un traje nuevo.
(I need to buy *fabric* to make myself a new suit)

40   La falta

Una **falta** can mean: 'a lack, need, absence, shortage, or shortcoming.'

La **falta** de oxígeno hace difícil vivir en Marte.
(The *lack* of oxygen makes it difficult to live on Mars)

▶ However, if you want to say:

fault ⇨ **la culpa**

El accidente no fue **culpa** de nadie.
(The accident was nobody's *fault*)

*Learn the expressions: **la falta de ortografía** (spelling mistake); **sin falta** (without fail); **hacer falta** (to be necessary)

41   La firma

Una **firma** is a handwritten signature.

> Se dice que la **firma** de uno refleja su personalidad.
> (One's *signature* is said to reflect one's personality)

▶ However, if you want to say:

firm ⇨ **la compañía, la empresa** (smaller)

> Microsoft es una **compañía** extremadamente rentable.
> (Microsoft is an extremely profitable *firm*)

42   El fracaso

Un **fracaso** is not a noisy quarrel on the street, but a failure or disaster.

> La fiesta fue un **fracaso** porque llovió a cántaros.
> (The party was a *disaster* because it rained cats and dogs)

▶ However, if you want to say:

fracas ⇨ **el altercado, la reyerta**

> Hubo un **altercado** el viernes por la noche delante de la discoteca.
> (There was a *fracas* on Friday night in front of the disco)

43   La ganga

Una ganga does not mean 'a gang.' It means 'a bargain' or an item sold at a reduced price.

> Siempre hay **gangas** en los mercadillos de Madrid.
> (The flea market of Madrid is always full of *bargains*)

▶ However, if you want to say:

gang ⇨ **la banda (de criminales), la pandilla (de niños)**

> La obra *West Side Story* trata de **bandas** rivales de Nueva York.
> (*West Side Story* is about rival *gangs* in New York)

44   La goma

Goma does not mean 'gum.' It means 'rubber' or 'eraser.'

> Necesito un lápiz que tenga **goma** para poder borrar.
> (I need a pencil with an *eraser*)

▶ However, if you want to say:

gum ⇨ **el chicle, la goma de mascar** (in some Latin American countries)

> No permito que mastiquen **chicle** en mi clase.
> (I don't allow *gum* chewing in my class)

*Learn the word: **las encías** (gums in one's mouth)

Exercises (Part 1)

EXERCISE 1. Fill in the blanks with the most appropriate word.

1 El cardiólogo me ha recomendado que haga _____ todos los días.
   a) ejército   b) ejercido   c) ejercicio   d) ejerciendo

2 ¿Has comprado _____ de helio para el cumpleaños de tu prima?
   a) los bolos   b) los globos   c) los balones   d) las bolas

3 ¿Dónde está _____ del edificio? No me acuerdo.
   a) la partida   b) la pálida   c) la salida   d) el éxito

4 _____ principal de la novela es un caballero andante llamado Don Quijote.
   a) La personalidad   b) El carácter   c) El personaje   d) La persona

5 En el terremoto de Pakistán hubo muchas _____.
   a) casualidades   b) víctimas   c) vencidas   d) confidencias

6 Antes de meter la camisa en la lavadora, lava los puños y el _____.
   a) coronario   b) cuello   c) cuerno   d) collar

7 Éste es tu último año de bachillerato. ¿A qué _____ quieres ir el año que viene?
   a) colegio   b) universidad   c) escuela   d) colegiata

8 Para guardar los apuntes de la universidad necesitas una _____.
   a) papeleta   b) caldera   c) papelera   d) carpeta

9 ¡Esa chaqueta es una auténtica _____ porque es de marca y además es preciosa!
   a) ganga   b) tanga   c) banda   d) manga

10 Tenemos que comprar 6 metros de _____ para hacerte el vestido.
   a) vela   b) fábrica   c) tela   d) estela

11 Era cantante de ópera y ahora estudia para ser _____ de orquesta.
   a) domador   b) conductor   c) acomodador   d) director

12 ¿Ya se sabe cuándo va a llegar _____ de medicinas para la Cruz Roja?
   a) el carga   b) el cargado   c) el cargo   d) el cargamento

13 Pepe y Pepa se enzarzaron en _____ sin ningún motivo en medio de la calle.
   a) un debate   b) una manifestación   c) una discusión   d) un argumento

14 Tuve yo _____ de que Jaime no viniera a la fiesta. Se me olvidó decírselo.
   a) la falla   b) la culpa   c) la falta   d) el fracaso

15 Debería ir al dentista lo antes posible porque me duelen mucho _____.
   a) las gomas   b) los chicles   c) las bocas   d) las encías

16 ¿Te apetece tomar _____? No gracias, no puedo porque tengo que conducir.

   a) una copa   b) una jarra   c) una taza   d) un vaso

17 En Río de Janeiro se encuentra _____ de fútbol más grande del mundo.

   a) el ruedo   b) la arena   c) el estadio   d) el campamento

18 No te olvides _____ de crédito cuando vayas a salir de compras por Nueva York.

   a) el tarjetón   b) la cartilla   c) la carta   d) la tarjeta

19 Al final no pudo venir a la reunión porque tenía _____ muy importante.

   a) un comprometido   b) un compromiso   c) un comestible
   d) un comprendido

20 _____ de ayer por la noche despertó a toda la familia a las 4:00 de la mañana.

   a) El alternado   b) El fracaso   c) El altercado   d) El argumento

EXERCISE 2. Connect each word with its most logical pair.

   Example: alfombra + Aladín

1	carbón	a.	anuncio
2	firma	b.	¡perdón!, ¡lo siento muchísimo!
3	colegio	c.	armas
4	collar	d.	Boston College
5	publicidad	e.	mineral
6	fábrica	f.	de los diputados
7	manifestación	g.	de abogados
8	asignatura	h.	de prensa
9	etiqueta	i.	de una película, novela, etc.
10	cuello	j.	robo, pelea, asesinato, etc.
11	universidad	k.	de perlas
12	argumento	l.	precio (vestido)
13	dibujos animados	m.	protesta
14	delincuencia	n.	de la camisa
15	disculpa	o.	bolígrafo
16	bufete	p.	de comida rápida
17	conferencia	q.	geometría, latín, matemáticas, etc.
18	ejército	r.	Trinity School
19	congreso	s.	producción
20	bufet	t.	el ratón Mickey, el pato Donald, etc.

EXERCISE 3. Insert the word from the box that best corresponds to each definition

el cargamento • la casualidad • el bachillerato • el altercado • la carpeta • la apología • el carácter • la cuestión • la desgracia • el delito • el campamento • la copa • la ganga • la confidencia • el argumento

1 Asunto o tema del que se trata. Dificultad, duda, pregunta o problema.

_____

2 Modo de ser y de comportarse. La personalidad de una persona.

_____

3 Asunto o trama de una obra literaria, cinematográfica, teatral, etc. Razonamiento usado para demostrar algo o convencer a alguien.

_____

4 Suceso que causa dolor, daño o perjuicio.

_____

5 Combinación de circunstancias que caracterizan un acontecimiento imprevisto.

_____

6 Discurso de palabra o por escrito, en defensa o alabanza de personas, ideas o cosas.

_____

7 Estudios de enseñanza secundaria anteriores a los superiores y título académico que se obtiene al terminar dichos estudios.

_____

8 Especie de cartera o estuche que consiste en dos partes unidas por uno de sus lados que sirve para guardar papeles.

_____

9 Acción de comunicar algo en secreto o de manera reservada a alguien.

_____

10 Tipo de vaso, generalmente acampanado y sostenido sobre un pie, que se usa para beber.

_____

11 Cosa ventajosa y muy conveniente que se consigue sin esfuerzo o a muy bajo precio.

_____

12 Acción o conducta voluntaria castigada por la ley.

_____

13 Conjunto de instalaciones donde acampan excursionistas, militares, etc.

_____

14 Disputa acalorada y violenta.

_____

15 Conjunto de mercancías que carga o que lleva una embarcación, camión, tren, etc.

_____

Mastering false friends: nouns (Part 2)

45   La gripe

La gripe is a flu or influenza. Please note that in Colombia and Mexico it is known as *la gripa*.

> Tuve suerte; toda la oficina tuvo la **gripe** excepto yo.
> (I was lucky; everyone in the office got the *flu* except me)

▶ However, if you want to say:

> *gripe* ⇨ **la queja**

> ¿Cuál es tu **queja**?
> (What's your *gripe*?)

46   La grosería

Although this word ends in the suffix *–ía*, which sometimes indicates a store, like *panadería* (bakery), *carnicería* (butcher's), etc., it is not a store of any kind. It simply means 'rudeness or vulgarity.'

> Ese hombre malhumorado siempre dice **groserías**.
> (That moody guy always has *something rude* to say)

▶ However, if you want to say:

grocery store ⇨ **la tienda de comestibles o la tienda de ultramarinos** (Spain), **la bodega** (Cuba, Peru, Venezuela), **tienda de abarrotes** (Central America, Mexico).

> En Huesca se encuentra **la tienda de comestibles** más antigua de España.
> (In Huesca you can find the oldest *grocery store* in Spain)

47   El idioma

Un idioma is a synonym of the word **'lenguaje'** or 'language.'

> Pawel habla siete **idiomas** además de árabe.
> (Pawel speaks seven *languages* besides Arabic)

▶ However, if you want to say:

> *idiom* ⇨ **el modismo o la expresión idiomática**

> El **modismo** para 'to rain cats and dogs' es 'llover a cántaros'.
> ('Llover a cántaros' is the *idiom* for 'to rain cats and dogs')

48   **La ilusión**

Although **una ilusión** can also mean 'an illusion,' it is most commonly used to mean 'an excitement, thrill or dream.'

Mi sobrina me dijo que le hacía **ilusión** ir al zoo.
(My niece said that she was *excited* about going to the zoo)

La **ilusión** de mi vida es grabar un disco.
(My life's *dream* is to record a CD)

*Learn the expressions: **¡qué ilusión!** (how exciting!) / **hacerse ilusiones** (to build up one's hopes)

49   **La jarra**

Una jarra is not a jar. It is a pitcher, a jug (to serve something), a stein or a tankard (to drink from).

Para la receta necesito una **jarra** de cerveza y una de leche.
(For the recipe, I need a beer glass and a milk jug)

▶ However, if you want to say:

jar ⇨ **el bote, el tarro**

Compré un **bote** de mermelada de naranja.
(I bought a *jar* of orange marmalade)

 Note that *el jarro* also exists and means 'pitcher,' however it is less used than *la jarra*. And, from the same semantic family, *un jarrón* means 'a vase.'

50   **La jornada**

Una jornada refers to a working day.

Mi hermana trabaja a media **jornada**, no a **jornada** completa.
(My sister works *part-time*, not *full-time*)

▶ However, if you want to say:

journey ⇨ **el viaje**

Este año vamos a hacer un **viaje** a Turquía.
(This year we are taking a *trip* to Turkey)

51   **El jornal**

Un jornal means 'a day's pay;' but a more common word is **el salario** or **el sueldo** (salary)

El patrón le dio el **jornal** al trabajador.
(The boss gave the worker his *day's wages*)

▶ However, if you want to say:

> *journal* ⇨ **la revista de investigación**

> Mi amigo Héctor escribe para *BHS*, una prestigiosa **revista de investigación**.
> (My friend Héctor writes for *BHS*, a prestigious *journal*)

*Learn the word: **el jornalero** (day-laborer)

52   La jubilación

La jubilación in Spanish refers to both one's retirement and the pension received. As the word implies, it is often perceived in Hispanic cultures as a very positive stage of life.

> Mucha gente anhela la **jubilación**.
> (Many people look forward to *retirement*)

▶ However, if you want to say:

> *jubilation* ⇨ **el júbilo**
> *jubilee* ⇨ **el aniversario**

> El 5 de mayo en México hay **júbilo** y baile en la calles.
> (On May 5th there is *jubilation* and dancing in the streets of Mexico)

> Este sábado se celebra el vigésimo quinto **aniversario** de la reina.
> (This Saturday is the Queen's silver *jubilee*)

53   La lectura

Una lectura is the act of reading.

> La **lectura** de hoy es un cuento de Borges.
> (The *reading* for today is a story by Borges)

▶ However, if you want to say:

> *lecture* ⇨ **la conferencia**

> En la universidad los profesores dan **conferencias**.
> (College professors give *lectures*)

54   La letra

The word '**letra**' in Spanish refers to a letter of the alphabet: a, b, c, etc.

> El alfabeto español tiene una **letra** que no existe en inglés: la 'ñ'.
> (The Spanish alphabet has one *letter* that doesn't exist in English: the 'ñ')

▶ However, if you want to say:

> *letter* ⇨ **la carta**

Ahora la gente escribe más correos electrónicos y menos **cartas**.
(Nowadays people write more e-mails and fewer *letters*)

55   La librería

Una librería is not a library that lends books, but a store that sells books. In Spain this word also means 'bookshelf' (*estantería*), while in Latin America this piece of furniture is usually called **'un librero.'**

Puedes comprar *Speed Up Your Spanish* en la **librería** Juanito.
(You can buy *Speed Up Your Spanish* at the Juanito *bookstore*)

▶ However, if you want to say:

library ⇨ **la biblioteca**

Nuestra **biblioteca** municipal está en la calle 42.
(Our city *library* is on 42nd Street)

56   La linterna

Una linterna is not a lantern. It is a flashlight or a torch.

Necesito comprar pilas para mi **linterna**.
(I have to buy batteries for my *flashlight*)

▶ However, if you want to say:

lantern ⇨ **el farol**

La invención de la bombilla eléctrica hizo desaparecer los **faroles**.
(With the invention of the light bulb *lanterns* disappeared)

*Learn the expression: **marcarse un farol** (to bluff in a game)

57   La lujuria

La lujuria is lust, one of the seven capital sins.

La **lujuria** es tan mala como la envidia o la codicia.
(*Lust* is as bad as envy or greed)

▶ However, if you want to say:

luxury ⇨ **el lujo**

Si quieres un coche de **lujo** tienes que pagar un impuesto de **lujo**.
(If you want a *luxury* car, you have to pay a *luxury* tax)

58   La manifestación

While **una manifestación** is the equivalent of the English 'manifestation,' in Spanish it is most commonly used to refer to a demonstration or public display of group feelings.

Todos los días hay **manifestaciones** contra la guerra.
(Every day there are *demonstrations* against the war)

59   La máscara

Una máscara does not mean 'mascara.' It means 'a mask.'

En el baile de disfraces todo el mundo llevaba **máscaras**.
(At the costume ball everyone was wearing *masks*)

▶ However, if you want to say:

mascara ⇨ **el rímel**

Ella no sale a la calle sin pintura de labios ni **rímel**.
(She doesn't leave the house without putting on lipstick and *mascara*)

*Learn the expressions: **la mascarilla** (oxygen mask); **la careta** (a mask made out of paper or cardboard); **el antifaz** (an eye mask like the one Zorro wears)

60   El / la minorista

Like many words ending in **–ista** that identify professions, both masculine and feminine (*el / la* dentista, *el / la* periodista, *el / la* taxista, etc.), **minorista** means retailer, or retail used as an adjective.

Hay más comercio **minorista** en los pueblos que en las ciudades.
(*Retail* trade is more common in villages than in cities)

▶ However, if you want to say:

minority ⇨ **la minoría**

Los hispanos son ahora la **minoría** más grande de Estados Unidos.
(Hispanics are now the largest *minority* in the United States)

61   El motivo

Motivo does not really mean the same as its English cognate 'motive,' which normally carries a negative connotation or is used in a legal context.

¿Cuál es el **motivo** de tu visita a Venezuela?
(What is the *reason* of your visit to Venezuela?)

▶ However, if you want to say:

motive ⇨ **el móvil**

¿Cuál fue exactamente el **móvil** del asesino?
(What exactly was the killer's *motive*?)

*Learn the expression: **sin ningún motivo** (for no reason at all)

62 El negocio

Un negocio is a business, an economic transaction, or a deal.

Van a poner un **negocio** en el centro de Lima.
(They are setting up a *business* in downtown Lima)

▶ However, if you want to say:

negotiation ⇨ **la negociación**

Están en **negociaciones** sobre los sueldos del año que viene.
(They are in *negotiation* about next year's salaries)

63 La noticia

Una noticia is a piece of news: a report of recent events in newspapers or newscasts.

La **noticia** de la boda real dio la vuelta al mundo.
(The *news* of the royal wedding went around the world)

▶ However, if you want to say:

notice ⇨ **el aviso**

Hay un **aviso** en el diario acerca del concierto de rock.
(There's a *notice* in the newspaper about the rock concert)

64 El nudo

Un nudo has nothing to do with a nude or naked person. It is simply a knot, an interlacing of flexible parts.

Tengo que deshacer este **nudo** antes de atarme los cordones.
(I need to undo this *knot* before tying my shoe laces)

▶ However, if you want to say:

naked or nude ⇨ **desnudo**

Había un hombre **desnudo** corriendo en el maratón.
(A *naked* man was running in the marathon)

*Learn the expressions: **tener un nudo en la garganta** (to have a lump in one's throat)

65   La ocurrencia

Una ocurrencia is a witty remark, a bright idea, a wisecrack.

¡Tienes cada **ocurrencia**! ¡No vamos a bañarnos en noviembre!
(What a *bright idea* you have! We are not going to go swimming in November!)

▶ However, if you want to say:

occurrence ⇨ **el hecho, el acontecimiento, el suceso**

Una tormenta tropical no es un **hecho** frecuente en las Islas Canarias.
(Tropical storms are a rare *occurrence* in the Canary Islands)

66   El oficio

Un oficio is not an office, but a trade or occupation requiring manual or mechanical skill.

La carpintería es un **oficio** útil.
(Carpentry is a useful *occupation*)

▶ However, if you want to say:

office ⇨ **la oficina**

La oficina del director del banco está en el último piso.
(The bank manager's *office* is on the last floor)

67   La parada

Una parada is not a parade. It is a bus stop or metro stop.

La **parada** del autobús para ir al centro está en Broadway.
(The *bus stop* for going downtown is on Broadway)

▶ However, if you want to say:

parade ⇨ **el desfile**

Las calles están cerradas por el **desfile** de San Patricio.
(The streets are closed for the St. Patrick's Day *parade*)

68   La parcela

Una parcela is not a parcel. It is a plot of land.

Quisiera construir mi casa en esa **parcela** sobre la colina.
(I'd like to build my house on that *plot of land* on the hill)

▶ However, if you want to say:

parcel ⇨ **el paquete**

Mi tía me ha mandado un **paquete**. ¿Qué será?
(My aunt sent me a *package*. I wonder what it is)

69 **Los parientes**

Los parientes are not parents, but rather the extended family of aunts, uncles, cousins, grandparents, etc.

Mis **parientes** son mis abuelos, tíos, primos, etc.
(My *relatives* are my grandparents, uncles, cousins, etc.)

▶ However, if you want to say:

parents ⇨ **los padres**

Los **padres** quieren lo mejor para sus hijos.
(*Parents* want the best for their kids)

*Learn the Mexican expressions: **¡qué padre!** (how cool!) / **¡qué madre!** (bad luck!)

70 **El patrón**

Un patrón is a pattern or template used as a model for making things. The word is also used to refer to a boss, or the captain of a fishing, small trading, or pleasure boat, i.e., a skipper.

Necesito un **patrón** original para hacerme un vestido.
(I need an original *pattern* to make myself a dress)

En *Moby Dick,* Ahab es el **patrón** de un barco.
(Ahab was the *skipper* of a small boat in *Moby Dick*)

▶ However, if you want to say:

patron ⇨ **el patrocinador, el mecenas** (of the arts)

El **patrocinador** de la exposición es el multimillonario Bill Gates.
(The *patron* of the exhibition is the multimillionaire Bill Gates)

71 **La peculiaridad**

Una peculiaridad is a characteristic or a feature that makes a person unique or different. In Spanish, this word has retained its etymological meaning so it doesn't mean strange or weird.

El barco tiene la **peculiaridad** de ser automático.
(The boat has the special *characteristic* of being automatic)

▶ However, if you want to say:

peculiarity ⇨ **la rareza, la manía**

No siempre es así de amable, también tiene sus **rarezas**.
(He is not always so kind, he also has his *peculiarities*)

72   El personaje

Un personaje is not a real person, but a character in a novel play, movie, etc.

¿Quién es **el personaje** principal de *La Celestina*?
(Who is the main *character* of *La Celestina?*)

▶ However, if you want to say:

person ⇨ **la persona**

María es una buena **persona**, siempre ayuda a la gente.
(Maria is a good *person*, she is always helping people)

*Learn the expression: **ser todo un personaje** (to be quite a character)

73   El preservativo

Un preservativo is the usual word used in Spanish for a condom.

El uso del **preservativo** ha ayudado a reducir los casos de SIDA.
(*Condom* use has helped to reduce AIDS cases)

▶ However, if you want to say:

preservative ⇨ **el conservante**

La comida orgánica no tiene **conservantes**.
(Organic food doesn't have *preservatives*)

74   La receta

Interestingly enough, the word '**receta**' in Spanish is used to refer to both a cooking recipe and also a medical prescription.

La **receta** del gazpacho no es complicada.
(The *recipe* for making a gazpacho is not complicated)

▶ However, if you want to say:

receipt ⇨ **un recibo**

Para devolver la falda necesitas el **recibo**.
(To return the skirt you will need the *receipt*)

75   La recolección

Una recolección means the harvest. A synonym would be '**una cosecha.**'

La **recolección** de la uva empieza en septiembre.
(The grape *harvest* begins in September)

▶ However, if you want to say:

> *recollection* ⇨ **el recuerdo**

> No tengo **recuerdos** de mi país natal.
> (I have no *recollection* of my native country)

*Learn the expression: **la época de la cosecha** (harvest time)

76   El resorte

Un resorte has nothing to do with a resort. It is a mechanical spring, an elastic device that recovers its original shape when released.

> A este viejo reloj le falta un **resorte**.
> (This old clock needs a new *spring*)

▶ However, if you want to say:

> *resort* ⇨ **el complejo turístico, la estación balnearia o de esquí**

> Este verano vamos a un **complejo turístico** en Cancún.
> (This summer we are going to a *resort* in Cancun)

77   La reunión

Although **una reunión** can refer to a *family reunion* ⇨ **una reunión familiar**, it usually simply means a get together or meeting.

> A las dos tenemos una **reunión** de profesores.
> (At two o'clock we have a teachers' *meeting*)

▶ However, if you want to say:

> *reunion* ⇨ **el reencuentro**

> ¿Vas a asistir al **reencuentro** de los ex-alumnos de la universidad?
> (Are you going to the alumni *reunion*?)

78   La ropa

The word **ropa** refers to clothing, and is generally used in its singular.

> Tenemos que comprar **ropa** nueva para el viaje.
> (We have to buy new *clothes* for the trip)

▶ However, if you want to say:

> *rope* ⇨ **la cuerda**

> Necesito una **cuerda** para tender la ropa.
> (I need a *rope* to hang out the clothes)

*Learn the expression: **la ropa interior** (underwear)

79   La sopa

Do not think of soap but of soup.

> En invierno no hay nada mejor que una buena **sopa** caliente.
> (In winter there is nothing better than some good, hot *soup*)

▶ However, if you want to say:

soap ⇨ **el jabón**

> Utilizo un **jabón** especial porque tengo la piel sensible.
> (I use a special *soap* for sensitive skin)

*Learn the expressions: **estar hasta en la sopa** (to be everywhere) / **ponerse como una sopa** (to get soaked)

80   Los suburbios

These are not suburbs for the middle classes, but slums where there is poverty and social disorganization.

> Los **suburbios** de la ciudad son bastante peligrosos.
> (The city *slums* are quite dangerous)

▶ However, if you want to say:

suburbs ⇨ **la zona residencial, las afueras**

> Vive en la mejor **zona residencial** de Filadelfia.
> (He lives in the best *suburb* of Philadelphia)

81   El suceso

This word has nothing to do with success. Rather, it is a noteworthy happening, usually a tragic one.

> Ese **suceso** trágico ocurrió en una discoteca.
> (The tragic *event* took place in a disco)

▶ However, if you want to say:

success ⇨ **el éxito**

> La fiesta fue un gran **éxito**.
> (The party was a smashing *success*)

*In a newspaper you can find a section called **sucesos** (accident and crime reports)

82   El sujeto

This word does not refer to school subjects, but to the subject of a sentence. It can also sometimes be used to refer to an individual or person.

El **sujeto** de la frase: "yo tengo hambre" es "yo".
(The *subject* of the sentence "I am hungry" is "I")

Yo no me fiaría de él, es un **sujeto** sospechoso.
(I wouldn't trust him, he is a suspicious *individual*)

▶ However, if you want to say:

school subject ⇨ **la asignatura, la materia**

Para mí, la **asignatura** más difícil es química.
(My most difficult *subject* is chemistry)

subject (meaning theme) ⇨ **el tema, el asunto**

El **tema** del programa de hoy es el medio ambiente.
(The *subject* of today's program is the environment)

83 El/la teniente

Un/a teniente is not a tenant. It is a lieutenant in the armed forces.

El **teniente** habló con el coronel, quien habló con el general.
(The *lieutenant* spoke to the colonel, who spoke to the general)

▶ However, if you want to say:

tenant ⇨ **el/la inquilino/a**

¿Usted es un **inquilino** o es el propietario del apartamento?
(Are you a *tenant* or the owner of your apartment?)

84 El tópico

Un tópico is a hackneyed theme, a cliché. However, in some Latin American countries **un tópico** means the same thing as in English, i.e., 'the subject of a discourse or a conversation.'

Pensar que todos los españoles son morenos, bajitos y que bailan flamenco es un **tópico**.
(It's a *cliché* to think that all Spaniards are short, dark and dance Flamenco)

▶ However, if you want to say:

topic ⇨ **el tema**

Nuestro **tema** de hoy es cómo mejorar las ventas.
(Our *topic* for today is how to improve sales)

*Learn the medical expression: **uso tópico** (for external use)

85   La trampa

Una trampa is a trap, not a tramp or homeless person.

Lo engañaron y cayó en la **trampa** fácilmente.
(They lured him into the *trap* very easily)

▶ However, if you want to say:

tramp ⇨ **el vagabundo, el indigente**

Oxford es la ciudad de Inglaterra con el mayor número de **vagabundos**.
(Oxford is the city with the largest number of *tramps* in England)

*Learn the expression: **tender una trampa** (to lay / set a trap)

86   La tuna

Very popular in Spain, **una tuna** is a group of wandering singers dressed as medieval troubadours. Its members, called **tunos**, are traditionally university students.

La **tuna** apareció debajo de mi balcón para hacerme una serenata.
(The *minstrels* appeared under my balcony to serenade me)

▶ However, if you want to say:

tuna ⇨ **el atún**

En Inglaterra es común encontrar bocadillos de **atún** con pepino sin pelar.
(It is common in England to find *tuna* sandwiches with unpeeled cucumber)

87   La vacuna

This has nothing to do with a vacuum cleaner, but instead means 'a vaccine.'

Necesitamos una **vacuna** eficaz contra el SIDA.
(We need an effective *vaccine* against AIDS)

▶ However, if you want to say:

vacuum cleaner ⇨ **la aspiradora**

Compré una **aspiradora** para limpiar la alfombra.
(I bought a *vacuum cleaner* to clean the carpet)

*Learn the verb: **vacunarse** (to get oneself vaccinated)

88   El vaso

Un vaso is simply a tumbler, goblet or glass, not a vase.

Los **vasos** de cristal duran más, pero son difíciles de reciclar.
(Crystal *glasses* last longer, but they are harder to recycle)

▶ However, if you want to say:

vase ⇨ **el jarrón, el florero**

¡Qué horror! ¡El niño me ha roto el **jarrón** chino!
(How awful! The child has broken my Chinese *vase*!)

 ## *Exercises* (Part 2)

EXERCISE 4. Fill in the blanks with the most appropriate word.

1   Un buen marinero sabe hacer muchos tipos de _____.
    a) desnudos   b) mudos   c) nudos   d) rudos
2   Antes de sentarse a la mesa hay que lavarse las manos con _____.
    a) jarrón   b) jabón   c) jamón   d) jalón
3   Como soy periodista, este año voy a asistir a una _____ de prensa
    en Dinamarca.
    a) reunión   b) lectura   c) conferencia   d) lección
4   Tengo que comprar un libro antes de que cierren _____.
    a) la biblioteca   b) la librería   c) la sastrería   d) la estantería
5   El ayuntamiento le vendió una pequeña _____ de tierra para que
    cultivara vegetales.
    a) patera   b) panera   c) parranda   d) parcela
6   Para amarrar el barco al muelle necesitamos una _____ muy gruesa.
    a) ropa   b) cuerda   c) cuenta   d) roca
7   Si estás enfermo lo mejor es tomar un tazón de _____ caliente.
    a) sola   b) sonda   c) sosa   d) sopa
8   Su familia no debe ser muy rica porque vive en _____ de la ciudad.
    a) una zona residencial b) la orilla   c) un suburbio   d) una madriguera
9   Tengo dos _____, una buena y una mala. ¿Cuál quieres oír primero?
    a) notificadas   b) noticias   c) conocidas   d) coincidas
10 El _____ de la conferencia de hoy es "La reproducción de la rana".
    a) temario   b) sujeto   c) temático   d) tema
11 Comprar un Ferrari es _____ que no me puedo permitir.
    a) una lujuria   b) una culpa   c) un lujo   d) una luxación
12 Celebraron el gordo de la lotería con _____ y alegría.
    a) jubilación   b) jubilados   c) jubileo   d) júbilo
13 Los niños llevaban _____ de papel para la noche de San Juan.
    a) farolas   b) bombillas   c) faroles   d) faros
14 Pronto se va a celebrar _____ de los puertorriqueños que viven en
    Nueva York.
    a) la parada   b) el desfiladero   c) la llamada   d) el desfile

15 Últimamente sólo como comida orgánica sin _____ ni colorantes.

   a) conservados   b) preservativos   c) conservantes   d) conservas

16 Ha llegado por correo _____ de Japón pero no sabemos para quién es.

   a) un paquete   b) una parcela   c) una letra   d) una recolección

17 Vi al médico pero se me olvidó pedirle _____ para poder comprar el medicamento.

   a) la prescripción   b) el recibo   c) la receta   d) el recibidor

18 Hay que comprar _____ de mermelada de fresa para el desayuno.

   a) una bota   b) una jarra   c) un jarro   d) un bote

19 Para hablar bien una lengua extranjera hace falta saber utilizar _____.

   a) idiomáticos   b) modismos   c) idiomas   d) modistas

20 No aguanto al _____ del piso de arriba. Siempre escucha música a las 3:00 de la mañana.

   a) teniente   b) inquisidor   c) inquilino   d) tenante

EXERCISE 5. Connect each word with its most logical pair.

   Example: alfombra + Aladín

1	complejo turístico	a.	parada
2	tópico	b.	venta al por menor
3	cuerda	c.	mala educación
4	ilusión	d.	de riñón
5	parientes	e.	cosecha
6	vacuna	f.	barco
7	aviso	g.	razón
8	reunión	h.	periódico
9	sujeto	i.	receta
10	vaso	j.	guitarra, violín
11	noticia	k.	del club de español
12	grosería	l.	atún
13	patrón	m.	contra la gripe, las paperas, el sarampión, etc.
14	cólico	n.	tener ganas de hacer algo
15	pez	o.	de agua, leche, zumo, etc.
16	médico	p.	yo, tú, él, etc.
17	autobús	q.	Cancún (México)
18	motivo	r.	¡atención!, ¡no fumar!
19	recolección	s.	la tía Enriqueta
20	minorista	t.	¡todos los hombres son iguales!

EXERCISE 6. Insert the word from the box that best corresponds to each definition

los personajes • la máscara • el recibo • la librería • el oficio • el jornal • el suceso • la jornada • el preservativo • el motivo • la ocurrencia • la trampa • los parientes • la reunión • la lectura

1 Tienda donde se venden libros. Mueble con estanterías para colocar libros.

   _____

2 Trabajo que requiere esfuerzo físico o habilidad manual y para el cual no hacen falta estudios teóricos superiores. Cualquier profesión.

   _____

3 Algún evento importante o de interés. También, un delito, accidente, o algún hecho dramático o desafortunado.

   _____

4 Conjunto de personas que se juntan para tratar un asunto concreto.

   _____

5 Cada uno de los protagonistas de una obra literaria, una película, etc.

   _____

6 Acción de leer. Aquello que se lee. Interpretación de una obra, especialmente literaria.

   _____

7 Se dice de las personas de la misma familia.

   _____

8 Objeto con el que una persona se cubre la cara para no ser reconocida o protegerse de gases tóxicos.

   _____

9 Dinero que recibe un trabajador por cada día de trabajo.

   _____

10 Duración del tiempo diario o semanal de un trabajador.

   _____

11 Idea inesperada o repentina; pensamiento o dicho original y gracioso.

   _____

12 Plan para engañar a alguien. Cualquier medio o dispositivo para cazar animales con artificio o engaño.

   _____

13 Funda de goma que se usa durante la realización del acto sexual para evitar la fecundación o la transmisión de enfermedades.

   _____

14 Aquello que hace que alguien actúe de cierta forma. Causa o razón que mueve una acción.

   _____

15 Escrito o resguardo firmado en que se declara haber recibido dinero, una mercancía u otra cosa.

   _____

EXERCISE 7. Fill in the blanks with the appropriate nouns.

Ayer tuvimos una (1)_____ (get-together) familiar después de volver del (2)_____ (parade) de San Patricio, pero el verdadero (3)_____ (reason) de la celebración fue el cumpleaños de mi hermano, que se estaba recuperando de una fuerte (4)_____ (flu). Vinieron muchos (5)_____ (relatives), algunos amigos, y hasta apareció mi (6)_____ (boss). Después de ir al médico a buscar una (7)_____ (prescription), le preparé a mi hermano una excelente (8)_____ (soup) de pollo y fideos, que me salió tan buena que no tuvo ninguna (9)_____ (gripe) al respecto. A los demás les serví un gazpacho que hice con la (10)_____ (recipe) de mi tía Marta, una ensalada de (11)_____ (tuna) que compré en la (12)_____ (grocery store) de enfrente de casa, un delicioso pan orgánico sin (13)_____ (preservatives) y un (14)_____ (jar) de mermelada de albaricoque. Mi hermanito se tomó un (15)_____ (glass) de leche, y nosotros los adultos bebimos tres enormes (16)_____ (pitchers) de cerveza. La fiesta fue un (17)_____ (success), a pesar de que mi hermano no se sentía bien del todo, y le hizo mucha (18)_____ (excitement, thrill) el regalo de (19)_____ (clothes) de deporte que le compré para el equipo de béisbol.

 Notes

4 Mastering false friends: adjectives and adverbs

Students of Spanish find these adjectives and adverbs difficult to remember. Some of them may have more than one meaning. Therefore, try to learn all the meanings of each adjective, as well as its corresponding adverb.

1   En absoluto

En absoluto does not mean 'absolutely,' but rather its opposite, 'absolutely not,' 'not at all,' or 'by no means.'

> No me gustó esa película **en absoluto**.
> (I didn't like that movie *at all*)

▶ However, if you want to say:
absolutely ⇨ **absolutamente, completamente, totalmente, realmente**

> Es **absolutamente** imposible llegar al monte Everest en coche.
> (It is *absolutely* impossible to reach Mount Everest by car)

*Learn the expressions: **¡desde luego!, ¡faltaría más!** (absolutely!)

2   Actual
Actualmente

The adjective **actual** and its corresponding adverb **actualmente** do not mean 'real' or 'in reality.' What they mean is 'now.' Both express contemporariness or connection with the present time.

> El precio **actual** del petróleo perjudica al consumidor.
> (The *current* price of oil burdens the consumer)

> **Actualmente** hay una guerra en Irak.
> (*At present* there is a war in Iraq)

▶ However, if you want to say:
actual ⇨ **real, verdadero**
actually ⇨ **realmente, en realidad**

> Aunque Mickey Mouse habla, no es una persona **real**.
> (Although Mickey Mouse speaks, he is not an *actual* person)

> **En realidad**, todos queremos tener éxito en la vida.
> (*Actually*, all of us want to be successful in life)

3   Alterado

Although **alterado** can be used to mean 'altered,' it is mostly used to refer to someone being angry, upset or very nervous.

> Después de la reunión Pedro salió muy **alterado**.
> (Pedro came out of the meeting very *upset*)

▶ However, if you want to say:
altered ⇨ **modificado**

La información fue **modificada** por la agencia de noticias.
(The information was *altered* by the news agency)

*Learn the words: **la reforma** (an alteration to a building, to a religion, to a government policy); **el arreglo** (an alteration to a garment)

4 Anciano

Anciano does not mean 'ancient,' but rather 'elderly,' or 'an elderly person.'

Ese **anciano** necesita un bastón para caminar.
(That *elderly* gentleman needs a walking stick in order to walk)

▶ However, if you want to say:
ancient ⇨ **antiguo**

Esa casa **antigua** era de mi tatarabuelo.
(That *ancient* house belonged to my great grandfather)

 Note that if the adjective **antiguo** comes before a noun, it means 'previous or former' e.g. **mi antigua escuela** (my former school). If it comes after, it means 'ancient or old' e.g., **una escuela antigua** (an old school).

*Learn the expressions: **la Roma antigua** (ancient Rome); **la Grecia antigua** (ancient Greece); **la historia antigua** (ancient history)

5 Bizarro

Bizarro is an adjective not often used, yet often confused with 'bizarre.' It simply means 'brave, gallant or high-spirited' (*valiente*).

El bombero estuvo **bizarro** durante el fuego.
(The firefighter was *brave* during the fire)

▶ However, if you want to say:
bizarre ⇨ **extraño**

Esa chica tiene un comportamiento **extraño**.
(That girl exhibits *bizarre* behavior)

6 En blanco

The word **'blanco'** means 'white,' as in **blanco y negro** (black and white). But **'en blanco'** means 'blank.'

Mi tío me dio un cheque **en blanco** por mi cumpleaños.
(My uncle gave me a *blank* check for my birthday)

▶ However, if you want to say:
to draw a blank ⇨ **quedarse en blanco**

Me quedé **en blanco** cuando la maestra me hizo una pregunta.
(When the teacher asked me a question, I *drew a blank*)

*Learn the expressions: **una cinta, un CD, un DVD virgen, etc.** (a blank tape, CD, DVD, etc.), but **una página en blanco** (a blank sheet or paper). **El blanco** also means 'a target' or 'bull's eye.'

7   Blando

Blando does not mean 'bland.' It means 'soft' or 'tender' as well as 'lenient' when referring to a person.

Esta carne está **blanda** y deliciosa.
(This meat is *tender* and delicious)

▶ However, if you want to say:
bland ⇨ **soso, insulso**

Alberto es un poco **soso** para ser presidente del club del humor.
(Alberto is a little *bland* to be the president of the comedy club)

La comida aquí es un poco **sosa**, pero no nos da tiempo de ir a otro sitio.
(Food here is a little *bland*, but there's no time to go somewhere else)

*Learn the expressions: **blando de corazón** (sentimental, tender-hearted); **ponerse blando** (to go soft)

8   Bravo

Bravo has nothing to do with 'brave.' It means 'fierce or wild,' as well as 'angry.'

Mi perro es **bravo**, pero nunca ha mordido a nadie.
(My dog is *fierce*, but he has never bitten anyone)

No te pongas **bravo** conmigo; no he hecho nada.
(Don't get *angry* with me; I haven't done anything)

▶ However, if you want to say:
brave ⇨ **valiente**

Los toreros tienen que ser **valientes** para enfrentarse al toro.
(Bullfighters have to be *brave* to confront bulls)

*Learn the expressions: **el mar bravo** (the rough sea); **¡bravo!** (well done!; after a good performance)

9   Cándido

This is not a synonym of 'honest.' It means 'innocent.'

Cleopatra no fue una mujer **cándida**.
(Cleopatra was not an *innocent* woman)

▶ However, if you want to say:
candid ⇨ **sincero**

> Soy una persona **sincera** y te estoy diciendo la verdad.
> (I am a *candid* person, and I'm telling you the truth)

10 Casual
Casualmente

The adjective **casual** and its corresponding adverb **casualmente** often do not correspond to 'casual' or 'casually' in Spanish. Both refer to the unexpected, the element of chance.

> Nos conocimos en un encuentro **casual**.
> (We met through a *chance* encounter)

> **Casualmente** llevaba un paraguas cuando empezó a llover.
> (*By chance,* I had an umbrella with me when it started to rain)

▶ However, if you want to say:
a casual meeting ⇨ **un encuentro casual / fortuito**
a casual visit ⇨ **una visita ocasional / casual**
a casual job ⇨ **un trabajo eventual**
casual clothes ⇨ **ropa informal**
casually ⇨ **de modo informal**

> Jaime viste un tanto **informal**.
> (Jaime is *casual* with the clothes he wears)

> En la fiesta todo el mundo estaba vestido **de modo informal**.
> (At the party everyone was dressed *casually*)

*Learn the expression: **ropa de sport o informal** (casual clothes)

11 Colorado

Colorado means 'tinged with red' or 'of a reddish color.'

> Marta se puso **colorada** cuando se vio en la televisión.
> (Marta *blushed / turned red* when she saw herself on TV)

▶ However, if you want to say:
colored ⇨ **de color**

> La niña llevaba un vestido **de color** azul.
> (The girl wore a blue colored dress)

*Learn the expression: **ponerse colorado** (to blush)

12   Comprensivo

This adjective does not mean 'complete' or 'comprehensive.' It means 'understanding.'

> Juan es muy **comprensivo** con las personas con problemas.
> (Juan is very *understanding* with people with problems)

▶ However, if you want to say:
comprehensive ⇨ **completo, exhaustivo**

> El médico me hizo un examen **completo**.
> (The doctor gave me a *comprehensive* check up)

13   (Estar) constipado

This word in Spanish has nothing to do with one's digestion. It means 'to be congested.'

> Siempre estoy **constipado** en el invierno.
> (I am always *congested* in winter)

▶ However, if you want to say:
constipated ⇨ **estreñido**

> Estoy **estreñido** porque me he comido una caja entera de bombones.
> (I am *constipated* because I ate a whole box of chocolates)

*Learn the expression: **coger un constipado** (to catch a cold)

14   Conveniente

Something that is **conveniente** is something that is advisable, suitable, useful or advantageous.

> Es **conveniente** que guardes cama con esa fiebre.
> (It is *advisable* for you to stay in bed with that fever)

▶ However, if you want to say:
convenient ⇨ **cómodo** (handy, close), **práctico**

> Nos resulta muy **cómodo** tener la escuela tan cerca de casa.
> (It's *convenient* having the school so near)

*Learn the expression: **sería conveniente ...** (it would be a good idea to ...)

15   Crudo

Although **el crudo** is also used in Spanish to refer to crude oil, this word does not typically mean 'crude' or 'rude,' but simply 'raw' or 'undercooked.'

> Este pollo está **crudo**. ¡Al horno!
> (This chicken is *undercooked*. Into the oven!)

► However, if you want to say:
crude ⇨ **grosero, ordinario**

> Luis es **grosero**; no tiene modales.
> (Luis is *crude*; he has no manners)

16 Culto

The adjective **culto** is used to refer to a very educated and cultured person.

> Fátima es muy **culta**: habla cinco idiomas y toca el violín.
> (Fátima is very *educated*: she speaks five languages and plays the violin)

► However, if you want to say:
a cult ⇨ **la secta, el culto (religioso)**

> Formar parte de una **secta** siempre es peligroso.
> (To belong to a *cult* is always dangerous)

*Learn the expression: **rendir culto** (to worship)

17 Destituido

Destituido is an adjective which means to be dismissed or removed from a position.

> Fue **destituido** de su cargo por desviar fondos a una cuenta suiza.
> (He was *removed from* his office for diverting funds to a Swiss bank account)

► However, if you want to say:
destitute ⇨ **indigente, necesitado**

> Nosotros siempre ayudamos a las personas **necesitadas**.
> (We always help *destitute* people)

18 Educado

The adjective **educado** is used to refer to a person who is not only educated but also considerate, well-mannered, tactful, deferential or polite.

> Hay que ser **educado** con las personas mayores.
> (One has to be *polite* with the elderly)

► However, if you want to say:
educated ⇨ **culto,**

> No es necesario asistir a la universidad para ser **culto**.
> (One does not need to go to college to be *well-educated*)

*Learn the expression: **ser un/a maleducado/a** (to be rude or ill-mannered)

19 En efectivo

If you are asked to pay **en efectivo**, you will have to pay cash.

> En esta tienda se paga **en efectivo**, no con tarjeta de crédito.
> (In this store you have to pay *cash*, not with a credit card)

▶ However, if you want to say:
in effect, in fact ⇨ **en efecto, de hecho**

> **En efecto**, no podemos salir porque está lloviendo a cántaros.
> (*In fact*, we can't go out because it's raining cats and dogs)

*Learn the expression: **hacer efectivo** (to carry out)

20 (Estar) embarazada

This word has nothing to do with being embarrassed. It means 'to be pregnant.' Consequently, it is only used in its feminine form: **embarazada**.

> Estoy **embarazada** de siete meses.
> (I'm seven months *pregnant*)

▶ However, if you want to say:
embarrassed ⇨ **(estar or sentirse) avergonzado**

> Estoy **avergonzado** por (Me da vergüenza) el mal comportamiento de Carlos.
> (I'm *embarrassed* by Carlos' bad behavior)

*In many Latin American countries the most common expression is:
embarrassed ⇨ **(dar) pena**

> *Me da pena* el comportamiento de Carlos.
> (I'm *embarrassed* by Carlos' bad behavior)

21 Emocionante
Emocionado

Emocionante means that something is exciting, thrilling or moving; whereas a person is **emocionado / a**.

> Para algunos la corrida de toros puede ser muy **emocionante**.
> (A bullfight can be very *exciting* for some people)

> María estaba muy **emocionada** con la boda de su hijo.
> (María was very *excited* with her son's wedding)

▶ However, if you want to say:
emotional ⇨ **emotivo**

> El viaje a la luna fue un evento **emotivo**.
> (The trip to the Moon was an *emotional* event)

22 Envidioso

Envidioso does not mean 'invidious.' It means 'envious' or 'jealous.'

> Hay mucha gente **envidiosa** de la buena fortuna de otros.
> (There are lots of people who are *envious* of the good fortune of others)

▶ However, if you want to say:
invidious, injurious, obnoxious ⇨ **odioso**

> Ese sinvergüenza constantemente dice cosas **odiosas**.
> (That scoundrel constantly makes *invidious* comments)

*Learn the expression: **estar en una posición ingrata** (to be in an invidious position)

23 Equivocado

Equivocado simply means 'to be mistaken,' 'to be wrong' or 'incorrect.'

> Me subí al metro **equivocado** y terminé en Yonkers.
> (I took the *wrong* subway and I ended up in Yonkers)

▶ However, if you want to say:
equivocal, ambiguous ⇨ **equívoco**

> El ministro dio un informe **equívoco** sobre los impuestos.
> (The minister gave an *equivocal* statement about taxes)

24 Escolar

The adjective **escolar** does not mean 'scholar,' but rather 'something having to do with school.'

> Durante el año **escolar** vamos a viajar a Paraguay.
> (During the *school* year we will travel to Paraguay)

▶ However, if you want to say:
scholar ⇨ **erudito**

> Carlos Fuentes es un hombre **erudito** además de ser escritor.
> (Carlos Fuentes is a *scholar* as well as a writer)

*Learn the expression: **la edad escolar** (school age)

25 Eventual

Eventualmente

Eventual is not translated as 'eventually.' Rather, it refers to something that is incidental or temporary.

> No es un trabajo fijo sino **eventual**.
> (It's not a permanent job, but a *temporary* one)

► However, if you want to say:
eventual ⇨ **final**
eventually ⇨ **finalmente, al final**

> El resultado **final** de la inversión dependerá del mercado.
> (The *eventual* result of the investment will depend on the market)

> **Al final** conseguí abrir la caja fuerte.
> (I *eventually* managed to open the safe)

26 Excitado

Excitado means 'aroused, sexually excited.' It can also be used in the sense of 'very nervous' or 'agitated.'

> ¡No tomes más café! Estás demasiado **excitado**.
> (Don't drink any more coffee! You are too *nervous*)

► However, if you want to say:
excited ⇨ **entusiasmado, emocionado**

> La niña está muy **entusiasmada** con su fiesta de cumpleaños.
> (The little girl is very *excited* about her birthday party)

27 Fastidioso

When using **fastidioso** think about something tedious. The word does not mean 'fastidious,' but rather 'causing vexation, irritation or annoyance.'

> Es un proyecto **fastidioso** porque lleva mucho tiempo.
> (The project is *annoying* because it takes a lot of time)

► However, if you want to say:
fastidious ⇨ **meticuloso**

> Juan es perfeccionista y **meticuloso** en su trabajo.
> (Juan is perfectionist and *fastidious* in his job)

28 Gracioso

Gracioso in Spanish is used to characterize someone as funny. It has nothing to do with charm or gracefulness.

> Javier es muy **gracioso**. Siempre está contando chistes.
> (Javier is very *funny*. He is always telling jokes)

► However, if you want to say:
gracious ⇨ **gentil, cortés**

Tomar el té es una manera **gentil** de hacer negocios.
(Tea drinking is a *gracious* way to do business)

29   Grande

While sharing a common etymology, **grande** does not mean 'grand.' It means 'big,' 'large' or it can also mean 'tall.'

La Casa Blanca es una casa muy **grande**.
(The White House is a very *big* house)

▶ However, if you want to say:
grand ⇨ **grandioso, imponente, ambicioso** (plan, scheme)

Además de ser grande, la Casa Blanca es **imponente**.
(Besides being big, the White House is also *grand*)

Note that if the adjective **grande** is placed before a noun, it normally means 'great': **Juan es una gran persona** (Juan is a great person); and if it is placed after, it means 'big': **Juan es una persona grande** (Juan is a big person). Also note that the short form **gran** is used when the adjective is placed before both masculine and feminine nouns: **Oxford es una gran universidad** (Oxford is a great university).

*Learn the expressions: **a gran escala** (on a grand scale); **los grandes almacenes** (a department store); **un piano de cola** (a grand piano); **pasarlo en grande** (to have a great time)

30   Grato

Grato is used to characterize something as 'pleasant or enjoyable,' and it is used in formal contexts.

Nos es **grato** comunicarle que ha ganado el Premio Planeta.
(We are *pleased* to inform you that you have been awarded the Planeta prize)

▶ However, if you want to say:
great ⇨ **genial, gran / grande, excelente**

Es un **gran** artista y un tipo **excelente**.
(He is a *great* artist and a *great* guy)

Note the expression: 'that's great!' changes depending on where you are. In Spain people say **¡qué bien!**, **¡genial!**, **¡estupendo!** or **¡guay!**; in most of Latin America **¡chévere!** is used; and in Mexico it is: **¡qué padre!**, **padre** or **padrísimo**.

*Learn the expression: **Gran Bretaña** (Great Britain); **los Grandes Lagos** (the Great Lakes); **el área metropolitana de Londres** (Greater London); **recibir una grata impresión** (to get a pleasing impression); **un montón de** or **muchísimo/a** (a great deal of).

31 Grueso

Grueso means 'thick' or 'stout' for a person.

> Estás un poco **grueso**; deberías comer menos y hacer más ejercicio.
> (You are *stout*, you should eat less and exercise more)

▶ However, if you want to say:
gross ⇨ **asqueroso**

> La comida en este restaurante me parece **asquerosa**.
> (I find the food in this restaurant *gross*)

*Learn the expression: **el producto interior bruto** (gross domestic product)

32 Intoxicado

Intoxicado is not used in Spanish to mean 'drunk,' but simply to refer to someone as 'poisoned.'

> Descubrieron que el hombre estaba **intoxicado** por arsénico.
> (They discovered that the man was *poisoned* with arsenic)

▶ However, if you want to say:
intoxicated ⇨ **ebrio, en estado de embriaguez, borracho**

> El conductor estaba **ebrio** cuando chocó contra el árbol.
> (The driver was *intoxicated* when he collided with a tree)

33 Largo

Largo does not mean 'large.' It means 'long,' both in terms of space and time.

> El examen duró un **largo** rato.
> (The exam lasted a *long* time)

> El conflicto puede ir para **largo**.
> (The conflict may last a *long* time)

▶ However, if you want to say:
large ⇨ **grande, extenso, amplio**

> El Golden Gate es un puente muy largo y muy **grande**.
> (The Golden Gate is a very long bridge, and a very *large* one)

·*Learn the expressions: **¡largo de aquí!** (clear out!, get out of here!); **pasar de largo** (to pass by someone without taking note); **a lo largo y a lo ancho de** (across, throughout); **a lo largo del camino** (along the way)

34 Mayor

The adjective **mayor** can be translated as 'older, larger, bigger,' depending on the context.

> María es **mayor** que su hermano, pero él es más alto.
> (María is *older* than her brother, but he is taller)

▶ However, if you want to say:
mayor ⇨ **el alcalde / la alcaldesa**

> El **alcalde** de Nueva York se presenta para presidente.
> (The *mayor* of New York is running for president)

*Learn the expressions: **cuando sea mayor** (when I grow up); **ser mayor de edad** (to be an adult); **el hermano mayor** (eldest brother); **las personas mayores** (the elderly); **vender al por mayor** (to sell wholesale)

35 Peculiar

In Spanish the adjective **peculiar** has retained its etymological use. It is used to mean 'characteristic or distinctive,' not 'strange or weird.'

> Miguel tiene una manera **peculiar** de bailar.
> (Miguel has a *distinctive* way of dancing)

▶ However, if you want to say:
peculiar ⇨ **extraño, raro**

> Me siento un poco **raro**.
> (I am feeling somewhat *peculiar*)

36 Raro

Although **raro** can also be used to mean 'rare,' most commonly it refers to something that is strange, unusual or odd.

> ¿No es un poco **raro** que no haya nadie en el cine?
> (Isn't it *odd* that there is no one in the cinema?)

▶ However, if you want to say:
rare ⇨ **poco común, poco frecuente**

> El kotuku es un pájaro **poco común** en Nueva Zelanda.
> (One *rarely* sees the kotuku bird in New Zealand)

*Learn the expression: **¡qué raro!** (how peculiar!); **sentirse raro** (to feel unwell)

37   Relativo

This word has nothing to do with relatives or family. It refers to something that is relative in the sense of 'not being absolute.'

> La riqueza es algo **relativo**, depende más de saber contentarse que del dinero.
> (Wealth is something *relative*, it depends more on mindset than on money)

▶ However, if you want to say:
relative ⇨ **pariente**

> Aunque nos parecemos, Penélope Cruz y yo no somos **parientes**.
> (Although there is a resemblance, Penélope Cruz and I are not *relatives*)

*Learn the expression: **en lo relativo a …** (regarding …)

38   Relevante

Relevante in Spanish refers to something important, or of significant worth or consequence.

> El abogado defensor presentó datos **relevantes** a la inocencia de su cliente.
> (The defense attorney presented *crucial* data in establishing his client's innocence)

▶ However, if you want to say:
relevant ⇨ **pertinente, adecuado, relacionado con**

> Para la tesis, el estudiante tendrá que elegir un tema **pertinente**.
> (For the thesis, the student will have to select a *relevant* topic)

39   Sano

This adjective means 'healthy,' or 'in good health.' It has nothing to do with being sane.

> Es **sano** comer frutas y vegetales diariamente.
> (It's *healthy* to eat fruit and vegetables every day)

▶ However, if you want to say:
sane ⇨ **cuerdo**

> Al final del libro, Don Quijote comienza a estar **cuerdo**.
> (At the end of the novel, Don Quixote starts to become *sane*)

*Learn the expressions: **estar sano y salvo** (to be safe and sound); **hacer vida sana** (to have a healthy lifestyle)

40 Sensible

Una persona sensible experiences feelings and sensations deeply. Such a person is easily impressed or moved, and has feelings that are easily hurt.

> Tengo los dientes muy **sensibles** al frío.
> (My teeth are very *sensitive* to the cold)

▶ However, if you want to say:
sensible ⇨ **sensato, prudente**

> Ella es muy **sensata** y sabe lo que quiere.
> (She is very *sensible* and knows what she wants)

*Learn the expressions: **lo sensato ...**, **lo que tiene sentido hacer ...** (the sensible thing to do ...); **un documento confidencial** (a sensitive document)

41 Terrorífico

This adjective is used to describe terror or apprehension. It does not mean 'terrific.'

> Las novelas de Poe se desarrollan en un ambiente **terrorífico**.
> (Poe's novels take place in a *terrifying* setting)

▶ However, if you want to say:
terrific ⇨ **fenomenal, genial, estupendo**

> Es una idea **fenomenal** ir mañana a la playa.
> (It's a *terrific* idea to go to the beach tomorrow)

42 Último
Últimamente

The adjective **último** and its corresponding adverb **últimamente** do not mean 'ultimate' or 'ultimately.' Both indicate that something is at the end, lowest in rank, or most recent.

> ¿Ya viste la **última** moda para este verano?
> (Did you see the *latest* fashion for this summer?)

> **Últimamente** la economía chilena ha crecido mucho.
> (*Lately* the Chilean economy has grown a lot)

▶ However, if you want to say:
ultimate ⇨ **final, principal, fundamental**
ultimately ⇨ **al final, finalmente, en última instancia**

> Nuestra meta **final** en el país es establecer una democracia.
> (Our *ultimate* goal in the country is to establish a democracy)

Finalmente Estados Unidos tendrá que firmar el tratado de Kioto.
(*Ultimately* the United States will have to sign the Kyoto treaty)

*Learn the expressions: **ir a la última** (to wear the latest fashion); **a últimos de mes** (at the end of the month); **estar en las últimas** (to be on one's deathbed or to be down to one's last penny)

43 Vicioso

Vicioso does not mean 'aggressive or hostile,' but rather 'depraved or dissolute.'

Un comportamiento **vicioso** siempre es incorrecto.
(*Depraved* behavior is always unacceptable)

► However, if you want to say:
vicious ⇨ **fiero, agresivo**

Los perros dóberman son muy **fieros** y peligrosos.
(Dobermans are *vicious* and dangerous dogs)

*Learn the expression: **tener muy mal genio** (vicious temper)

 ## Exercises

EXERCISE 1. Fill in the blanks with the most appropriate word.

1 Ella siempre piensa antes de actuar; la verdad es que es muy _____.
   a) sencilla b) sensata c) sensible d) semilla
2 Tengo que hacer un análisis _____ de los detalles que aparecen en esta novela.
   a) comprensible b) comprensivo c) completo d) comprendido
3 Para estar _____ hay que hacer ejercicio todos los días.
   a) santo b) sano c) saldo d) salto
4 Durante el año _____ vamos a ir a Perú con el club de español.
   a) escuela b) escolarizar c) escollar d) escolar
5 El profesor es muy _____, y entenderá por qué llegaste tarde.
   a) comprensivo b) comprendido c) conocido d) comprometido
6 ¿Es usted la _____ persona de la cola?
   a) final b) terminal c) finita d) última
7 La carne está _____. ¿Me podría traer otro trozo más hecho?
   a) creída b) cruda c) culta d) colorada
8 Eres la más inteligente de la clase. Tus ideas siempre son _____.
   a) terroríficas b) geniales c) terribles d) raras
9 María está muy _____ porque por fin vamos a ir a la piscina.
   a) fastidiada b) entusiasmada c) excitada d) embarazada

10 El cable no es muy _____; habrá que comprar otro.

   a) grande   b) grato   c) largo   d) gran

11 No tienes razón. Estás totalmente _____.

   a) equivocando   b) equívoco   c) constipado   d) equivocado

12 Como no había estudiado, dejó todas las respuestas del examen _____.

   a) de blanco   b) el blanco   c) blanco   d) en blanco

13 Andrés es muy _____. Siempre está contando chistes.

   a) gentil   b) gracioso   c) emotivo   d) bizarro

14 En vez de un 'sí' o un 'no,' me dio una respuesta un tanto _____.

   a) modificada   b) equívoca   c) indigente   d) ebria

15 Cuando la profesora me preguntó, me puse _____ como un tomate.

   a) colocado   b) colorado   c) de color   d) corolario

16 Creo que ha discutido con el jefe, porque ha salido del despacho bastante _____.

   a) alterado   b) sano   c) alternado   d) cuerdo

17 Vivir en el centro de la ciudad siempre es más _____ que vivir en las afueras.

   a) cómodo   b) relevante   c) sensato   d) pertinente

18 La policía le paró por conducir _____ y no llevar carnet de conducir.

   a) intoxicado   b) ebrio   c) embelesado   d) envenenado

19 Los alumnos de historia se quedaron _____ después de ver la Mezquita de Córdoba.

   a) emocionados   b) apabullados   c) emotivos   d) excitados

20 La vida no siempre es _____ de rosa, por eso hay que valorar las cosas positivas.

   a) en color   b) de olor   c) a color   d) de color

21 En la Grecia _____ se organizaron los primeros Juegos Olímpicos.

   a) anciana   b) antepasada   c) vieja   d) antigua

22 A Pepe le encantan las galletas con kétchup, pero a mí me parece algo _____.

   a) gracioso   b) asqueroso   c) grueso   d) grasoso

EXERCISE 2. Connect each word with the ones that have the opposite meaning.

Example: culto ≠ inculto, ignorante

1	valiente	a.	blando, mullido
2	informal	b.	insensato, imprudente
3	completo	c.	multimillonario, opulento
4	educado	d.	delgado, fino
5	entusiasmado	e.	con un cheque, con tarjeta de crédito
6	raro	f.	cocido, hecho
7	grande	g.	maleducado, grosero
8	fastidioso	h.	aburrido, monótono
9	largo	i.	menor, inferior
10	cuerdo	j.	inconveniente, poco útil
11	fiero	k.	cobarde, gallina
12	sensato	l.	formal, serio
13	crudo	m.	incompleto, sin terminar
14	en efectivo	n.	pequeño, minúsculo
15	sano	o.	loco, lunático
16	último	p.	agradable, ameno
17	mayor	q.	enfermo, indispuesto
18	indigente	r.	corto, breve
19	conveniente	s.	normal, común
20	duro	t.	primero, inicial
21	grueso	u.	manso, tranquilo

EXERCISE 3. For each underlined word or phrase on the left, choose the word on the right with the closest meaning, and rewrite the entire expression with the appropriate agreement.

Example: los dientes + sensible (los dientes sensibles)

1	Estar muy nervioso	a.	indigente _____
2	Una dieta equilibrada	b.	graciosa _____
3	Un niño con buen comportamiento	c.	fastidioso _____
4	Tener un trabajo temporal	d.	sano _____
5	De ninguna manera	e.	pregunta _____
6	Un encuentro inesperado	f.	colorado _____
7	Pagar en metálico	g.	en absoluto _____
8	Estar en estado	h.	peculiar _____
9	Juan tiene la gripe	i.	relevante _____
10	Una cuestión que no es absoluta	j.	blando _____
11	Un hermano antipático	k.	excitado _____

12　De ahora

13　Un estudiante que sabe mucho

14　Un tipo muy característico

15　Una última duda

16　Una hermana que es la primera hija

17　Ponerse rojo como un pimiento

18　Una historia muy divertida

19　Una persona necesitada

20　Un hecho importante

21　Una almohada mullida

l.　estar constipado _____

m.　eventual _____

n.　actual _____

o.　en efectivo _____

p.　educado _____

q.　relativo _____

r.　mayor _____

s.　culto _____

t.　casual _____

u.　embarazada _____

EXERCISE 4, Complete the following story with words that you have learned in this chapter.

Querida Julia:

¡No sabía que tus (1)_____ (parents) eran tan (2)_____ (polite)! Fue un (3)_____ (real) placer para mí pasar un rato con ellos. Hablamos de mil cosas: de historia (4)_____ (ancient), de arte, y de todo lo (5)_____ (relevant) con la vida moderna. Además de ser tan (6)_____ (cultured), tu madre es muy (7)_____ (sensitive) y (8)_____ (understanding). Les conté que me sentía un tanto desesperada y que había estado muy (9)_____ (upset) porque había sido (10)_____ (fired) de mi trabajo por estar (11)_____ (pregnant) porque mi jefa es una muy (12)_____ (envious), y tampoco se puede decir que sea una persona demasiado (13)_____ (sane).

Tu madre me animó mucho; me dijo cosas (14)_____ (funny) para hacerme reír, y tu padre me hizo comprender que no debía preocuparme (15)_____ (at all). Que lo (16)_____ (advisable) era cuidar del bebé, y que me podían ayudar porque, (17)_____ (by chance), necesitaban a alguien como yo para trabajar en su galería de arte. Cuando oí esto, me quedé boquiabierta. No sabía si ponerme (18)_____ (blushed) o sentirme (19)_____ (embarrassed), o besarle los pies a estas dos (20)_____ (great) personas, quienes (21)_____ (in fact) me van a ayudar a salir de un gran apuro. ¡Gracias Julia por animarme a que hablara con ellos!

Cariñosamente,

Tu amiga Marina

5 Verb pairs and other misused words

This chapter discusses various Spanish verbs and other words that appear similar but have different meanings. In the second part of the chapter we focus on verbs that are differentiated by prefixes that have a direct impact on their meaning.

One verb in English – two verbs in Spanish

Ser and estar (to be)

Confusion often arises with the use of the Spanish verbs 'ser' and 'estar,' as in English both are translated as the verb 'to be.' Traditionally, there has been an attempt to explain the difference between these two verbs by speaking about 'permanent' vs. 'temporary' states or conditions. However, this is not always the case and can be misleading.

Rather, when trying to identify which verb you have to use, think of what you are expressing or communicating. Generally speaking, **ser** is used to describe, define or characterize a person, thing or place. It can be used to refer to occupations or professions, to identify nationality or origin, or to tell the time or date.

By contrast, **estar** is used to describe physical, mental or emotional states, as well as expressing location, and describing an ongoing action through the present progressive tense.

The uses of these verbs are not limited to these contexts, and there are also many idiomatic expressions and special cases that mean different things depending on whether 'ser' or 'estar' is used. For example, 'ser listo,' means 'to be clever' whereas 'estar listo' means 'to be ready.'

You will also see that in some instances both 'ser' and 'estar' can be used to speak about prices, dates, professions, etc., which is typically the domain of 'ser.' Therefore, pay close attention to the shades of meaning that can be expressed in these cases with 'estar.' For example, we say: 'soy profesor' which identifies a profession, but '(ahora) estoy de profesor,' which means that for the time being 'I am working as a teacher.'

As a preliminary step, the following mnemonic device will help you to recognize different concepts that 'ser' and 'estar' can express.

> **Mnemonic device**
> It is important to focus on the communicative functions of **ser** and **estar** when trying to choose which one to use.
>
> | | ser | | estar |
> |---|---|---|---|
> | **D** | Description | **H** | Health |
> | | Juan es alto, delgado guapo e inteligente. | | Juan está cansado y resfriado. |
> | **O** | Occupation | **E** | Emotions |
> | | Juan es policía. | | Juan está nervioso y preocupado. |
> | **N** | Nationality | **L** | Location |
> | | Juan es cubano. | | Juan está en Zaragoza. |
> | **T** | Time | **P** | Present progressive |
> | | Son las dos en punto. Es la una y cuarto. | | Juan está comiendo. |

Note that while 'estar' is used to indicate location, e.g., 'estoy en casa' (I am at home), there is one exception to this rule, and that is when talking about an event taking place somewhere. In that case 'ser' is used since it means to 'take place' or 'to be held,' e.g., 'La conferencia es en la universidad' (The lecture is taking place at the university).

Below is an overview of the most common uses of 'ser' and 'estar' with examples.

SER

1 Identity:

Hola. Soy Juan, el hermano de Miguel. Y tú, ¿quién eres?
(Hello. I am Juan, Miguel's brother. And who are you?)

- ¿Quién es? - Soy yo, Ana.
(Who is it? It is me, Ana)

2 Occupation:

Soy profesora.
(I am a teacher)

3 Nationality, origin, religion, ideology:

Juan y Felipe son cubanos / de Cuba.
(Juan and Felipe are Cuban / from Cuba)

En España la mayor parte de la población es católica.
(In Spain, the majority of the population is Catholic)

Sus artículos periodísticos son de derecha, pero sus novelas son más bien de izquierda.
(His press articles are right-wing, but his novels are rather left-wing)

4 Material:

Tienes un bolso precioso. Es de piel, ¿verdad?
(Your bag is very nice. It is leather, isn't it?)

5 Possession, affiliation, authorship:

¿Es tuyo ese coche? No, ese coche es de mi hermano. El mío está en el garaje.
(Is that car yours? No, that car is my brother's. Mine is in the garage)

Antes era del Barça, pero ahora soy del Real Madrid.
(I used to support Barça, but now I support Real Madrid)

Ese cuadro es de Goya.
(That painting is a Goya)

6 Purpose, recipient:

¿Son para mí estas flores? ¡Qué detalle! Muchísimas gracias.
(Are these flowers for me? How sweet! Many thanks)

Las lenguas son para aprender y no para dividir a la gente.
(Languages are to be learned and not to divide people)

7 To cost:

¿A cómo es el kilo de cerezas?
(How much is a kilo of cherries?)

 'Estar' is also possible but the meaning changes slightly:

¿A cómo está el kilo de cerezas?
(How much is a kilo of cherries now?)

8 To mean 'to take place,' 'to be held,' i.e., *suceder*, *acontecer*, *tener lugar*, *celebrarse*:

¿Dónde es el concierto? Es en el pabellón de deportes.
(Where is the concert? It is at the sports centre)

9 In mathematical operations:

Dos y dos son cuatro.
(Two plus two is four)

Diez menos dos son ocho.
(Ten minus two is eight)

Tres por tres son nueve.
(Three times three is nine)

Doce entre cuatro son tres.
(Twelve divided by four is three)

10   Passive voice (passive of action):

Esta iglesia fue construida en el siglo XII.
(This church was built in the 12th century)

Cuando explotó la bomba, el presidente fue protegido por los guardaespaldas.
(When the bomb exploded, the president was protected by the bodyguards)

11   Impersonal verb:

Time

Son las cuatro.
(It is four o'clock)

Day of the week, date, season, part of the day, expression of time, etc.

Hoy es martes, 2 de abril.
(Today is Tuesday, April 2nd)

Es primavera.
(It is spring)

Es de día / de noche.
(It is daytime / night time)

Es temprano / tarde.
(It is early / late)

12   Expressions with ser:

Sea como sea = no matter what

Tengo que aprobar el examen de conducir sea como sea.
(I have to pass the driving test no matter what)

Érase una vez = Once upon a time

Érase una vez una princesa que vivía en un castillo…
(Once upon a time, there was a princess who lived in a castle…)

Es que … = the thing is that … it's just that …

– Te he estado llamando al móvil toda la mañana.
– Es que se me olvidó encenderlo después de la reunión.

(I have been calling your cell phone all morning)
(The thing is, I forgot to switch it on after the meeting)

O sea = that is to say, in other words, so

O sea, hace un mes más o menos.

(That is to say, a month ago more or less)

O sea que no te interesa.

(In other words, you are not interested)

O sea que al final no fuiste.

(So you didn't go in the end)

No ser para menos = with good reason

El año 2005 fue tachado de nefasto. No fue para menos. Todas las cosechas se echaron a perder.

(2005 was considered disastrous. And with good reason. All the crops were completely destroyed)

No vaya a ser que + subjunctive = just in case

Voy a llevarme un paraguas. No vaya a ser que se ponga a llover.

(I am going to take an umbrella just in case it starts raining)

¿Qué es de ...? = is used to enquire about the state of a person or something

¿Qué es de Pedro? Hace mucho tiempo que no lo veo.

(How is Pedro? I have not seen him for a while)

Ser de + infinitive (esperar, etc) = one would expect, it is expected that ...

Con unos carnavales tan populares, es de esperar que el despliegue policial se intensifique.

(With the carnival being so popular, it is to be expected that the police presence will increase)

ESTAR

1 **Physical location of something or someone:**

– ¿Dónde estás?

– Estoy en la universidad.

(Where are you?)

(I am at the university)

2 **Estar de + noun (temporary occupation):**

– ¿A qué se dedica tu hermano mayor?

– Ahora mismo está de profesor en una academia de Alicante.

(What does your oldest brother do?)

(At the moment he is a teacher at a language school in Alicante)

3   With adjectives that indicate states of mind: *triste, preocupado, contento, enfadado, cansado, harto, disgustado, etc.*

SER is used with adjectives that define the personality of a subject: *serio, inteligente, tímido, callado, sociable, abierto, cariñoso, trabajador, atento, cordial, agradable, maleducado, etc.* However, when there is a contrast with what is normally the case, ESTAR is used:

> Alejandro es un tipo muy raro.
> (Alejandro is very strange guy)

> Alejandro está muy raro.
> (Alejandro is very strange lately; he's been acting in a very strange way)

> Normalmente Pedro es una persona muy callada, pero hoy está muy hablador.
> (Normally Pedro is a very quiet person, but today he is very talkative)

4   With some adverbs (*bien, mal, etc.*) or adverb phrases:

> Tu examen está muy bien. ¡Enhorabuena!
> (Your exam paper is very good. Congratulations!)

5   With the following adjectives/participles: *abierto, cerrado, lleno, vacío, desnudo, vestido, acostumbrado (a), seguro (de), interesado (en), orgulloso (de), convencido (de), harto (de), capacitado (para), solo, acompañado, vivo, muerto, etc.*

> Estoy harta de este trabajo.
> (I am fed up with this job)

> La puerta está abierta.
> (The door is open)

> La botella está vacía.
> (The bottle is empty)

6   With adjectives that express sensory experiences:

> La sopa estaba fría y la carne estaba saladísima.
> (The soup was cold and the meat was very salty)

7   To indicate partial quantities: (while 'ser' is used to indicate total quantities):

> En esta clase somos 20 alumnos, pero hoy sólo estamos 15.
> (We are/There are 20 students in this group, but today there are only 15 of us)

8   Estar + soltero, casado, separado, divorciado, viudo (although 'ser' can also be used with these adjectives).

9 **Date:**
  - ¿A qué día estamos hoy?
  (What day is it today?)

  - Hoy estamos a martes 2 de abril.
  (Today is Tuesday, April 2nd)

 Also possible with 'ser:'
  ¿Qué día es hoy?
  (What day is it today?)

10 **Temperature:**
  – ¿A cuántos grados estamos?
  – Estamos a 34 grados.

  (How many degrees is it today?)
  (It's 34 degrees)

11 **Passive voice (passive of state):**
  La luz está encendida.
  (The light is turned on)

  Cuando explotó la bomba, el presidente estaba protegido por los
  guardaespaldas.
  (When the bomb exploded, the president was already protected by the
  bodyguards)

12 **Gerund (to form the progressive tense)**
  Estoy leyendo un libro.
  (I am reading a book)

Mnemonic device
Remember the following rhyme: **how you feel** and **where you are** always
take the verb **estar**!

13 **Expressions with estar:**
¿Estamos? (or ¿Estáis?, ¿Estás?, ¿Están?, etc.) = Do you understand? All
right?
  A las nueve en casa, ¿estamos?
  (You must be home by nine. All right?)

Estar al + infinitve = to be about to

Miguel está al llegar / al caer.

(Miguel is about to arrive)

Estar con + noun / pronoun = to be on somebody's side, to agree with somebody, to support somebody

Muchos me dijeron que estaban conmigo, pero que preferían no votar.

(Many told me that they supported me, but that they would rather not vote)

Estar de + noun = to be occupied with something or doing something

Estar de viaje = to be away on a trip

Estar de vacaciones = to be on holiday

Estar de compras = to be shopping

Estar de broma = to be joking

Estar de charla = to be talking / chatting

Estar para + infinitive = to be about to

Estoy para salir.

(I am about to leave)

No estar para + noun/infinitive = not to be in the mood or situation to do something

No estoy para bromas/chistes

(I am not in the mood for jokes)

Me gustaría comprarme un coche, pero ahora mismo no estoy ni para comprarme una bicicleta.

(I would like to buy a car, but right now I cannot even afford to buy a bicycle)

Estar que + clause = to feel as if

Estoy que no me tengo en pie / que me caigo de sueño = I am exhausted, very tired, sleepy

Estoy que me muero de hambre = I am starving

Estoy que salto de alegría = I am ecstatic

Estoy que ardo / muerdo / trino = I am in a very bad mood

Estoy que me muero de nervios = I am extremely nervous

Estoy en cama. Estoy que me muero = I am in bed. I feel awful

Estos días estoy que no paro = Over the last few days I have not stopped / I have been extremely busy.

Many adjectives change their meaning depending on whether they are used with 'ser' or 'estar.'

Ser (emphasizes the notion of description or classification)	Estar (emphasizes the notion of state)
abierto (social) Miguel es un chico muy abierto. Habla con todo el mundo. (Miguel is a very open boy. He talks to everyone)	**abierto** (open) ¿Estará abierto el kiosco de la esquina a estas horas? (Will the news kiosk on the corner be open at this time of day?)
aburrido (boring) El profesor de matemáticas es tan aburrido que dos de los estudiantes se quedaron dormidos en su clase. (The math teacher is so boring that two of the students fell asleep in his class)	**aburrido** (bored) Estoy aburridísimo. No sé qué hacer. (I am very bored. I do not know what to do)
alto (tall, high) **bajo** (short) Mi hermano es muy alto, y yo soy más bajo que él. (My brother is very tall, and I am shorter than him)	**alto** (high; volume of a TV, radio, etc.). **Estar alto** also means "to be tall" in the sense of "having grown up a lot" since the last time we saw that person (normally a child) **bajo** (low; volume of a TV, radio, etc.) La tele está muy alta. ¡Bájala un poco, por favor! (The TV is very loud. Turn it down a bit, please!)
atento (attentive; considerately attending to the comfort or wishes of others) Nuestro nuevo profesor es un hombre muy atento y educado. (Our new teacher is a very attentive and polite man)	**atento** (attentive; paying close attention) El oído humano no puede estar atento a más de una conversación. (Human hearing cannot pay attention to more than one conversation at the same time)
bueno (good) Sé bueno y haz los deberes. (Be good and do the homework) Esta novela es muy buena. Tienes que leerla. (This novel is very good. You must read it)	**bueno** (tasty; appetizing; attractive) La sopa está muy buena. ¿La has hecho tú? (The soup is very good. Did you make it?) Ricky Martin baila muy bien ¡y está muy bueno! (Ricky Martin dances very well and is very hot!)

Ser (emphasizes the notion of description or classification)	Estar (emphasizes the notion of state)
cansado (tiring) Fue un viaje muy cansado. (It was a very tiring journey)	**cansado** (tired) Estoy muy cansado y tengo hambre. (I am very tired and I am hungry)
católico (Catholic) Creo que ella es católica. (I think she is Catholic)	**no estar católico** (unwell) (old-fashioned) Hoy no estoy muy católico. (I am feeling unwell today)
decidido (resolute) Es muy decidido, nunca tiene miedo. (He is very resolute, he's never afraid)	**decidido** (decided) Está decidido. Nos casaremos el viernes. (It's decided. We'll get married on Friday)
despierto (clever, bright) Emilio es un chico muy despierto. (Emilio is a very bright boy)	**despierto** (awake) ¿Estás despierto? (Are you awake?)
interesado (self-interested) – Eugenia sale con un directivo de empresa que tiene mucho dinero. – ¿Y sale con él por eso? – No. Eugenia no es nada interesada. (Eugenia is dating a very wealthy company director. Is she dating him because of that? No. Eugenia is not a person that is interested in self-gain)	**interesado (en / por)** (interested) La empresa gallega está interesada en la apertura de nuevos mercados. (The Galician company is interested in opening new markets)
listo (clever) Mi sobrino es muy listo. Sabe multiplicar y dividir mucho mejor que su hermano mayor. (My nephew is very clever. He knows how to multiply and divide much better than his older brother)	**listo** (ready) ¿Estás lista? Tenemos que irnos dentro de cinco minutos. (Are you ready? We must leave in five minutes)

Ser (emphasizes the notion of description or classification)	**Estar** (emphasizes the notion of state)
malo (bad) Es una película malísima. (It is a very bad film) ¡Qué malo eres! (You are so bad!)	**malo** (ill, sick) ¿Estás malo? (Are you ill?)
molesto (irritating, annoying; uncomfortable; awkward) Se produjo un silencio molesto. (There was an awkward silence)	**molesto** (upset, angry) Estaba molesta porque pensaba que ese cargo debía haber sido para ella. (She was upset because she thought that the job should have been given to her)
orgulloso (proud) (pejorative) Es demasiado orgulloso y poco humilde. (He is too proud and not very humble)	**orgulloso** (proud of something / someone) Está muy orgulloso de su hermana mayor. (He is very proud of his older sister)
verde (green; dirty, obscene) No le escuches, es un viejo verde. (Don't listen to him, he is a dirty old man)	**verde** (unripe) Esta pera está verde, pero ésa está madura. (This pear is unripe, but that one is ripe)
vivo (clever, sharp) Mi marido es muy vivo y puso todo nuestro dinero a nombre de nuestras hijas. (My husband is very sharp and put all our money in our daughters' names)	**vivo** (alive) Estoy viva y coleando. (I am alive and kicking)

Mnemonic device

Remember the following sentence: "Cuando un plátano **es verde**, significa que **está verde**" (When a banana is green it means that it is not ripe).

Exercises

EXERCISE 1. Choose the correct form of each verb.

1   El concierto (es / está) en la catedral que (es / está) en la Plaza Mayor.

2   ¿(Serás / Estarás) listo a las 10:00? Sí, pero no (soy / estoy) nada despierto después de la siesta de dos horas que he dormido.

3   La botella (es / está) de cristal y (es / está) bastante antigua, pero parece que (es / está) completamente vacía.

4   No (es / está) posible. (Es / Está) invierno y (somos / estamos) a 18 grados centígrados.

5   ¿Sabes de quién (es / está) ese coche? –No lo sé, pero aquellos policías (son / están) a punto de ponerle una multa.

6   Creo que Jorge no (es / está) cubano, sino dominicano; pero ahora no (es / está) de peluquero, sino de cocinero.

7   Este sobre no (es / está) para mí, pero (es / está) un poco roto.

8   Me parece que Pedro (es / está) un poco aburrido. –¡Qué va! Lo que le pasa (es / está) que (es / está) un poco cansado y también que (es / está) malo.

9   Este tomate (es / está) rojo, pero por el sabor diría que no (es / está) nada maduro.

10 ¿A qué día (somos / estamos) hoy? –Hoy (es / está) jueves, pero parece como si (fuera / estuviera) lunes.

11 Hoy no he ido a la universidad porque (soy / estoy) enfermo y (he sido / he estado) todo el día en la cama.

12 ¿(Eres / Estás) del Madrid o del Barcelona? No (soy / estoy) de ninguno de los dos equipos sino del Betis.

EXERCISE 2. Choose the correct form of the verb in the following story.

"Trabajar o no trabajar: ésa es la cuestión"

Margarita, que (es / está) una persona muy viva, (es / está) mi cuñada. El domingo (fui / estuve) en su casa y me dijo que últimamente (era / estaba) trabajando demasiado, que (era / estaba) muy cansada, y que por lo tanto le gustaría (ser / estar) sin trabajar y sin hacer nada durante un tiempo para (ser / estar) un poco más libre y poder disfrutar de la vida. En ese momento pensé que mi amiga (era / estaba) en lo cierto ya que, después de todo, la vida no (es / está) sólo trabajo. Yo le dije que (era / estaba) de acuerdo, que eso (es / está) verdad, y que (es / está) bueno no hacer nada durante un tiempo para darse cuenta de lo que uno realmente quiere hacer. Pues hoy (es / está) martes, (eran / estaban) las 5:30 de la mañana y Margarita ya me (era / estaba) llamando para decirme que ahora (es / está) aburrida de no trabajar. Yo (era / estaba) medio dormida, no (era / estaba) para bromas a esas horas y colgué y desconecté el teléfono para que no llamara más. Así (es / está) la vida. Unos se conforman con lo que (son / están) y otros no (son / están) nunca satisfechos con lo que tienen.

EXERCISE 3. Create sentences using **ser** or **estar** with one item from each column. Please note that in two cases you can use either **ser** and **estar**.

1	El profesor de matemáticas		mía.
2	La puerta		vacío.
3	Esta bicicleta		en el Círculo de Bellas Artes.
4	Aquel señor		de piel.
5	Este niño		enferma.
6	El tren		abierta.
7	El bacalao		lunes.
8	Mi abuela	**es / está**	salado.
9	Su hermana		muy ligero.
10	Mi móvil		viuda.
11	Su bolso		abogado.
12	La conferencia		muy travieso.
13	Hoy		encima de la mesa.
14	El libro		encendida.
15	La televisión		muy aburrido.

EXERCISE 4. In all of the following sentences except one, **ser** / **estar** has been used incorrectly. Correct the mistakes and find the one sentence that is completely accurate. Pay close attention to the meaning of each sentence.

1   Tu habitación es muy desordenada. Por favor, ordénala ahora mismo.

   _____

2   Soy abogado de profesión, pero ahora mismo soy de camarero en una cafetería.

   _____

3   El examen de español está en el aula principal. Procura no llegar tarde.

   _____

4   No te preocupes por él. Es acostumbrado a tratar con gente difícil.

   _____

5   ¿Te ha tocado la lotería? Eres de broma, ¿no?

   _____

6   Voy a estudiar bien el subjuntivo. No vaya a ser que sea en el examen.

   _____

7   ¿Están para mí estas flores? ¡Qué sorpresa!

   _____

8   Soy que me muero de hambre. ¿Te apetece que vayamos a comprar un bocadillo?

   _____

9   ¿A qué día estamos hoy? Hoy estamos a 1 de septiembre.

   _____

10 ¿Todavía es vivo el autor de esta novela?

   _____

11 El tren es a punto de salir.

   _____

12 Mañana seré en Madrid a media tarde, a no ser que haya problemas con el transporte.

   _____

13 Oye, ¿qué está de tu hermana? Hace siglos que no la veo.

   _____

14 Este jarrón no está de plástico. Está de cristal de roca.

   _____

15 Últimamente eres muy raro, ¿no?

   _____

Saber and conocer (to know)

Spanish verbs 'saber' and 'conocer' create difficulties for English speakers. Both verbs usually translate into English as 'to know' but cannot normally be used interchangeably. Below is a summary of the main uses of 'saber' and 'conocer' in Spanish.

Remember that these verbs are regular in the present tense, except for the first person singular 'yo' forms: 'sé' and 'conozco.'

SABER

1   **'Saber' means 'to know a fact or have information about something,' 'to have a good command of a language or subject,' or 'to be aware of something through observation, enquiry or information.'**

   ¿**Sabes** cuál es la capital de Ecuador? – Sí, claro que lo **sé**. Es Quito.
   (Do you know what the capital of Ecuador is? Of course I do. It is Quito)

   ¿**Sabes** a qué hora empieza la película?
   (Do you know what time the film starts?)

   Sé que está por aquí, pero no me acuerdo exactamente de la dirección.
   (I know it's somewhere around here, but I can't remember the exact address)

Sé japonés, pero no **sé** chino.
(I know Japanese but I do not know Chinese)

2 **'Saber' means 'having the ability or to know how to do something.' In English this verb is normally translated as 'to be able to' or 'to know how to.'**

¿**Sabes** conducir?
(Can you drive?)

¿**Sabes** nadar?
(Can you swim?)

¿**Sabes** tocar la guitarra?
(Can you play the guitar?)

¿**Sabes** cambiar la rueda de un coche?
(Do you know how to change a tire?)

3 **'Saber de' means 'to be aware of the situation or state of a person or thing' or 'having knowledge or information concerning someone or something.'**

¿**Sabes** algo **de** Miguel?
(Have you heard from Miguel?)

Sé de un dentista muy bueno.
(I know of a very good dentist)

Although in this case you can also say:

Conozco a un dentista muy bueno.
(I know a very good dentist)

Note that the preposition 'a' is required in this case in Spanish.

4 **Expressions with 'saber':**
¡Yo qué sé! / **¡Qué sé yo!** = how am I supposed to know; I haven't a clue!
¿Cómo se llega al Paseo de Sagasta? ¡Qué sé yo! ¡No soy de aquí!
(How does one get to Paseo de Sagasta? How am I supposed to know? I'm not from here!)

¡Quién sabe! / **¡Vete a saber!** / **¡Vaya usted a saber!** / **¡Sabe Dios!** / **¡Dios sabe!** = Who knows! God knows!
¿Sabes si él se va a casar con ella? ¡Sabe Dios!
(Do you know if he's going to marry her? Who knows!)

Saber de buena tinta = to have it on good authority
Yo sé de buena tinta que le compró un anillo de diamantes.
(I have it on good authority that he bought her a diamond ring)

Saber de qué pie cojea = to know somebody's weaknesses

Mi cuñada sabe de qué pie cojea su marido; lo sabe manejar muy bien.

(My sister-in-law knows her husband's weaknesses; she knows how to handle him very well)

CONOCER

1 **'Conocer' means 'to be familiar or acquainted with a person, place or thing.'**

Conozco Granada, pero no **conozco** Sevilla.

(I know (have been to) Granada, but I do not know (have not been to) Seville)

¿**Conoces** a mi primo el cantante?

(Do you know / Have you met my cousin the singer?)

– ¿Os **conocéis**? – Sí, hombre, nos **conocemos** desde hace mucho tiempo.

(Do you know each other? Yes, of course. We have known each other for ages)

– ¿**Conoces** a Javier Marías? – No lo **conozco** en persona, pero **sé** quién es y **conozco** su obra.

(Do you know Javier Marías? I do not know him personally, but I know who he is and I am familiar with his work)

No **conozco** muy bien su discografía, pero los temas que he oído de él me han encantado.

(I am not familiar with his discography, but I really liked the recordings that I have heard)

Conozco bien el funcionamiento de mi empresa.

(I am very familiar with the workings of my company)

2 **Expressions with 'conocer':**

Se conoce que = It seems that; it's well known that

Se conoce que él es muy buen cocinero y repostero.

(It's well known that he is a very good cook and pastry maker)

Conocer (algo) como la palma de la mano = to know something inside out / like the back of one's hand

Conozco Madrid como la palma de mi mano. Viví allí durante veinte años.

(I know Madrid like the back of my hand. I lived there for twenty years)

Conocer (a alguien) **de vista** = to know somebody by sight

Yo nunca he hablado con esa chica. La conozco sólo de vista.

(I've never talked to that girl. I only know her by sight)

Conocer el percal = to know the score or what's what

Ya sé lo que va a suceder; conozco el percal.
(I know the score; I already see what's going to happen)

Dar a conocer = to announce
Las dos familias dieron a conocer el compromiso de sus hijos.
(The two families announced the engagement of their children)

Darse a conocer = to make oneself known
Ella se dio a conocer en la sociedad por su talento de pianista.
(She made herself known in society through her talent at the piano)

Saber and conocer in the past tense

Note that both **saber** and **conocer** change their meanings in the past tense:
Saber
In the preterite it generally means: 'to find out.'

No **supe** que se había ido hasta dos meses después.
(I did not know (find out) he had left until two months later)

In the imperfect it simply means 'to know' in the same sense as in the present.

¿**Sabías** que Marta es la mujer de Antonio?
(Did you know that Marta is Antonio's wife?)

Conocer
In the preterite it means: 'to meet someone for the first time.'

Conocí a mi marido hace diez años en Filadelfia.
(I met my husband ten years ago in Philadelphia)

In the imperfect it simply means 'to know' in the same sense as in the present.

No **conocía** la música de Falla hasta que me regalaste un CD.
(I did not know Falla's music until you gave me the CD)

 Exercises

EXERCISE 5. Choose the correct form of the verb.

1   No (sé / conozco) a nadie que (sepa / conozca) de literatura lo que tú
    (sabes / conoces).
2 . Hace años (sabía / conocía) Lima como si fuera limeño, pero ahora no
    (sabría / conocería) cómo llegar a Miraflores.

3   Cuando uno es niño no (sabe / conoce) lo que quiere y siempre pregunta todo lo que no (sabe / conoce).

4   (Supe / Conocí) a Alberto cuando era aprendiz de chef, y ya entonces (sabía / conocía) cocinar muy bien.

5   No (sabría / conocería) decirte si era catalán o no, porque no (sé / conozco) el acento catalán.

6   No (sé / conozco) decirle que no a la gente, pero siempre (sé / conozco) qué es lo que debo hacer.

7   Ya (sabía / conocía) yo que (sabrías / conocerías) una buena galería de arte.

8   Miguel no (sabe / conoce) la pintura de Sorolla, por eso le quiero regalar un libro para que (sepa / conozca) su obra.

9   No (sé / conozco) a este escritor y tampoco (sé / conozco) si venden sus libros aquí.

10   Nos (supimos / conocimos) hace dos años por casualidad, pero todavía no (sé / conozco) dónde vive.

11   No (sabía / conocía) que (sabías / conocías) tan bien a mi jefa.

12   En aquella época no (sabía / conocía) hablar sueco, pero ahora (sé / conozco) a muchos suecos y hablo bastate bien su lengua.

13   (Supe / Conocí) que había una manifestación en el centro porque (sabía / conocía) quién la organizaba.

14   Hace tiempo que (sé / conozco) a Marta, pero no (sabía / conocía) que era de origen uruguayo.

15   ¿(Sabes / Conoces) un buen restaurante colombiano? No, pero (sé / conozco) dónde hay uno brasileño que no está nada mal.

Pedir and preguntar (to ask)

Both 'pedir' and 'preguntar' translate into English as 'to ask,' but the contexts in which these verbs are used vary significantly.

PEDIR

We use 'pedir' when we want to ask for something or request something.

Pídele que te preste su coche.
(Ask him if you can borrow his car / Ask him for his car)

Pídele el dinero o no te lo devolverá.
(Ask him for the money or he won't give it back to you)

PREGUNTAR

'Preguntar' is used when we want to ask something or ask a question.

Pregúntale la hora. **Pregúntale** qué hora es.
(Ask him for the time. Ask him what time it is)

Consider the contrast between the following two sentences:

Le **pregunté** a mi profesora **si** me podía dar el resultado de mi examen.
(I asked my teacher **if** she could give me the result of my exam)

But:

Le **pedí** a la profesora **el resultado de mi examen**.
(I asked my teacher **for** the result of my exam)

Or:

Le **pedí** a mi profesora **que me diera el resultado de mi examen**.
(I asked my teacher **to** give me the result of my exam)

Tocar and jugar (to play)

When we play a sport we use 'jugar.' When we play an instrument we use 'tocar.'
Remember that you must insert the preposition 'a' between the verb 'jugar' and
the sport or game that follows.

Toco el piano y la flauta desde los seis años.
(I have been playing the piano and the flute since I was six)

Me encanta **jugar** al tenis. Es mi deporte favorito.
(I love playing tennis. It is my favorite sport)

Mnemonic device
Remember that the verb 'tocar' literally means 'to touch.' This obviously will
help you remember its meaning when you play an instrument, since you
actually need to 'touch' an instrument with your hands in order to be able to
play it: "Es imposible **tocar** el violín y el piano a la vez, a no ser que tengas
cuatro manos" (It's impossible to play the violin and the piano at the same
time, unless you have four hands).

On pronominal verbs and their meaning

In Spanish there are a number of verbs that have different meanings depending on whether they are used in their pronominal form (i.e. with me, te, se, etc.), or not. Let us have a look at some of the most important verbs that follow this pattern.

Quedar and quedarse

Both 'quedar' and 'quedarse' can be used in Spanish with the meaning of 'to remain in a particular state or situation.' However, there are many instances where these verbs are not interchangeable. Pay close attention to the different meanings.

QUEDAR

Quedé con Miguel para ir a ver el partido de béisbol.
(I arranged to meet Miguel to go to see a baseball game)

No **quedan** huevos.
(There are no eggs left / remaining)

Quedan dos semanas para las vacaciones de verano.
(There are two weeks to go before the summer holidays)

Ese vestido **te queda** (te sienta) muy bien.
(That dress fits you very well)

Quedamos en comprar la casa a principios de año.
(We agreed to buy the house at the beginning of the year)

Marín **queda** a cinco kilómetros aproximadamente de Pontevedra.
(Marín is situated approximately 5 kilometers from Pontevedra)

Al final todo **quedó** en nada.
(In the end it all came to nothing)

Le regalé unos bombones y **quedé** de maravilla.
(I gave her a box of chocolates and made a very good impression)

QUEDARSE

¿Hasta cuándo **te quedas** en Valencia?
(How long are you staying in Valencia for?)

No va a dormir en un hotel; **se queda** en casa de un amigo.
(He is not going to sleep at a hotel, he'll be staying at a friend's house)

Se quedó viuda a los cuarenta años.
(She was left a widow at the age of forty)

Probablemente **te quedes** calvo cuando seas mayor.
(You will probably go bald when you are older)

Cuando oyó la noticia en la televisión, **se quedó** de piedra.
(When he heard the news on the television, he was stunned)

Me quedé dormido en el sofá.
(I fell asleep on the sofa)

¿Puedo **quedármelo**?
(Can I keep it?)

Me he quedado sin dinero.
(I have run out of money)

Other noteworthy examples

Verb	Pronominal form
acordar (to agree)	**acordarse (de)** (to remember)
Acordamos ir a México para las vacaciones de Pascua. (We agreed to go to Mexico for Easter vacation)	¿**Te acordaste de** llamar a tus padres? (Did you remember to call your parents?)
comportar (to entail)	**comportarse** (to behave)
El acuerdo **comporta** un pago mensual. (This agreement entails a monthly payment)	Si **os comportáis** bien os llevaré al circo. (If you behave, I'll take you to the circus)
dedicar (to dedicate; to devote)	**dedicarse a** (to do something for a living; to devote oneself to)
Luisa le **dedicó** su colección de poemas a su hermano. (Luisa dedicated her collection of poems to her brother)	Quiero **dedicarme** a pintar retratos. (I want to devote myself to painting portraits)
desprender (to detach; to give off)	**desprenderse de** (to part with; to get rid of; to infer, to deduce)
Desprendí los botones de un viejo suéter y los cosí en mi blusa. (I detached the buttons from an old sweater and sewed them on my blouse) Esta flor **desprende** un olor agradable. (This flower gives off a pleasant scent)	Quiero **desprenderme de** esa vieja silla. (I want to get rid of that old chair) De sus palabras **se desprende** que no tiene razón. (From his words one can deduce that he is wrong)

Verb	Pronominal form
disponer (to arrange; to stipulate); **disponer de** (to have at one's disposal) **Dispuso** todo para el viaje en un periquete. (He got everything ready for the journey in a jiffy) Ese hombre **dispone de** recursos interminables. (That man has unlimited resources at his disposal)	**disponerse a** (to prepare to) Ella **se dispuso a** viajar alrededor del mundo. (She prepared herself to travel around the world)
echar (to throw; to put; to pour; to fire; to post); **echarle la culpa a** (to blame) El jefe se equivocó con el presupuesto y **le echó la culpa** al contable. (The boss made a mistake in the budget and blamed the accountant) ¿Puedes **echar** estas cartas al correo? (Can you put these letters in the post for me?) (See chapter 6 for more expressions with 'echar')	**echarse** (to lie down); **echarse a** (to start doing something); **echarse a perder** (to go bad, to be ruined) La comida **se echó** a perder; la voy a tirar. (The food went bad; I will throw it out) Estaba muy cansado y **se echó** en una hamaca. (He was very tired and he lay down on a hammock)
empeñar (to pawn) Tuvimos que **empeñar** el reloj del abuelo para pagar el alquiler. (We had to pawn grandpa's watch to pay the rent)	**empeñarse en** (to insist on, to persist in; to strive to) Ese joven **se empeña en** querer ser médico. (That young man insists on becoming a doctor)
encargar (to order; to ask; to put in charge) Puesto que no hay nada que comer, **encargaré** una pizza. (Since there's nothing to eat, I'll order a pizza) Pese a ser novato, le **encargaron** el proyecto. (In spite of his being inexperienced, they put him in charge of the project)	**encargarse de** (to take care of, to be responsible for; to deal with something) No te preocupes, yo **me encargo de** los niños. (Don't worry, I'll take care of the kids) Ella **se encarga de** las facturas de la empresa. (She deals with the invoicing for the company)

Verb	Pronominal form
encontrar (to find)	**encontrarse** (to feel, to be located);
No sé dónde puse mi cartera, pero no la **encuentro**.	**encontrarse con** (to bump into, to run into)
(I don't know where I put my wallet, but I can't find it)	¿Cómo **te encuentras**?
No lo **encuentro** tan interesante como dice la gente.	(How are you feeling?)
(I don't find it as interesting as other people do)	Mi colegio **se encuentra** en el mismo centro de Londres.
	(My school is located right in the center of London)
	Ayer **me encontré con** tu hermana en el teatro.
	(Yesterday I ran into your sister at the theatre)
fiar (to sell on credit; to put on the slate)	**fiarse de** (to trust)
Si quieres sacar más dinero siempre puedes **fiarlo**.	No creo que pueda **fiarme de** ese abogado.
(If you want to obtain more money for it, you can always sell it on credit)	(I don't think I can trust that lawyer)
fijar (to fix; to set)	**fijarse** (to pay attention, to listen carefully, to look at; to notice)
Vamos a **fijar** las reglas del juego.	¿Te **fijaste** en sus zapatos rojos de charol?
(Let's set the rules of the game)	(Did you notice her red patent leather shoes?)
	¡**Fíjate** y no te distraigas!
	(Pay attention and don't get distracted)
hacer (to do, to make)	**hacerse** (to get, to become; to pretend)
Quiero **hacer** una torta de avellana y crema batida.	¿Dónde está el taxi? ¡**Se está haciendo** tarde!
(I want to make a hazelnut and whipped cream torte)	(Where is the taxi? It's getting late!)
(See chapter 6 for more expressions with 'hacer')	Esto **se está haciendo** pesado. ¡Vámonos!
	(This is becoming tedious. Let's go!)

Verb	Pronominal form
incorporar (to add; to incorporate) Al reescribir el ensayo, **incorpora** las correcciones del profesor. (As you rewrite your essay, incorporate your teacher's corrections)	**incorporarse** (to sit up); **incorporarse a** (to join; to start work) Al ver a su hijo, la madre **se incorporó**. (Upon seeing her son, the mother got up)
ir (to go) Ayer **fuimos** a patinar sobre hielo. (Yesterday we went ice skating)	**irse** (to leave, to go away) El huésped vino tarde y **se fue** temprano. (The guest came late and left early)
negar (to deny) ¡Hijo mío, no te puedo **negar** nada! (I can't deny you anything, my child!)	**negarse a** (to refuse to) Ella **se negó a** dejar a su perro con ese hombre. (She refused to leave her dog with that man)
ocurrir (to happen) Según Bernarda, en su casa no ha **ocurrido** nada. (According to Bernarda, nothing happened in her house) ¿Qué **ocurre**? (What's the matter?) Lo que **ocurre** es que no tengo suficiente dinero. (The thing is that I don't have enough money)	**ocurrírsele a alguien** (to occur to someone) **Se me ocurre** que si hace sol podríamos ir al parque. (It occurs to me that if it's sunny, we could go to the park) A él no **se le ocurrió** la idea. (The thought did not occur to him) No **se me ocurre** ninguna solución fácil. (I can't think of an easy solution)
pasar (to come in; to happen; to drop in; to go past; to go by; to pass; to go through; to transfer something from one person to another; to give (a message); to show (a film); to spend (time); to let off; to cease; etc.) Anoche **pasaron** una buena película por la tele. (They showed a good film on TV last night) ¿Qué **ha pasado**? (What's the matter?)	**pasarse** (to go too far; to go off (food); to forget); **pasárselo bien** / **mal** (to have a good/bad time); **pasarse de** bueno, generoso, etc. (to exceed in a quality) ¡Con ese comportamiento insolente, **te pasaste** de la raya! (With that insolent behavior, you really went too far!) Perdona, **se me pasó** decírtelo. (I am sorry, I forgot to mention it to you)

Verb	Pronominal form
portar (to carry) (old-fashioned) Portar significa lo mismo que llevar pero ya no se usa. ('Portar' means the same as 'llevar', but it is no longer used)	**portarse** (to behave) Con ese maestro los alumnos **se portan** muy bien. (With that teacher the students behave very well)
prestar (to lend) Aquí tienes el dinero que me **prestaste** la semana pasada. (Here's the money you lent me last week)	**prestarse a** (to lend itself to; to offer) Este lugar **no se presta** para fiestas. (This place does not lend itself to parties) **Se prestó a** ayudarme sin que se lo pidiera. (He offered to help me without my having asked him)
resignar (to give up, to relinquish) Debido al escándalo, **resignó** de su cargo como diplomático. (Because of the scandal, he relinquished his position as a diplomat)	**resignarse a** (to resign oneself to) Todos tenemos que **resignarnos** a que va a hacer mal tiempo. (We all have to resign ourselves to the bad weather)
rendir (to bear fruit); **rendir homenaje** (to pay tribute) Una tierra sin abono no **rinde** una buena cosecha. (Soil without fertilizer doesn't yield a good crop)	**rendirse** (to surrender; to give up) En la vida uno no debe **rendirse** nunca. (In life one should never give up)
valer (to cost, to be worth; to be fit for a purpose); **no valer para nada** (to be completely useless) ¿Cuánto **vale** eso? (How much does that cost?) **Vale** la pena visitar Granada y entrar en la Alhambra. (It is worth visiting Granada and going to la Alhambra)	**valerse (de)** (to resort to somebody or something for a particular purpose); **no poder valerse por sí mismo** (not to be able to cope by oneself) Aun teniendo 90 años mi abuelita **se vale** por sí misma. (Even at the age of 90, my grandma is able to cope on her own)
volver (to come back, to return); **volver a + infinitive** (to do something again) Te pido que no **vuelvas** a hacerme eso. (I'm asking you not to do that again)	**volverse** (to turn back; to become, to get, to turn) Al oír su voz, ella **se volvió** y lo miró. (Upon hearing his voice, she turned around and looked at him)

Exercises

EXERCISE 6. Choose the verb that best fits the meaning of the sentence.

1   (Acuerda / Acuérdate) de cerrar la puerta cuando salgas.
   _____

2   Es importante advertir de los riesgos que (comporta / se comporta) el tabaco.
   _____

3   En cuanto llegué al hotel, me (deshice / hice) de la maleta para que no la encontrara la policía.
   _____

4   La lámpara (desprendió / se desprendió) del techo y afortunadamente no le cayó a nadie encima.
   _____

5   Cada vez leemos menos y (nos dedicamos / dedicamos) más horas a ver la televisión.
   _____

6   Como el director (negó / se negó) a recibirnos, fuimos atendidos por su secretaria.
   _____

7   Los niños (se portaron / portaron) de maravilla. Se nota que están muy bien educados.
   _____

8   Tienes mala cara. ¿(Encuentras / Te encuentras) mal?
   _____

9   ¿Quién (va a encargar / se va a encargar) de preparar el menú para la cena de Nochevieja?
   _____

10   Como no encontraba trabajo, (ocurrió / se le ocurrió) poner un anuncio en la prensa.
   _____

11   Este párrafo es muy ambiguo y (se presta / presta) a confusión.
   _____

12   Doce países de América (acordaron / se acordaron) fomentar la educación intercultural.
   _____

13   Miles de argentinos (se rindieron / rindieron) homenaje a los desaparecidos durante la dictadura.
   _____

14 Para poder financiar su última película, el director salvadoreño (empeñó / se empeñó) su casa.

_____

15 No (te hagas / hagas) el tonto. Sabes muy bien de lo que te estoy hablando.

_____

16 Saúl y Marcos (incorporaron / se incorporaron) a la reunión media hora tarde.

_____

17 Para sacarme un sobresueldo, los fines de semana (me dedico / dedico) a la compraventa de pisos.

_____

18 Por la manera en la que (comporta / se comporta), yo diría que a Juanito le gusta Marisol.

_____

19 (Se valió / valió) de todas sus amistades para conseguir un trabajo.

_____

20 En la madrugada de ayer, los rebeldes (rindieron / se rindieron) y entregaron las armas.

_____

Verbs and their derivatives (Part 1)

This section deals with verbs and verb stems of Latin origin, around which a series of derivative verbs are formed, and discusses their variations and shades of meaning. Some of these verbs are differentiated by their prefixes, which have a direct influence on meaning.

1   –ceder

acceder – anteceder – ceder – conceder – interceder – preceder – proceder – retroceder – suceder

acceder (to accede; to enter a place), **anteceder** (to precede), **ceder** (to hand over; to give up), **conceder** (to grant, to award, to give; to agree; to concede, to admit or acknowledge something as true or correct), **interceder** (to intercede), **preceder** (to precede), **proceder** (to proceed), **retroceder** (to move back, to retreat), **suceder** (to happen; to succeed; to take over an office, post, etc.; to come next in order after something or somebody).

Abrí las ventanas para ventilar la habitación y _____ a hacer la cama.
a) precedí   b) sucedí   c) procedí   d) concedí

2 –coger

acoger(se) – coger – encoger(se) – escoger – recoger – sobrecoger

acoger(se) (to receive, to welcome, to take in; to protect; to admit, to accept, to approve; **acogerse a** (una ley, etc.) = to invoke for oneself the benefits and rights granted by a law, etc. (to avail oneself of, to exercise one's right to), **coger** (to take, to catch, to pick up); **encoger(se)** (to shrink; **encogerse de hombros** = to shrug one's shoulders), **escoger** (to choose), **recoger** (to pick up; to tidy up, to clear up; **recoger la mesa** = to clear the table; **recogerse** = to retire, to go to bed; **recogerse el pelo** = to put one's hair up), **sobrecoger** (to come upon somebody suddenly and unexpectedly; **sobrecogerse** = to become surprised or intimidated).

Durante el verano hay familias españolas que _____ a niños saharauis.

a) cogen   b) acogen   c) escogen   d) encogen

3 –currir

concurrir – discurrir – escurrir – incurrir – ocurrir – recurrir– transcurrir

concurrir (to congregate, to gather, to convene; to agree, to coincide; to contribute; to take part in a competition), **discurrir** (to walk or run continuously through a place; to invent; to infer, to speculate; to go by (time); to flow, to run (water, air, oil, etc.); to reflect, to think, to talk about something), **escurrir** (to strain, to drain); **escurrir el bulto** = to evade (a task, risk, commitment, etc.); **escurrirse** = to slip; to flee, **incurrir (en)** (to commit, to perform (a crime, error, etc.); to incur), **ocurrir** (to occur), **recurrir (a)** (to resort to, to turn to; to appeal against), **transcurrir** (to go by, when referring to time).

Primero lavas la ensalada, luego la _____ y después la cortas a trozos con el cuchillo.

a) discurres   b) escurres   c) recurres   d) concurres

4 –decir

bendecir – contradecir(se) – decir – desdecir – maldecir – predecir

bendecir (to bless), **contradecir(se)** (to contradict), **decir** (to say, to tell), **desdecir** (**desdecir de** = not to be as good as; not to match; **desdecirse** = to retract), **maldecir** (to curse), **predecir** (to predict).

Note that the verbs that end in **–decir** are irregular in the preterite: *dije, dijiste, dijo, dijimos, dijisteis, dijeron*. The same pattern with the letter [j] is applicable to the rest of the verbs above. Also note that the third person plural is 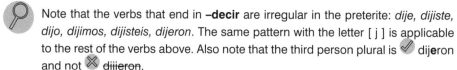 dije̶ron and not ⊗ dijieron.

Se levantó de repente, _____ a los cuatro vientos y golpeó la mesa con el puño.

a) maldijo   b) bendijo   c) predijo   d) desdijo

5 **–ducir**

aducir – conducir – deducir – inducir – introducir(se) – producir – reducir – reproducir – seducir – traducir

aducir (to adduce, to cite (reasons, examples, etc.) as evidence or proof), **conducir** (to drive; to guide, to direct; to lead), **deducir** (to deduce, to conclude (that), to infer), **inducir** (to induce, to persuade or use influence on; to cause or bring about), **introducir(se)** (to insert, to put in; to introduce, to cause to experience for the first time; to bring in, to establish), **producir** (to produce, to make, to grow, to yield), **reducir** (to reduce), **reproducir** (to reproduce), **seducir** (to seduce), **traducir** (to translate).

Note that the verbs that end in **–ducir** are irregular in the preterite: *conduje, condujiste, condujo, condujimos, condujisteis, condujeron*. The same pattern with the letter [j] is applicable to the rest of the verbs above. Also note that the third person plural is ✓ conduj**e**ron and not ✗ ~~condujieron~~.

_____ que no vendrías porque eran las 10:30 y no habías aparecido.

a) Aduje   b) Produje   c) Reproduje   d) Deduje

6 **–ferir**

conferir – diferir – inferir – interferir(se) – preferir – proferir – referir(se) – transferir

conferir (to confer), **diferir** (to defer, to postpone; to be different; to disagree), **inferir** (to infer), **interferir(se)** (to interfere), **preferir** (to prefer), **proferir** (to utter), **referir(se)** (to refer; **en lo que se refiere a** = as far as x is concerned, as for x), **transferir** (to transfer).

Es mejor dialogar y llegar a un acuerdo que _____ constantemente de lo que opinan los demás.

a) conferir   b) inferir   c) preferir   d) diferir

7 **–formar**

conformar – formar – informar(se) – reformar – transformar(se) – uniformar(se)

conformar (to agree; to give shape to something; **conformarse con** = to be content with), **formar** (to form; to train; to educate; to form up), **informar(se)** (to inform), **reformar** (to reform), **transformar(se)** (to transform, to convert), **uniformar(se)** (to unify, to standardize; to give the same uniform to the members of a body or community).

Van a _____ a los guardias del ministerio para que todos vayan vestidos iguales.

a) conformar   b) uniformar   c) reformar   d) transformar

8 –hacer

hacer – deshacer(se) – rehacer

hacer (to do, to make), **deshacer(se)** (to undo; to unpack (one's suitcase); to wreck, to ruin, to break; to break down; to break up, to divide into; **deshacerse de** = to get rid of, to part with, **deshacerse en** (elogios, alabanzas, agradecimientos, aplausos, explicaciones, etc.) = to be full of, **rehacer** (to redo; to reform; to restore, to rebuild (**rehacer su vida** = to rebuild one's life) **rehacerse** = to regain (strength, serenity, courage, self-esteem, etc.).

Gracias a una donación anónima van a poder _____ el muelle que está junto al acantilado.

   a) hacer   b) rehacer   c) deshacerse   d) deshacer

9 –hibir

cohibir(se) – desinhibir(se) – exhibir – inhibir(se) – prohibir

cohibir(se) (to inhibit, to restrain or hinder), **desinhibir(se)** (to lose one's inhibitions), **exhibir** (to exhibit), **inhibir(se)** (to inhibit; to restrain or hinder; to prevent the performance of; to stop, to prevent), **prohibir** (to prohibit, to forbid).

Su recibimiento tan caluroso me _____ y ruborizó. Me puse rojo como un tomate.

a) cohibió   b) prohibió   c) desinhibió   d) exhibió

10 –meter

acometer – arremeter – cometer – comprometer – entrometer(se) – meter(se) – prometer – someter(se)

acometer (to undertake; to charge; to suddenly appear, to strike)**, arremeter (contra)** (to charge, to attack), **cometer** (to commit (a crime); to make (an error)**, comprometer** (to compromise, to injure one's name, reputation, etc.; **comprometerse** = to commit oneself; to get engaged)**, entrometer/se** (to interfere, to meddle), **meter(se)** (to put in; to get involved), **prometer** (to promise)**, someter(se)** (to subjugate, to submit; to undergo).

El entrenador del equipo de fútbol no se pudo contener y _____ contra el árbitro.

a) acometió   b) prometió   c) arremetió   d) sometió

11 –mitir

admitir – dimitir – emitir – omitir – permitir – readmitir – remitir – retransmitir – transmitir

admitir (to admit; to accept; to allow or suffer), **dimitir** (to resign), **emitir** (to utter; to give off; to broadcast; to issue), **omitir** (to omit, to leave out), **permitir** (to allow, to permit), **readmitir** (to readmit, to reemploy), **remitir** (to send; to refer; to free of an obligation; to postpone or cancel, **remitir(se)** = to subside, **remitirse** = to refer to what has been said or done, or will be said or done), **retransmitir** (to broadcast), **transmitir** (to transmit, to pass on).

No hace falta que pongas tu número de teléfono en la encuesta, lo puedes
_____.

a) admitir   b) transmitir   c) remitir   d) omitir

12 –nunciar

anunciar – denunciar – enunciar – pronunciar – renunciar

anunciar (to announce), **denunciar** (to report; to denounce, to deplore or
condemn), **enunciar** (to state), **pronunciar** (to pronounce; to determine, to
resolve; to highlight, to stress; **pronunciarse** = to declare oneself (in favor or
against something or somebody), **renunciar (a)** (to relinquish).

En polaco existen sonidos que son muy difíciles de _____.

a) anunciar   b) denunciar   c) pronunciar   d) renunciar

13 –partir

compartir – impartir – partir – repartir

compartir (to share), **impartir** (to communicate (information), to teach (a class);
to give or bestow), **partir** (to divide, to split, to break open, to crack), **repartir** (to
hand out; to share, to divide amongst).

Los sábados por la mañana _____ propaganda para promocionar su grupo
de rock.

a) reparte   b) parte   c) imparte   d) comparte

Exercises

EXERCISE 7. Fill in the blanks with the most appropriate word.

1 Barack Obama _____ a George Bush como presidente de EE.UU.
   a) accedió   b) sucedió   c) concedió   d) intercedió
2 El ministro _____ ante la justicia para que pusieran en libertad a uno
   de sus colaboradores.
   a) accedió   b) procedió   c) concedió   d) intercedió
3 A la competición _____ más de 68 películas de todos los países del
   mundo.
   a) escurrieron   b) incurrieron   c) ocurrieron   d) concurrieron
4 A mí no se me ocurre qué regalarle, _____ tú algo a ver si tienes más
   suerte.
   a) escurre   b) discurre   c) incurre   d) concurre
5 El meteorólogo _____ que llovería antes del mes de abril.
   a) se desdijo   b) bendijo   c) se contradijo   d) predijo
6 La violencia no _____ a nada bueno.
   a) conduce   b) produce   c) reduce   d) deduce

7 Cuando termines de cenar, _____ la mesa, por favor.

a) recoge b) acoge c) sobrecoge d) encoge

8 El activista político _____ insultos y agredió al policía.

a) confirió b) prefirió c) difirió d) profirió

9 Algunos _____ la playa y otros la montaña. Es cuestión de gustos.

a) infieren b) refieren c) difieren d) prefieren

10 Después de reconocer que había estado robando pelotas, _____ como presidente del club de tenis.

a) acometió b) arremetió c) sometió d) dimitió

11 No nos _____ con un empate. Queremos ganar el partido.

a) informamos b) conformamos c) reformamos d) uniformamos

12 ¿Quién no ha _____ errores alguna vez? Al fin y al cabo, errar es humano.

a) acometido b) arremetido c) sometido d) cometido

13 Tras las fuertes lluvias del lunes pasado, la población necesita alimentos y materiales de construcción para _____ sus viviendas.

a) deshacer b) rehacer c) deshacerse de d) hacer

14 Me quejé al encargado y éste _____ de hombros sin saber qué hacer.

a) se escogió b) se sobrecogió c) se encogió d) se acogió

15 Según un estudio reciente, una buena higiene bucal no siempre _____ la caries dental.

a) cohíbe b) exhibe c) desinhibe d) inhibe

16 Mi compañera de piso siempre se _____ en todos los entresijos de mi vida.

a) arremete b) acomete c) entromete d) somete

17 _____ a su vecino por no querer bajar el volumen de la televisión.

a) Enunció b) Pronunció c) Denunció d) Anunció

18 Por la indumentaria, _____ que se trataba de un empleado del Ministerio de Defensa.

a) induje b) deduje c) aduje d) seduje

19 No pongas las luces antiniebla cuando vayas en caravana porque podrías deslumbrar al conductor que te _____ .

a) sucede b) precede c) concede d) retrocede

20 El patrón está obligado a _____ a los trabajadores una vez que finalice la huelga.

a) remitir b) dimitir c) readmitir d) omitir

21 _____ que era su último día en la empresa porque había aceptado una oferta de trabajo de la competencia.

a) Enunció b) Renunció c) Anunció d) Denunció

22 Como es tradición, el cura _____ con agua bendita a los animales el día de San Blas.

a) predijo b) desdijo c) bendijo d) maldijo

23   Por fin se _____ al inglés la novela *Ecuador, el velo se levanta* de la
     escritora ecuatoriana Rocío Durán Barba.
     a) ha reproducido   b) ha producido   c) ha conducido   d) ha traducido
24   En el libro no voy a _____ nada. Salvo lo excesivamente trivial.
     a) transmitir   b) omitir   c) emitir   d) remitir
25   Si no te importa, corta la tarta y _____ entre los invitados.
     a) pártela   b) repártela   c) impártela   d) compártela

Verbs and their derivatives (Part 2)

14   –poner

> anteponer – componer – contraponer – deponer – descomponer(se)
> – disponer – exponer – imponer(se) – interponer – oponer(se) – poner –
> posponer – predisponer(se) – presuponer – proponer – recomponer – reponer
> – sobreponer(se) – superponer – suponer – yuxtaponer

anteponer (to put before or in front of), **componer** (to make up, to constitute; to compose: (1) to produce or create a musical or literary work; (2) to put together or make up by combining; to put in proper order; to tidy up; to repair; **componerse de** = to be made up of), **contraponer** (to compare with something different; to place against something else to hinder or obstruct its effect), **deponer** (to depose: (1) to remove from an office or position, esp. one of power or rank; (2) to testify or give evidence on oath, esp. when taken down in writing; to put down; to claim), **descomponer/se** (to decompose, to break down or be broken down; to break up or separate into constituent parts; to stop working properly; to mess up), **disponer** (to arrange, to set out; to determine, to stipulate), **disponerse a** = to get ready to, to make preparations to), **exponer** (to expose; to display; to put forward); **exponerse a** = to expose oneself to, to be subject or susceptible (to an attack, criticism, etc.), **imponer(se)** (to impose; **imponerse** = to win), **interponer** (to place amongst things or people; to exert one's influence in favor of someone; to file, to make, to lodge (an appeal, a complaint, etc.); **oponer(se)** (to oppose), **poner** (to put), **posponer** (to postpone), **predisponer(se)** (to predispose); **presuponer** (to presuppose, to take for granted), **proponer** (to propose (idea, project), to offer for consideration), **recomponer** (to recompose, to mend, to repair), **reponer** (to replace; to restore to a former rank or condition; to replenish; to reply), **reponerse** (to recover from; to calm down), **sobreponer** (to place over something else), **sobreponerse** (to get over, to recover from), **superponer** (to superimpose, to place over something else), **suponer** (to suppose), **yuxtaponer** (to juxtapose).

Por fin ha podido _____ sus cuadros y esculturas en un famoso museo de la capital.

a) posponer   b) exponer   c) suponer   d) yuxtaponer

15 –prender

> aprender – comprender – desprender(se) – emprender – prender – reprender – sorprender

aprender (to learn), **comprender** (to understand), **desprender(se)** (to detach; to give off; **desprenderse de** = to get rid of, to part with), **emprender** (to undertake), **prender** (to arrest, to apprehend, to grip), **reprender** (to scold, to tell off), **sorprender** (to surprise).

Me _____ el día de mi cumpleaños con una cena en mi restaurante favorito.

a) comprendió   b) emprendió   c) sorprendió   d) prendió

16 –scribir

> adscribir – circunscribir(se) – describir – escribir – inscribir(se) – prescribir – proscribir – suscribir – transcribir

adscribir (to ascribe; to enroll), **circunscribir(se)** (to circunscribe, to restrict within limits; to draw a line round), **describir** (to describe), **escribir** (to write), **inscribir(se)** (to register, to enroll; to inscribe, to engrave), **prescribir** (to prescribe), **proscribir** (to proscribe, to prohibit, to outlaw, to exile), **suscribir** (to subscribe: (1) to sign; (2) to give support or approval; **suscribirse** = to pay a subscription for consecutive issues of a magazine, newspapers, etc.), **transcribir** (to transcribe).

Afortunadamente podremos _____ la conferencia porque la grabamos en vídeo.

a) suscribir   b) transcribir   c) describir   d) adscribir

17 –seguir

> conseguir – perseguir – proseguir – seguir

conseguir (to achieve, to get, to obtain, to manage to), **perseguir** (to pursue, to follow), **proseguir** (to carry on), **seguir** (to follow, to continue, to resume).

Si quieres que la receta te salga bien, tendrás que _____ mis explicaciones paso a paso.

a) seguir   b) perseguir   c) proseguir   d) conseguir

18 –sentir

> asentir – consentir – disentir – sentir

asentir (to agree, to consent; to nod), **consentir** (to consent), **disentir** (to dissent, to disagree), **sentir** (to feel, to regret, to be sorry about).

No tienes que _____ que siempre tengas que hacer tú todas las tareas domésticas.

a) consentir   b) asentir   c) disentir   d) sentir

19 –sistir

asistir – consistir – desistir – insistir – persistir – resistir(se) – subsistir

asistir (to attend; to help; to look after), **consistir** (to consist of; to lie; to involve), **desistir** (to give up), **insistir** (to insist), **persistir** (to persist), **resistir(se)** (to resist), **subsistir** (to subsist).

El niño no dejaba de _____. Quería que su madre le comprara un helado de vainilla.

a) desistir   b) consistir   c) insistir   d) subsistir

20 –stituir

destituir – instituir – restituir(se) – sustituir

constituir (to constitute), **destituir** (to dismiss; to deprive of), **instituir** (to institute), **restituir/se** (to restore), **sustituir** (to substitute, to replace).

No te preocupes, si continúas afónico te puedo _____ un par de días hasta que te pongas bien.

a) restituir   b) destituir   c) instituir   d) sustituir

21 –tener

atenerse – detener(se) – mantener – obtener – retener – sostener – tener

atenerse a (to abide by, to comply with, to stick to, to observe), **detener(se)** (to stop, to detain)**, mantener** (to maintain), **obtener** (to obtain), **retener** (to retain), **sostener** (to hold; to support), **tener** (to have).

Si no sigues mi consejo tendrás que _____ a las consecuencias.

a) atenerte   b) obtenerte   c) retenerte   d) sostenerte

22 –tocar

retocar(se) – trastorcar – tocar

retocar(se) (to touch up), **trastocar** (to disrupt), **tocar** (to touch, to play an instrument).

Había ido a la peluquería, pero aun así no paraba de _____ el moño delante del espejo.

a) retocarse   b) retocar   c) trastocar   d) tocar

23 –traer

abstraer – atraer – contraer – distraer(se) – extraer – retraer(se) – sustraer – traer

abstraer (to abstract; to ignore; **abstraerse** (to detach oneself mentally), **atraer** (to attract), **contraer** (to contract; **contraer matrimonio** = to get married), **distraer(se)** (to distract; to entertain), **extraer** (to extract), **retraer(se)** (to retract),

sustraer (to subtract), **sustraerse** (to to detach oneself from an obligation, plan, etc.), **traer** (to bring).

Note that the verbs that end in **–traer** are irregular in the preterite: *traje, trajiste, trajo, trajimos, trajisteis, trajeron.* The same pattern with the letter [j] is applicable to the rest of the verbs above. Also note that the third person plural is ✓ traj**e**ron and not ✗ ~~trajieron~~.

Recuerde venir en ayunas para que le podamos _____ sangre y hacer el análisis.

a) contraer   b) extraer   c) abstraer   d) distraer

24 –venir

> contravenir – convenir – intervenir – prevenir – provenir – sobrevenir – venir

contravenir (to contravene), **convenir** (to agree; to gather; to be useful, appropriate, convenient, to be best to), **intervenir** (to intervene), **prevenir** (to prevent), **provenir** (to come from, to originate), **sobrevenir** (to occur; to suddenly strike), **venir** (to come).

Le _____ ir aprendiendo un poco todos los días porque va a ser el nuevo director.

a) contraviene   b) viene   c) conviene   d) proviene

25 –vivir

> convivir – desvivirse – malvivir – revivir – pervivir – sobrevivir – vivir

convivir (to live with, to coexist, to exist side by side), **desvivirse (por)** (to be devoted to; to go out of one's way to, to do one's utmost to), **malvivir** (to struggle to make ends meet), **revivir** (to relive; to revive), **pervivir** (to remain); **sobrevivir** (to survive), **vivir** (to live).

Algunos animales pueden _____ a las bajas temperaturas del Polo Norte.

a) convivir   b) malvivir   c) desvivir   d) sobrevivir

26 –vocar

> convocar – invocar – provocar – revocar

convocar (to call, to convene), **invocar** (to invoke), **provocar** (to cause; to provoke), **revocar** (to revoke).

Como no apagues ahora mismo la hoguera vas a _____ un incendio a gran escala.

a) convocar   b) invocar   c) provocar   d) revocar

Exercises

EXERCISE 8. Fill in the blanks with the most appropriate word.

1 Después del susto se _____ bebiendo unos sorbos de café.
   a) descompuso b) compuso c) recompuso d) expuso

2 Me _____ mucho que no viniera a la reunión. Espero que no le haya pasado nada.
   a) aprendió b) sorprendió c) comprendió d) reprendió

3 El otro día por fin _____ a hacer el pino.
   a) emprendí b) aprendí c) comprendí d) reprendí

4 Te hace falta más personalidad. Te tienes que _____ más delante del consejo.
   a) reponer b) disponer c) anteponer d) imponer

5 Argentina ha _____ un tratado de libre comercio con Chile.
   a) transcrito b) inscrito c) prescrito d) suscrito

6 El periódico _____ una querella por calumnias contra un conocido periodista español.
   a) impuso b) interpuso c) predispuso d) propuso

7 Einstein se fue a Estados Unidos y _____ su labor investigadora.
   a) transcribió b) prosiguió c) consiguió d) persiguió

8 José Echegaray _____ en 1904 el primer Premio Nobel de literatura en lengua española.
   a) mantuvo b) obtuvo c) retuvo d) sostuvo

9 A la edad de 5 años W. A. Mozart ya era capaz de leer y de _____ música.
   a) proponer b) componer c) contraponer d) exponer

10 Para hacer el mosaico tienes que _____ pequeñas piezas de diversos colores formando dibujos.
   a) oponer b) proponer c) componer d) yuxtaponer

11 El que no avise con tiempo no _____ la invitación.
   a) seguirá b) proseguirá c) conseguirá d) perseguirá

12 El niño _____ con la cabeza y reconoció que se había comido la tableta de chocolate.
   a) consintió b) disintió c) sintió d) asintió

13 _____ que estás al corriente de los últimos acontecimientos.
   a) Presupongo b) Supongo c) Predispongo d) Interpongo

14 No saben cómo, pero _____ una rara enfermedad durante su viaje por el desierto.
   a) sustrajo b) atrajo c) extrajo d) contrajo

15 El presidente de la compañía fue _____ por un delito de malversación de fondos.

a) destituido   b) restituido   c) instituido   d) constituido

16   Yo venía _____ a ver a un humorista lleno de vida, y me encontré a un actor con poca gracia y salero.

a) antepuesto   b) propuesto   c) compuesto   d) predispuesto

17   El médico le ha _____ que haga reposo y que beba mucha agua.

a) prescrito   b) adscrito   c) inscrito   d) proscrito

18   El hotel _____ de dos grandes salas para bodas, comuniones y bautizos.

a) dispone   b) predispone   c) compone   d) expone

19   Para _____ ser el número uno de la carrera, estudió día y noche y no vio la televisión.

a) perseguir   b) seguir   c) conseguir   d) proseguir

20   Los médicos en EE.UU. tienen que _____ español por exigencias del mercado.

a) emprender   b) prender   c) aprender   d) sorprender

21   Inmediatamente _____ su actitud colérica y adoptó otra sumisa.

a) impuso   b) depuso   c) repuso   d) supuso

22   Ya no quedan yogures. Hay que _____ los productos lácteos antes de que lleguen más clientes.

a) componer   b) exponer   c) recomponer   d) reponer

23   No dejó de hablar. _____ hasta convencerme.

a) Persistió   b) Asistió   c) Consistió   d) Desistió

24   Picasso se _____ a que su cuadro fuera trasladado a España durante la dictadura.

a) expuso   b) opuso   c) dispuso   d) propuso

25   En Oaxaca _____ en armonía numerosas tribus indígenas que todavía conservan sus costumbres ancestrales.

a) desviven   b) reviven   c) conviven   d) malviven

 Notes

6 Common verb phrases and idiomatic expressions

IR DE GUATEMALA A GUATEPEOR = TO GO FROM BAD TO WORSE

Idiomatic expressions are a vital part of the Spanish language. Often colorful and spirited, one could say they are the 'salt and pepper' of language. However, since they do not translate literally, they can be a challenge to learn. This chapter also includes many everyday phrases, which are not necessarily idiomatic expressions but are very important to know as well.

Following, you will find expressions introduced by the verbs **caer**, **dar**, **echar**, **haber**, **hacer**, **ir**, **poner**, **salir**, **tener** and **venir**. Since there are many expressions with these verbs in Spanish, we have given priority to the most useful and relevant ones.

Expressions with caer, dar, echar, haber and hacer

1 **Caer** literally means 'to fall,' but it takes on several different meanings in the following expressions.

caer bien / mal ⇨ to like / dislike someone

> Yo le caigo bien a mi profesor de español. Pero él me cae mal a mí.
> (My Spanish teacher likes me. But I don't like him)

Note that this expression follows the same structure as the verb 'gustar'

caer (muy) bajo ⇨ to sink (very) low

> Ese hombre rico y poderoso ha caído muy bajo.
> (That rich and powerful man has sunk very low)

caer del cielo ⇨ to be heaven-sent; at just the right moment

> La oferta de trabajo le ha caído del cielo.
> (He has received a job offer just at the right moment)

caer enfermo, caer en cama ⇨ to become ill

> No tuvimos clase porque el profesor cayó enfermo.
> (We didn't have class because the teacher became ill)

caer en la cuenta de ⇨ to see the point of; to get it; to realize

> No caigo en la cuenta de por qué tú tienes éxito con las chicas y yo no.
> (I don't get why you are successful with girls and I'm not)

caer (en algo) ⇨ to be able to remember something

> ¡Ahora caigo! Fue el domingo y no el sábado cuando te vi.
> (Now I remember! It was on Sunday, not on Saturday, when I saw you)

caer en saco roto ⇨ to go unheeded; to be ignored

> Las advertencias sobre el terremoto cayeron en saco roto.
> (The earthquake warnings went unheeded)

caer sobre, encima ⇨ to fall; to pounce on

> El paracaidista cayó sobre el edificio.
> (The parachutist fell onto the building)

Ese loco me cayó encima y comenzó a pegarme.
(That crazy man pounced on me and began to beat me up)

caer una maldición   ⇨   to be cursed

Ha caído una maldición. Ya son cinco los profesores que están enfermos.
(Five teachers are now sick, victims of a curse)

caer una tormenta   ⇨   to storm

Cayó una tormenta y después hubo un apagón.
(First there was a storm and then a blackout)

caerse al suelo   ⇨   to fall to the ground

¡Qué vergüenza! En la recepción me caí al suelo.
(How humiliating! At the reception I fell on the floor)

caerse de sueño   ⇨   to feel sleepy, to be unable to keep one's eyes open

Estoy tan cansado que me caigo de sueño.
(I am so tired that I am falling asleep)

caérsele a uno la cara de vergüenza   ⇨   to blush deeply with shame, to feel extremely embarrassed

Cuando se enteró de que lo había visto bailar, se le cayó la cara de vergüenza.
(When he found out that I had seen him dance, he was extremely embarrassed)

caiga quien caiga   ⇨   even if it means that heads will roll

Seguiremos investigando lo sucedido caiga quien caiga.
(We will keep on investigating even if it means that heads will roll)

2   **Dar** literally means 'to give,' but it is a very versatile verb that is also used in many expressions.

dar a luz   ⇨   to give birth
dar la luz   ⇨   to turn the light on

Ayer mi tía dio a luz a un bebé.
(My aunt gave birth to a baby yesterday)

¿Puedes dar la luz? No veo nada.
(Can you turn the light on? I can't see anything)

dar con algo / alguien   ⇨   run into something / somebody; to meet by chance

Ayer di con Silvia en la farmacia.
(Yesterday I ran into Silvia at the pharmacy)

dar de comer / beber ⇨   to give food / drink
En la conferencia darán de comer y de beber.
  (There will be food and beverages at the lecture)

dar el alta ⇨   to discharge
darse de alta / de baja ⇨   to join; to become a member / to unsubscribe

  Mi hermana sale hoy del hospital. Le han dado el alta.
  (My sister is coming home from the hospital. They discharged her today)

  Se ha dado de alta en el partido ecologista.
  (He has joined the Green Party)

dar de sí ⇨   to stretch
dar el sí ⇨   to say 'yes;' to grant; to consent

  Los zapatos nuevos aprietan un poco, pero luego dan de sí.
  (New shoes pinch a little, but then they stretch out)

  Cuando el joven le pidió la mano, ella le dio el 'sí'.
  (When the young man asked for her hand in marriage, she said 'yes')

dar ejemplo ⇨   to set an example

  Son los líderes los que tienen que dar ejemplo.
  (It is the leaders who should set an example)

dar en el blanco ⇨   to hit the mark; to hit home
no dar una ⇨   to get everything wrong

  Con esa respuesta el estudiante dio en el blanco.
  (With that answer the student hit the mark)

  En el examen oral ese chico haragán no dio una.
  (In the oral exam that lazy kid got everything wrong)

dar la cara ⇨   to face up to something

  Alguien tiene que dar la cara.
  (Someone has to face up to the situation)

dar la lata ⇨   to pester somebody

  No voy a comprarte el helado. ¡Deja de dar la lata!
  (I am not going to buy you an ice cream. Stop being a pest!)

dar guerra ⇨   to wage war; to torment; to be very troublesome

  Cuando mi hijo era adolescente me dio mucha guerra.
  (As a teenager my son was a lot of trouble)

darle la mano a alguien ⇨ to shake hands

Vi a mi profesor en la calle y nos dimos la mano.
(I saw my teacher on the street and we shook hands)

dar el brazo a torcer ⇨ to give in, to change one's mind

He tomado la decisión y no voy a dar el brazo a torcer.
(I have made my decision and I'm not going to change my mind)

dar las gracias ⇨ to thank

Tengo que darte las gracias por las flores.
(I need to thank you for the flowers)

dar los buenos días ⇨ to say good morning

Es tan maleducado que no da ni los buenos días.
(He's so rude he doesn't even say 'good morning')

dar la enhorabuena ⇨ to congratulate

Tenemos que darle la enhorabuena a Alejandro por su promoción.
(We have to congratulate Alejandro on his promotion)

dar el pésame ⇨ to give / to offer one's condolences

Voy a darle el pésame a Juana por la muerte de su tía.
(I'm going to give Juana my condolences for her aunt's death)

dar la talla (estar a la altura de las circunstancias) ⇨ to be up to the task
or challenge

Le faltaba experiencia, no daba la talla.
(He lacked experience; he wasn't up to the task)

dar para ⇨ to be enough

Los cien dólares que me mandaste no dan para el alquiler.
(The $100 you sent me are not enough to pay the rent)

dar por (darle a uno por hacer algo) ⇨ to get it into one's head to do
something, to take to something

A mi amiga le ha dado por hacer gimnasia todos los días.
(My friend has taken it into her head to do gymnastics every day)

dar por hecho ⇨ to take for granted

En la vida no se puede dar nada por hecho.
(In life you can't take anything for granted)

dar que pensar   ⇨   to make one think

> Lo que me dijiste anoche me dio que pensar.
> (What you told me last night made me think)

dar un paseo / una vuelta   ⇨   to go for a walk or a ride; or to take a stroll

> Mis amigos se fueron a dar un paseo por el parque.
> (My friends went for a walk in the park)

dar un golpe / una puñalada   ⇨   to hit / stab somebody

> En *West Side Story* un pandillero le da una puñalada a otro.
> (In *West Side Story* one gangster stabs another)

dar voces   ⇨   to call or cry out

> Al ser atacada, la chica dio voces.
> (Upon being attacked, the girl cried out)

me da vergüenza / pena *(Latin America)*   ⇨   it embarrasses me

> Me da vergüenza mi comportamiento de borracho.
> (I'm embarrassed about my drunken behavior)

me da risa   ⇨   it makes me laugh

> Los recuerdos de nuestros días en el bachillerato siempre me dan risa.
> (To think of our high school days always makes me laugh)

me da miedo   ⇨   it frightens me

> A mí no me da miedo viajar en el metro de noche.
> (Travelling on the subway at night doesn't frighten me)

dar gato por liebre   ⇨   to cheat or con someone (literally: to give a cat instead of a hare)

> ¡Esto no es un kilo de uvas! ¡Me han dado gato por liebre!
> (This is not a kilo of grapes! I got cheated!)

3   **Echar** literally means 'to throw,' but its meaning varies in a number of expressions.

echarse a + infinitive   ⇨   to start to do something (often unexpected)

> Se echó a cantar, después se echó a reír y de repente se echó a llorar.
> (She started singing, she burst into laughter and suddenly she burst into tears)

echar(se) a correr   ⇨   to run away

> Cogió el bolso de la señora y se echó a correr.
> (He took the lady's bag and ran away)

echar(se) a perder ⇨   to spoil (food); to fall through (plan)

Echaron a perder el plan por culpa de la prensa.
(The plan fell through because of the press)

No metimos la comida en la nevera y se echó a perder.
(We didn't put the food in the fridge and it spoiled)

echar abajo (echar por tierra) ⇨   to demolish; to bring down (government);
to ruin (a project)

Ayer echaron abajo el edificio viejo.
(Yesterday they demolished the old building)

El caso Watergate echó abajo al gobierno de Nixon.
(Watergate brought down the Nixon government)

echarse atrás ⇨   to lean backwards; to retract; to back out

Se echaron atrás y decidieron no comprar la casa.
(They backed out and decided not to buy the house)

echarse a un lado ⇨   to move aside

Échate a un lado que no veo la pantalla.
(Move to the side please, I can't see the screen)

echarse encima ⇨   to pounce on

Mi primo se me echó encima hecho una furia.
(My cousin pounced on me in a fit of rage)

echar al correo ⇨   to put in the mail

¿Puedes echar al correo esta carta?
(Can you put this letter in the mail?)

echarse a dormir (echarse una siesta) ⇨   to lie down; to take a nap

Después de comer es bueno echarse una siesta.
(After lunch it is a good habit to take a nap)

echar de menos (in Latin America, *extrañar*) ⇨   to miss something or
someone

Echo de menos a mis amigos del pueblo.
(I miss my friends from the village)

Extraño la comida de mi mamá.
(I miss my mom's food)

echar de comer ⇨ to feed (animals)

Está prohibido echar de comer a las palomas.
(It is forbidden to feed the pigeons)

echar flores ⇨ to flatter

El periodista le echó flores al presidente durante la conferencia.
(The journalist flattered the president during the lecture)

echarle la bronca a uno ⇨ to tell somebody off

La profesora me echó la bronca por no traer el libro.
(I was told off by the teacher for not having my textbook)

echar la culpa ⇨ to blame someone

Al final me echaron la culpa a mí.
(In the end they blamed everything on me)

echar mano de ⇨ to make use of
echar una mano ⇨ to lend a hand; to assist
echar el guante ⇨ to arrest or catch someone

Si no encuentras a un médico, echa mano de un curandero.
(If you cannot find a doctor, get a quack)

¿Puedes echarme una mano para pintar la casa?
(Can you lend me a hand to paint the house?)

Al final le echaron el guante al ladrón.
(Finally they arrested the thief)

echar raíces ⇨ to put down roots; to become established in a place; to settle

Esta planta no echará raíces hasta la primavera.
(This plant won't take root until the spring)

Se mudaron a Canadá donde echaron raíces.
(They moved to Canada and settled there)

echar chispas ⇨ to be furious; to be angry

Estaba tan enfadado que echaba chispas.
(He was so angry that he was hopping mad)

echar en cara, a la cara, en la cara ⇨ to reproach someone

Ella nos echó en cara que no le ayudáramos con la fiesta.
(She reproached us for not helping her with the party)

echar (tirar) la casa por la ventana ⇨ to spend money like water; to spare no expense

> Echaron la casa por la ventana y se compraron un coche nuevo.
> (They bought a new car, spending money like water)

echar un vistazo a ⇨ to have a look

> Voy a echarle un vistazo al periódico.
> (I am going to have a look at the paper)

echar a alguien a patadas ⇨ to kick someone out

> Le echaron a patadas por mal comportamiento.
> (He was kicked out for inappropriate behavior)

echar las cartas ⇨ to read somebody's fortune (in cards)

> Me echaron las cartas y me dijeron que me tocaría la lotería.
> (Someone read my fortune and said that I would win the lottery)

4   **Haber** functions as a verb, or as an auxiliary verb, or with various meanings in set expressions.

Used as a verb in the third person singular:
Hay = there is / there are (invariable in singular & plural)

> Hay quince alumnos en clase y hay solamente un profesor.
> (There are 15 students in class and there is only one teacher)

Used as an auxiliary:

> Hoy he visto a Juanita.
> (I have seen Juanita today)

Used in idiomatic expressions:
haber que + infinitive ⇨ to be necessary / essential

> Hay que estudiar para el examen de español.
> (It is necessary to study for the Spanish exam)

haber gato encerrado ⇨ there is something fishy; there's a skeleton in the closet

> Ahora entiendo por qué me habéis invitado; aquí hay gato encerrado.
> (There is something fishy about your inviting me)

Había una vez ... (Érase una vez ...) ⇨ Once upon a time ...

> Había una vez, una princesa que vivía en un castillo abandonado. Un buen día ...
> (Once upon a time there was a princess who lived in an abandoned castle. One day ...)

¡haberlo dicho! ⇨ why didn't you say so?

Si no tenías ganas de ir ¡haberlo dicho!
(If you didn't feel like going, why didn't you say so?)

de haberlo sabido ... ⇨ if only I'd known ...

De haberlo sabido, me habría comprado otro abrigo a mitad de precio.
(If only I had known, I would have bought another coat at half the price)

¿Qué hubo?
¿Qué hay?   ⇨   What's new?
¿Qué hay de nuevo?

No te he visto en mucho tiempo. ¿Qué hay de nuevo?
(I haven't seen you in ages. What's new?)

No hay de qué. ⇨ Don't mention it.

Juan: Gracias por tu ayuda con la mudanza.
(Thanks for your help with the move)

José: No hay de qué.
(Don't mention it)

¿Cuánto hay de ...? ⇨ How far is it from ...? (both distance and time)

¿Cuánto hay de Barcelona a Zaragoza? En coche hay unas 2 horas y media.
(How long does it take to go from Barcelona to Zaragoza? By car it's about 2
and a half hours)

5 **Hacer** means 'to do' or 'to make' and it is also used in many expressions.

hacer una pregunta ⇨ to ask a question

¿Te puedo hacer una pregunta después de la reunión?
(Can I ask you a question after the meeting?)

hace + time expression ⇨ ago

Hace tres años estuve en Granada para un congreso.
(Three years ago I went to Granada for a conference)

hacer caso de ⇨ to pay attention to

Haz caso de lo que te dice el profesor.
(Pay attention to what your teacher says)

hacer cola ⇨ to stand in line

Tendremos que hacer cola si queremos conseguir las entradas.
(We'll have to stand in line if we want to get the tickets)

hacer de ⇨ to work as; to act as

Para ganar algún dinero hace de canguro el fin de semana.
(To earn some money, she works as a babysitter on the weekends)

hacer de nuevo ⇨ to do again

Puesto que el experimento no ha dado resultado, tendremos que hacerlo de nuevo.
(Since the experiment has failed we will have to do it again)

hacer de las suyas ⇨ to be up to one's old tricks

El niño ha vuelto a hacer de las suyas y esta vez ha roto la puerta.
(The boy has been up to his old tricks and this time has broken the door)

hacer falta ⇨ to be in need of; to need

Me va a hacer falta dinero para pagar el alquiler.
(I am going to need money to be able to pay the rent)

hacer frente a ⇨ to face

El nuevo gobierno tendrá que hacer frente a la crisis económica.
(The new government will have to face the financial crisis)

hace fresco / frío / calor ⇨ it is chilly / cold / hot
hace buen / mal tiempo ⇨ the weather is good / bad

Hace buen tiempo; hace mucho calor para ser diciembre.
(The weather is good; it's very warm for December)

hacer juego ⇨ to match

Esta corbata te hace juego con los ojos.
(This tie matches the color of your eyes)

hacer un viaje ⇨ to take a trip

Van a hacer un viaje a la Patagonia este verano.
(This summer they are taking a trip to Patagonia)

hacer un pedido ⇨ to place an order

¿Ya has hecho el pedido por Internet?
(Have you already placed the order on-line?)

hacer la maleta ⇨ to pack (one's bag)

Tengo solamente una hora para hacer la maleta.
(I only have one hour to pack my suitcase)

hacer una visita   ⇨   to pay a visit

Mis padres me van a hacer una visita el mes que viene.
(My parents will be visiting me next month)

hacerse tarde   ⇨   to become late

Se está haciendo tarde; será mejor que nos demos prisa.
(It is getting late; we had better hurry up)

hacerse daño   ⇨   to hurt oneself

Se hizo daño con un martillo.
(He hurt himself with a hammer)

hacerse el tonto   ⇨   to play dumb

No te hagas el tonto, sabes a qué me refiero.
(Don't play dumb, you know what I'm talking about)

hacerse el sueco   ⇨   to pretend not to understand

Se hacía el sueco como si no supiera nada.
(He was pretending he didn't know anything)

 ## Exercises

EXERCISE 1. In the sentences below fill in the blanks with the correct idiomatic expressions with **caer**, **dar**, **echar**, **haber** and **hacer**.

1   ¿Te apetece _____ por el bosque?
    a) dar paseo   b) dar la vuelta   c) dar vueltas   d) dar una vuelta
2   Si tienes tiempo, ¿me podrías _____ estas cartas?
    a) echar al correo   b) echar a correr   c) echar el correo
    d) echar correo
3   A mí Pablo no me _____. Es antipático y engreído.
    a) cae en la cuenta   b) cae bien   c) cae enfermo   d) cae encima
4   Al principio no les gustaba vivir en Finlandia, pero ahora ya han

    _____.
    a) echado a reír   b) echado raíz   c) echado raíces   d) echado mano
5   En el último momento _____ y no firmaron el acuerdo para construir la fábrica.
    a) se echaron detrás   b) se echaron encima   c) se echaron atrás
    d) se echaron a un lado
6   Estábamos hablando de él, pero _____ y miraba hacia otro lado.
    a) se hacía el inglés   b) se hacía el sueco   c) se hacía el suizo
    d) se hacía el francés

7 Ayer cayó _____ de verano y no dejó de llover hasta las 3 de la madrugada.
   a) una tormenta   b) tormento   c) tormenta   d) un tormento

8 Si él, que conocía al comité, no se presentó para el cargo de presidente, es porque _____.
   a) había una vez   b) había gato encerrado   c) no había de qué
   d) había gato por liebre

9 Ella quiere _____ en su casa, no en el hospital.
   a) dar una luz   b) dar la luz   c) dar a luz   d) dar luz

10 Para el viaje me va a _____ más gasolina de lo que pensaba.
   a) hacer juego   b) hacer en falta   c) hacer falta   d) hacer de

11 _____ ir de vacaciones al pueblo. ¡Qué tiempos aquellos!
   a) Echo de siempre   b) Echo de atrás   c) Echo de menos   d) Echo de más

12 _____ para recoger la mesa y subirla a mi apartamento.
   a) Échame mano   b) Échame una mano   c) Échame la mano
   d) Échame las manos

13 Los presidentes de los países en conflicto se estuvieron _____, pero no llegaron a ningún acuerdo.
   a) echando honores   b) echando flores   c) echando chispas
   d) echando tulipanes

14 Si aquí te montas en un taxi y no preguntas cuánto te va a costar, te van a _____.
   a) dar liebre por gato   b) dar gamo por liebre   c) dar gato por liebre
   d) dar gata por liebre

15 El verano pasado mi padre cayó _____ y estuvo cinco meses hospitalizado.
   a) enfermo   b) encima   c) bien   d) mal

16 Habrá que comprar otra cuerda en la ferretería porque la que has comprado no _____.
   a) da por sí   b) da en sí   c) da de sí   d) da el sí

17 El primer ministro le _____ en señal de agradecimiento.
   a) dio la cara   b) dio un brazo   c) dio la espalda   d) dio la mano

18 Los zapatos tenían unos tacones tan altos que la modelo _____ durante el desfile de moda.
   a) se cayó al techo   b) se cayó mal   c) se cayó encima
   d) se cayó al suelo

19 _____ Juan por casualidad cuando estaba en el centro comercial.
   a) Di con   b) Di por   c) Di para   d) Di a

20 Estos pendientes te _____ con el vestido que te regalé.
   a) hacen juergas   b) hacen juegos   c) hacen juanetes   d) hacen juego

EXERCISE 2. Fill in the blanks by choosing the best idiomatic expression for each sentence from the box. Make changes accordingly.

> • caiga quien caiga • hacer una pregunta • dar por hecho • echar chispas •
> darse de alta • hacerse el sueco • echar a perder • hacer juego • caerse de
> sueño • de haberlo sabido • echar las cartas • dar para • echar flores
> • dar gato por liebre • haber gato encerrado •

1   Este vestido no es de marca. ¡Ni siquiera tiene etiqueta! Me
    _____.

2   Entró malhumorado y _____, como si fuera el peor día de su
    vida.

3   Deja ya de _____ al profesor. Por mucho que lo intentes, no te
    cambiará la nota.

4   No te _____, sabes perfectamente que estamos hablando de
    ti.

5   No sé cuánto dinero llevo, pero creo que no me va a _____
    comprarme otro helado.

6   Si quieres saber si te va a tocar la lotería, necesitas a alguien que te
    _____.

7   Ponte estos pendientes azules porque te _____ con el color
    de los ojos.

8   ¿Te puedo _____, aunque sea un poco personal?

9   Los periodistas van a investigar el escándalo hasta que se sepa la verdad:
    _____.

10 No hay que _____ que nos vayan a dar el premio, pero nuestro
    proyecto es el más innovador.

11 Aquí _____: son las 10 de la noche, es mi cumpleaños y no
    hay nadie en casa.

12 Si mezclas las prendas blancas con las de color vas a _____
    la ropa.

13 Mañana tengo que ir a la seguridad social para _____.

14 Durante la película estaba tan sumamente cansado que _____.

15 _____, habríamos reservado para más gente en el restaurante.

Expressions with ir, poner, salir, tener and venir

6 **Ir** literally means 'to go.' The following are some common uses of this verb.

ir a caballo ⇨   to ride on horseback

> Cuando era pequeño iba a caballo a la escuela.
> (When I was little, I used to go to school on horseback)

ir al grano ⇨   to get to the point

> ¡Ve al grano! Lo que quieres es que te suba la nota.
> (Get to the point! What you want is a better grade)

ir a lo suyo ⇨   to act selfishly

> Felipe siempre va a lo suyo; no hace caso a los demás.
> (Felipe always does his own thing; he doesn't care about anyone else)

ir a medias ⇨   to malfunction; to go Dutch

> Esta radio va a medias, unos días funciona y otros no.
> (This radio malfunctions; it works some days and not others)

> ¿Quién paga? Vamos a medias.
> (Who's paying? Let's go Dutch)

ir a pie ⇨   to walk; to go on foot

> Vivo muy cerca de la escuela, así que voy a pie.
> (I live very close to the school, so I walk there)

ir a una ⇨   to act together; harmoniously

> Vamos todos a una, como *Fuenteovejuna*.
> (Let's act together, like *Fuenteovejuna*)

ir bien ⇨   to be fine; to go well

> Por el momento todo va bien en la escuela. Espero que no haya problemas.
> (For the time being school is fine. I hope there won't be any problems)

ir de compras ⇨   to go shopping

> ¡Vamos de compras! Hay buenas rebajas en las tiendas.
> (Let's go shopping! There are some great sales in the stores)

ir de juerga ⇨   to go partying

> Vámonos de juerga hasta las seis de la mañana.
> (Let's go partying until 6:00 a.m.)

ir delante / por delante ⇨ to go in the front / ahead
ir detrás / por detrás ⇨ to go in the back / behind

En el coche yo voy delante y el bebé va detrás.
(In the car I go in the front and the baby in the back)

ir de Guatemala a Guatepeor ⇨ to go from bad to worse

Va de Guatemala a Guatepeor, con una C+ y ahora una D–.
(He is going from bad to worse, with a C+ and now a D–)

ir a por (ir a buscar) ⇨ to go for; to go get

Voy a por leche pues no hay para el desayuno.
(I'm going to get some milk since there is none for breakfast)

ir para (+ profesión) ⇨ to study to become

Va para médico.
(He's studying to become a doctor)

ir por cuenta de la casa ⇨ to be on the house

Esta sangría va por cuenta de la casa.
(This sangria is on the house)

ir sobre ruedas, ir viento en popa ⇨ to go smoothly

El nuevo proyecto va sobre ruedas; todo marcha a la perfección.
(The new project is going smoothly; everything is working perfectly)

irse deprisa, irse corriendo ⇨ to rush away; to leave in a hurry

María se fue deprisa para preparar la cena. Se fue corriendo.
(María left in a hurry to prepare dinner. She ran off)

írsele la cabeza a uno ⇨ to lose it; to be confused; to lose mental faculties

Es muy mayor, se le va la cabeza.
(He is very old, he is losing it)

¡Qué va! ⇨ Nonsense! No way!

El profesor de español es pelirrojo. ¡Qué va! Ése es el de matemáticas.
(The Spanish teacher is a redhead. No way! That's the math teacher)

¡Vaya! ⇨ Darn! You don't say!

El supermercado está cerrado. ¡Vaya! Tendremos que ir a un restaurante.
(The supermarket is closed. Darn! We'll have to go to a restaurant)

¡*Vaya con Dios!* ⇨   God be with you!

Adiós, amigo. ¡Vaya con Dios!
(Goodbye, my friend. May God be with you!)

A donde fueres haz lo que vieres ⇨   when in Rome, do as the Romans do

7   **Poner** literally means 'to put' or 'to place.' It is used in a variety of ways.

ponerse a + infinitive ⇨   to begin to

El bebé se puso a llorar.
(The baby started to cry)

poner al corriente ⇨   to inform; to keep someone posted

No te preocupes, te pondré al corriente de la situación.
(Don't worry; I'll keep you posted on the situation)

poner al día ⇨   to bring someone up to date; to give an update

¿Me puedes poner al día de cómo va la empresa?
(Can you give me an update on how the company is doing?)

poner al sol ⇨   to put something in the sun

Si pones la pintura al sol se secará antes.
(If you put the painting in the sun it will dry faster)

poner algo aparte ⇨   to set something aside

No te comas todo el chocolate; pon algo aparte para mañana.
(Don't eat up all the chocolate; put some aside for tomorrow)

ponerse de acuerdo ⇨   to reach an agreement

Estuvimos en la reunión cinco horas y no nos pusimos de acuerdo.
(We were in the meeting for five hours but didn't reach an agreement)

poner en un apuro ⇨   to put in a difficult situation

Mi hijo me puso en un apuro delante del jefe.
(My son put me in a difficult situation in front of my boss)

poner en duda ⇨   to cast doubt on; to question

Te conozco, por eso nunca pongo en duda tu integridad.
(I know you; therefore I never doubt your integrity)

poner en marcha ⇨   to start; to get going

Si quieres conducir, pon en marcha el motor.
(If you want to drive, start the engine)

poner las cartas sobre la mesa ⇨   to put one's cards on the table; to come clean

poner las cosas en claro ⇨   to clear things up; to explain

Ya basta de cuentos. Pon las cartas sobre la mesa.
(No more lies. Put your cards on the table)

poner la mesa ⇨   to set the table

Voy a poner la mesa para la cena.
(I am going to set the table for dinner)

poner énfasis en ⇨   to emphasize

Siempre pongo énfasis en el buen comportamiento.
(I always emphasize good behavior)

poner el reloj / despertador ⇨   to set the alarm clock

Voy a poner el despertador a las 6 de la mañana.
(I'm setting the alarm for 6 a.m.)

ponerse lejos / cerca ⇨   to place oneself far / close

Cuando voy al cine me pongo lejos de la pantalla.
(When I go to the movies I always sit far from the screen)

poner a alguien en su lugar ⇨   to put someone in his place

Se ha portado mal. Necesito ponerlo en su lugar.
(He has behaved badly. I need to put him in his place)

ponerse (un prenda de ropa) ⇨   to put on (a garment)

Ponte el vestido que te regaló tu tía.
(Put on the dress your aunt gave you)

poner el grito en el cielo ⇨   to complain bitterly; to hit the roof

Se dio cuenta de que se había olvidado las llaves y puso el grito en el cielo.
(She realized she had left the keys at home and hit the roof)

poner mala cara ⇨   to give a dirty look

Cuando le dije que no iríamos al cine puso mala cara.
(When I told her that we weren't going to the movies, she gave me a dirty look)

8 **Salir** literally means 'to leave' or 'to go out,' but in some expressions it has other meanings.

salir a ⇨ to take after (somebody); to resemble

> Este niño salió a su padre.
> (This kid takes after his father)

salir a la luz ⇨ to come to light; to become known

> El escándalo salió a la luz.
> (The scandal came to light)

salir al encuentro ⇨ to go to meet (en route)

> Voy a salir al encuentro de mi amigo antes de que llegue aquí.
> (I am going to meet my friend before he arrives here)

salir a pedir de boca ⇨ to turn out perfectly, without a hitch

> Organizamos el baile y todo salió a pedir de boca.
> (We organized the ball, and everything turned out perfectly)

salir adelante ⇨ to get by

> Ellos trabajan duro para salir adelante.
> (They work hard to get by)

salir bien / mal ⇨ to turn out well / badly

> ¿Cómo salió la operación? Salió bien.
> (How did the operation turn out? It turned out well)

salir con ⇨ to go out with; to date

> ¿Te gustaría salir conmigo este sábado por la noche?
> (Would you like to go out with me this Saturday night?)

salirse con la suya ⇨ to get one's way

> Él siempre se sale con la suya. ¡Estoy harta!
> (He always gets his way. I'm fed up!)

salir de ⇨ to leave (a place)
salir de viaje ⇨ to go away (on a trip)

> Salió del edificio por la puerta principal.
> (He left the building by the front door)

salir de un apuro ⇨ to get out of a jam

> Estoy mal. Tengo que salir de este apuro.
> (I'm not doing well. I have to get out of this jam)

salir ganando / perdiendo   ⇨   to come out better off; to lose out

No quiero salir perdiendo en este asunto.
(I don't want to lose out in this matter)

salir pitando   ⇨   to run away hastily and in confusion

Al oír la alarma, los ladrones salieron pitando.
(Upon hearing the alarm, the thieves ran away)

salir para   ⇨   to leave for

Salgo para Granada mañana.
(I'm leaving for Granada tomorrow)

salir por la tele   ⇨   to appear on TV

Ayer salió Javier Bardem por la tele.
(Yesterday Javier Bardem appeared on TV)

salirse del tema   ⇨   to digress
salir por peteneras   ⇨   to go off on a tangent

No te salgas del tema.Ve al grano.
(Don't beat about the bush. Get to the point!)

9   **Tener** means 'to have,' but it is also used in many expressions that take the verb 'to be' in English.

a) Expressions where 'tener' means 'to have' or a related concept:

tener que + infinitive   ⇨   to have to

Tengo que estudiar más.
(I have to study more)

tener un disgusto   ⇨   to have a falling out; to be upset about something

Tuve un disgusto con mi amigo Pedro.
(I had a falling out with my friend Pedro)

tener dolor de   ⇨   to ache; to hurt

Tengo dolor de garganta y tú tienes dolor de cabeza.
(My throat hurts and you have a headache)

tener ganas de   ⇨   to feel like; to be in the mood

No tengo ganas de trabajar.
(I don't feel like working)

tener un bebé ⇨ to give birth

Tiene cinco hijos y ayer tuvo otro bebé.
(She has five kids, and yesterday she had another baby)

tener lugar ⇨ to take place

La fiesta tuvo lugar en mi casa.
(The party took place in my house)

tener mala cara ⇨ to look bad; to look sick

Tienes mala cara. ¿No has dormido?
(You look bad. Haven't you slept?)

tener los nervios de punta ⇨ to be on edge

Tengo los nervios de punta por el examen de mañana.
(I'm on edge because of tomorrow's exam)

tener (algo) en la punta de la lengua ⇨ to have something on the tip of one's tongue

No recuerdo su nombre, pero lo tengo en la punta de la lengua.
(I don't remember her name, but I have it on the tip of my tongue)

no tener pelos en la lengua ⇨ not to mince words

No tiene pelos en la lengua. Dice lo que piensa.
(She doesn't mince words. She says what she thinks)

tener que ver con ⇨ to have to do with

No quiero tener nada que ver con ese hombre.
(I don't want to have anything to do with that man)

b) Expressions where 'tener' means 'to be':

tener ... años ⇨ to be ... years old

Tengo 25 años.
(I'm 25 years old)

tener calor / frío ⇨ to be hot / cold

Tengo mucho calor.
(I'm very hot)

tenerle celos a ⇨ to be jealous

Ella me tiene celos.
(She's jealous of me)

tener cuidado   ⇨   to be careful

Ten cuidado al cruzar la calle.
(Be careful when crossing the street)

tener la culpa de   ⇨   to be guilty of; to be at fault

No tengo la culpa de que hayas perdido el dinero.
(It's not my fault that you lost the money)

tener éxito   ⇨   to be successful

Todos queremos tener éxito en la vida.
(We all want to be successful in life)

tener hambre / sed   ⇨   to be hungry / thirsty

¿Tienes hambre o sed?
(Are you hungry or thirsty?)

tener madera de / para   ⇨   to have the makings of something; to have what it takes for something

Tiene madera de artista / Tiene madera para el arte.
(She's got the makings of an artist)

tener mucho mundo   ⇨   to be sophisticated; to be worldly-wise

Tiene mucho mundo porque ha viajado mucho.
(He is sophisticated because he has traveled a lot)

tener prisa   ⇨   to be in a hurry; to be in a rush

Tenemos prisa. ¡Apúrate!
(We are in a rush. Hurry up!)

tener razón   ⇨   to be right

¿Tengo razón o no? No la tienes.
(Am I right or not? You are wrong)

tener sueño   ⇨   to be sleepy
tener un sueño   ⇨   to have a dream

El chiquillo tiene sueño, ¡acuéstalo!
(The little one is sleepy. Put him to bed!)

Ayer tuve un sueño muy extraño.
(Yesterday I had a very strange dream)

tener suerte   ⇨   to be lucky

Ella no tiene suerte en este juego.
(She has no luck in this game)

tener vergüenza   ⇨   to be ashamed

Es un sinvergüenza, no tiene vergüenza de nada.
(He is a scoundrel; he's not ashamed of anything)

c) Many idiomatic expressions with **tener** express sensations and feelings:

tenerle miedo a + *noun*   ⇨   to be afraid of something or someone

Ella le tiene miedo a la oscuridad.
(She is afraid of the dark)

tener miedo de + *infinitive*   ⇨   to be afraid to do something

Tengo miedo de cometer un error.
(I am afraid to make a mistake)

tener confianza en   ⇨   to be confident; to trust

Tienes que tener más confianza en ti mismo.
(You have to be more confident in yourself)

tener en cuenta   ⇨   to take into account; to take into consideration

Debemos tener en cuenta que el estudiante no habla español.
(We have to take into account that the student doesn't speak Spanish)

10   **Venir** literally means 'to come,' but it is used in some expressions with other meanings.

venir a buscar   ⇨   to come and get someone

Te vengo a buscar a las 5 en punto.
(I am coming to get you at 5 o'clock sharp)

venir bien   ⇨   to fit; to do nicely; to be suitable

El abrigo que me regalaste me viene bien.
(The coat you bought me fits me nicely)

venir de   ⇨   to come from; to stem from; to originate

¿De dónde viene tu familia?
(Where does your family come from?)

venir de perilla, venir de perlas ⇨ to be just what one needs; to come in handy

Me viene de perilla (de perlas) quedarme en tu apartamento de la playa.
(To stay at your apartment on the beach is just what I need)

venirse abajo ⇨ to fall; to collapse; to crumble; to experience a breakdown

Cuando oyó la noticia, se vino abajo.
(When she heard the news, she collapsed)

la semana / el mes / el año que viene ⇨ next week / month / year

Nos vemos la semana que viene.
(We will see each other next week)

¡Venga! ⇨ Come on! Let's go!

¡Venga, señora! ¡Abra la cartera y deme su dinero!
(Come on, lady! Open your wallet and give me your money!)

Exercises

EXERCISE 3. In the sentences below fill in the blanks with the correc t expressions using ir, poner, salir, tener and venir.

1 El ministro puso _____ en la educación como la mejor manera de ayudar a los jóvenes.
 a) aparte b) en cuestión c) en duda d) énfasis

2 Anita _____ un vestido rojo y tacones muy altos.
 a) puso b) se puso c) se puso a d) puso se

3 Los pacientes deben tener _____ en el médico de cabecera.
 a) éxito b) vergüenza c) confianza d) suerte

4 Con el nuevo jefe la situación empeoró. De hecho, fuimos _____.
 a) bien b) a lo nuestro c) a medias d) de Guatemala a Guatepeor

5 Sé claro y directo. Ve _____ del asunto y no pierdas el tiempo.
 a) a lo tuyo b) sobre ruedas c) al grano d) a trancas y barrancas

6 Ana es bastante malpensada. Tiene _____ de todas las mujeres que trabajan con su marido.
 a) celos b) vergüenza c) pelos d) hambre

7 Lo siento mucho, pero yo no tengo _____ de que usted tenga que levantarse a las cuatro de la mañana.
 a) la madera b) la suerte c) la justicia d) la culpa

8 Lo que más odio es el bricolaje e ir _____.
 a) a compras b) en compras c) de compras d) para compras

9 Me temo que no puedo detenerme a hablar ahora. Tengo mucha
_____.

a) razón   b) suerte   c) prisa   d) valentía

10 Hay gente que no apoya la huelga porque tiene _____ a perder
su trabajo.

a) mundo   b) celos   c) confianza   d) miedo

11 El avión salió _____ La Habana con víveres para las víctimas
del huracán.

a) para   b) con   c) por   d) sin

12 Tengo _____. Me voy a tumbar un rato antes de que lleguen
los niños.

a) un sueño   b) el sueño   c) sueño   d) sueños

13 Afortunadamente, logró salir _____ con al apoyo de su familia.

a) adelante   b) perdiendo   c) con la suya   d) delante

14 Yo creo que este muchacho tiene _____ de periodista. Debería
dedicarse a escribir.

a) mundo   b) éxito   c) rabia   d) madera

15 ¿Te _____ que nos veamos el lunes a las nueve de la mañana?

a) sale bien   b) viene bien   c) hace bien   d) cae bien

16 Tengo _____ escribir no sólo cuentos, sino también una novela
entera.

a) gana de   b) ganas   c) ganas de   d) gana

17 Deberías llevar siempre algo de dinero en efectivo, lo suficiente para salir
de _____.

a) apuro   b) a un puro   c) a puros   d) un apuro

18 ¿Sabes que acabo de tener gemelos? _____ Esto sí que es
una agradable sorpresa.

a) ¡Vayas!   b) ¡Vaya!   c) ¡Va!   d) ¡Vayan!

19 Cuando nos metieron el quinto gol, el equipo entero se vino
_____.

a) al bajo   b) bajo   c) a bajo   d) abajo

20 Le cuesta andar, pero hay que tener _____ que tiene ochenta
años.

a) de cuenta   b) en la cuenta   c) en cuenta   d) a cuenta

21 ¿Cómo te va el negocio? Bien, bien. De momento, y si no hay imprevistos,
todo _____.

a) da sobre ruedas   b) viene sobre ruedas   c) va sobre ruedas
d) hace sobre ruedas

22 En cuanto me dio el billete falso se _____. Nunca más lo volví
a ver.

a) vino corriendo   b) fue corriendo   c) salió corriendo   d) dio corriendo

EXERCISE 4. Fill in the blanks by choosing from the box the best idiomatic expression for each sentence. Make changes accordingly.

• ir de Guatemala a Guatepeor • poner al sol • ir a medias • salir pitando •
venirse abajo • tener un sueño • venir a buscar • salir a • tener sueño •
poner mala cara • tener mala cara • salir a la luz • írsele la cabeza •
ir por cuenta de la casa • poner la mesa • venir de perlas •

1 No tienes que pagar nada, esta ronda _____.
2 Hoy por la tarde me voy de vacaciones, y en cuanto pueda voy a _____ del trabajo.
3 ¡Qué bien que no tengas nada que hacer el fin de semana! Me va a _____ para que me ayudes a limpiar en casa.
4 A pesar de sus contactos en el gobierno, su vida privada _____.
5 No sé qué le pasa a Isabel, pero _____. Espero que no haya cogido el mismo virus que yo.
6 Desde hace años _____: ser el capitán del equipo de rugby de la universidad.
7 El niño que viene de camino tiene que _____ padre, porque los otros cuatro son clavaditos a la madre.
8 Si me vas a _____ a casa, no te olvides de llegar puntual.
9 No le hagas mucho caso a mi abuelo. _____ un poco. Cosas de la edad.
10 Esto es increíble. Son las 6 de la tarde y ya _____.
11 Cuando vio la nota del examen _____. Llevaba dos años estudiando para ser juez.
12 No _____ y haz el favor de _____ cuanto antes.
13 Esta vez pago yo la comida, pero la próxima vez _____.
14 La toalla todavía está mojada. La _____ para que se seque antes.
15 La economía de este país no mejora. _____.

Por and para

Por and **para** can be tricky to learn. The following mnemonic devices and expressions will come in handy; they will help you to be more accurate with the language.

Mnemonic device[1]

Remember the acronyms REMEDIAB and PERFECT to distinguish when to use **por** or **para**

Por

R Razón (a causa de, motivo) (cause, reason why, on behalf of)

Se casó con ella **por** dinero. (He married her for her money)

Lo hice **por** ti porque tú no estabas. (I did it on your behalf because your weren't there)

E Espacio (movement through space; means of transport and communication)

Di un paseo **por** el parque. (I took a walk through the park)

Hablé **por** teléfono. (I talked on the phone)

Voy a Italia **por** (en) barco. (I'm going to Italy by boat)

M Medidas y monedas (measures and currencies, rate)

Se venden a tres dólares **por** kilo. (They are sold for 3 dollars a kilo)

El cambio está a 5 euros **por** 7 dólares. (The exchange is 5 euros for 7 dollars)

E Expresiones hechas (idiomatic expressions)

Por favor, **por** primera vez, **por** fin, etc. (Please, for the first time, finally, etc.)

D Duración del tiempo (time)

Estudié **por** (durante) veinte minutos. (I studied for 20 minutes)

I Intercambio (in exchange for)

Te doy esta manzana **por** tu sándwich. (I'll give you this apple for your sandwich)

Si no puedes hablar, lo haré **por** ti. (If you can't talk, I'll talk for you)

A Agente de la voz pasiva (passive voice)

La pirámide fue construida **por** los aztecas. (The pyramid was built by the Aztecs)

B Búsqueda (to look for)

Voy (a) **por** mi libro; voy (a) **por** un vaso de agua. (I'm going to find my book; to get a glass of water)

---

1 This mnemonic device has been adapted from the one created by Laura Gordon, teacher at the Trinity School in New York.

Para

P Propósito (purpose)

Estudiamos **para** el examen. (We study for the exam)

Voy a Zaragoza **para** aprender español. (I'm going to Zaragoza to learn Spanish)

E Empleo (work, employment)

Mi padre trabaja **para** la empresa Goya. (My father works for the Goya company)

R Recibe la acción (intended for, recipient of an action)

Esta carta es **para** ti. (This letter is for you)

El dinero es **para** comprar el pan. (The money is to buy bread)

F Fecha límite (deadline, future date or event)

El ensayo es **para** el jueves. (The deadline for handing in the essay is Thursday)

E Expresiones hechas (idiomatic expressions)

Para siempre, **para** variar, **para** colmo, etc. (Forever, for good, for a change, to make matters worse)

C Contraste o comparación (comparison or contrast, exception to a generalization, viewpoint)

Para ser el director general es muy joven. (For a director he is very young)

Para mí, esto no tiene sentido. (For me, this makes no sense)

T Towards – dirección o destino (direction)

El vuelo sale **para** Madrid a las dos. (The flight leaves for Madrid at 2:00)

Expressions with 'por'

en un dos por tres	right away, on the double, very quickly
hablar por alguien	to speak on behalf of someone, for someone
hablar por hablar	to talk for the sake of talking
hablar por señas	to speak in sign language
palabra por palabra	word for word
poner por las nubes	to praise to the skies
por adelantado	in advance
por ahora	for now, for the time being
por amor de Dios	for the love of God
por aquel entonces	at that time, in those times

por aquí / allí	around here / there
por casualidad	by chance
por ciento	percent
por cierto	by the way
por completo	completely
por correo	by mail
por culpa de	through the fault of, because of
por debajo de	under, beneath
por dentro / por fuera	inside / outside
por desgracia	unfortunately
por detrás de	behind
por difícil que sea	hard though it may be
por dónde	where, in what direction
por ejemplo	for example
por encima de (todo)	over, above (all)
por escrito	in writing
por eso	therefore, that's why
por favor	please
por fin	finally, at last
por la mañana, la tarde, la noche	in the morning, in the afternoon, at night
por las buenas o por las malas	like it or not
por lo general	generally
por lo menos	at least
por lo mismo	for that very reason
por lo pronto	for the time being
por lo que dicen	according to what they say
por lo tanto	therefore, so
por lo visto	apparently
por medio de	by means of
por mi parte	as far as I am concerned
por ningún lado	nowhere
por poco	almost
por primera vez	for the first time
porque	because
¿por qué?	why? for what reason?
por si acaso / por si las moscas	just in case

por su cuenta	on one's own
por suerte (por fortuna)	fortunately
por supuesto	of course, certainly
por teléfono / fax / correo electrónico	by phone / fax / email
por todas partes	everywhere
por todos lados	everywhere
por último	finally
por un lado ... / por otro lado ...	on the one hand ... / on the other hand ...
trabajar por cuatro	to work like a slave
de una vez por todas	once and for all

Expressions with 'para'

estar para	to be about to
para colmo (de males / de desgracias)	to make matters worse, on top of everything, to crown it all
para entonces	by that time
para esa época	by / for that time
para otra vez / para otra ocasión	for another occasion, next time
para que + subjunctive	so that, in order that
¿para qué? + indicative	why? for what purpose?
para siempre	forever, for good
para variar	for a change, to vary

Exercises

EXERCISE 5. Choose either 'por' or 'para' in the following sentences. Pay attention to the meaning expressed in each sentence.

1   Mi prima trabaja (por / para) una empresa sueca de reciclaje (por / para) muy poco dinero.
2   Te cambio mi amuleto de la suerte (por / para) el tuyo, pero si me lo das será mío (por / para) siempre.
3   Voy un momento a la tienda a (por / para) una barra de pan (por / para) si acaso.
4   Cuando paseábamos (por / para) el parque, vimos (por / para) casualidad un oso pardo que se había escapado del zoo.
5   Era muy bajo (por / para) ser jugador profesional de baloncesto, pero (por / para) esa época eso no era demasiado importante.
6   Tuvo que irse de viaje (por / para) motivos laborales, no (por / para) gusto.

7 (Por / Para) lo que dicen, la redacción es (por / para) mañana y no (por / para) pasado mañana.

8 El Chupa Chups fue inventado (por / para) un español, (por / para) eso su nombre viene del verbo 'chupar'.

9 (Por / Para) no hacer caso al médico se puso muy enfermo y (por / para) poco no lo cuenta.

10 (Por / Para) lo general, en el banco sólo te dan 10 pesos mexicanos (por / para) un dólar, pero yo te daré 12.

11 (Por / Para) mí que Jaime ha salido pronto de casa (por / para) llegar antes que nosotros.

12 ¿Ya han traído el paquete (por / para) Yolanda? (Por / Para) mí que sí, pero voy a preguntar (por / para) si acaso.

13 Cuando hablamos (por / para) teléfono, me dijo que estaría aquí (por / para) las 10:00.

14 (Por / Para) si las moscas, vamos a organizar una reunión rápida (por / para) que todo el mundo sepa qué es lo que hay que hacer de una vez (por / para) todas.

15 ¿No es demasiado joven (por / para) ser el campeón del mundo de sudoku? (Por / Para) mí que es superdotado.

16 Si al final no se te mejora la garganta, hablaré (por / para) ti en la conferencia. No te preocupes (por / para) eso.

17 Ya sabes que nos tienes aquí (por / para) cuando quieras venir y (por / para) lo que necesites.

18 (Por / Para) lo visto, (por / para) colgar la lámpara tendremos que hacer un agujero con un taladro (por / para) encima del techo.

19 (Por / Para) supuesto que tú eres la única razón de mi existencia: todo lo que hago, lo hago (por / para) ti.

20 Había mucha niebla (por / para) la tarde (por / para) ser el mes de junio, y (por / para) colmo de males, el chiquillo se perdió (por / para) el bosque (por / para) no seguir los consejos de los monitores y (por / para) no mirar la brújula de vez en cuando.

EXERCISE 6. Complete the following sentences with 'por' or 'para.'

1 El grupo de alumnos va a pasar _____ Salamanca _____ la noche _____ ver la ciudad iluminada.

2 Ahora voy a _____ una caja de aspirinas, pero no sé ni _____ dónde hay que ir, ni si hay una farmacia _____ esta calle.

3 _____ favor, profesor ¿Cuál es la tarea _____ el miércoles?

4 Este verano voy a trabajar en una empresa _____ adquirir experiencia, aunque sea _____ poco dinero.

5 La cocina ya está cerrada _____ pedir comida. Te has quedado sin cenar _____ no venir antes.

6 Voy al gimnasio tres veces _____ semana _____ levantar pesas y nadar en la piscina.

7 No es muy alto _____ jugar en la NBA, pero _____ lo visto juega muy bien.

8 ¡Vaya! _____ desgracia estas flores no son _____ mí. ¿ _____ quién serán?

9 Sí, _____ mí también es un gran tipo y habla muy bien, pero _____ mí que no venga porque aburre hasta a las piedras.

10 _____ si acaso, voy a poner a lavar la ropa _____ que le dé tiempo a secarse.

11 Aida está estudiando _____ ser abogada, pero _____ terminar los estudios todavía le quedan unos años.

12 ¡No tienes dinero _____ entrar al cine! Y entonces, ¿_____ qué están los amigos?

13 Todavía tengo las tortillas _____ hacer, pero _____ lo menos el postre ya lo he preparado esta mañana.

14 _____ fin me devolvió los $20 que me debía _____ el CD que me encargó.

15 Trabaja _____ su cuenta y _____ suerte no tiene que pedirle permiso a ningún jefe _____ cogerse vacaciones.

16 Gracias _____ haberme ayudado a pintar la casa. _____ favor, ¡qué cosas tienes!

17 Pedrito no pudo ir al colegio _____ el resfriado que tenía, y _____ colmo tampoco pudo salir de casa para ir al médico _____ la nieve.

18 Dijo el profesor: "_____ que lo sepan, yo no regalo las notas. Las notas tienen que ganárselas _____ difícil que les resulte".

19 _____ que no te pierdas, baja _____ la escalera y ve _____ detrás del edificio.

20 No lo hago _____ amor al arte. Lo hago _____ amor al dinero y _____ no tener que preocuparme en el futuro.

21 _____ lo visto, han convocado una huelga general _____ el lunes.

22 Recuerdo que lo vi _____ primera vez y _____ última vez _____ el centro de Buenos Aires.

23 Es una niña muy madura _____ su edad, pero _____ serte sincero, a veces es un poco repelente.

24 Si quiere alquilar el piso _____ vivir aquí con una boa, una tarántula y un perro, tendrá que pagar tres meses _____ adelantado.

25 Cuando voy _____ el bosque llevo siempre conmigo una linterna y un botiquín, _____ si acaso.

26 Llevar un hogar es un trabajo bastante duro _____ la mayoría de la gente que, _____ colmo de males y _____ desgracia, no está remunerado.

27 ¿No habrás visto _____ casualidad mis gafas en el salón? _____ mí que están en el jardín o _____ algún cajón.

28 i _____ fin estás aquí! _____ variar, podrías haber llegado puntual.

29 Se negó a ser apresado _____ las buenas, y al final lo detuvieron _____ las malas y _____ chorizo.

30 _____ insectos pesados los mosquitos. _____ si las moscas, ponte crema porque aquí están _____ todas partes.

EXERCISE 7. Fill in the blanks with the appropriate expression using 'por' or 'para.'

1 No encuentro mi libro de gramática _____ (anywhere).

2 _____ (Apparently) lo dejaste en casa de tu amiga Rita.

3 Mándeme su reclamación _____ (in writing) y lo pensaré.

4 _____ (We are about to) ir al aeropuerto para recoger a Marta.

5 Llevo mi pasaporte _____ (just in case) me lo piden.

6 ¿Tienes tu pasaporte también? _____ (of course) que lo tengo.

7 Mi padre no se encuentra muy bien _____ (unfortunately).

8 ¿ _____ (for what purpose) quieres que te deje el coche?

9 El me dictó la carta _____ (word for word).

10 Mi hijo se fue a vivir a Noruega _____ (for good).

11 Yo no lo he visto _____ (around here) desde hace tiempo.

12 Voy a llegar _____ (very quickly); ve poniendo los platos y los cubiertos.

13 _____ (Almost) me caigo con esos zapatos de tacón.

14 ¿Puedes _____ (speak on my behalf) en la reunión? Estoy un poco afónico.

15 _____ (Next time) acuérdate de traer tu propio libro a clase.

16 Últimamente me encuentro a Juan _____ (everywhere).

17 _____ (Hard though it may be), tengo que sacar sobresaliente en este examen.

18 Para entrar en el castillo tienes que ir _____ (behind) de la iglesia.

19 En el año 1958 visité Cuba _____ (for the first time).

20 Tendremos que madrugar, limpiar la casa y _____ (on top of everything), quitar las malas hierbas del jardín.

21 _____ (Above all) el gobierno quiere que las pensiones suban.

22 Quiero ir a otro restaurante esta noche _____ (for a change).

23 En esta época electrónica la gente envía pocas cartas _____ (by mail).

24 _____ (For the time being) estamos en contacto.

25 No nos va a dar tiempo a preparar chocolate con churros. Será mejor que lo dejemos _____ (for another occasion).

EXERCISE 8. Fill in the blanks with the appropriate expression using 'por' or 'para.'

"Mario el pesado"

El otro día fui al cine _____ (in the afternoon) y me encontré con Mario _____ (by chance). Era la primera vez que lo veía en mucho tiempo, y _____ (fortunately) lo reconocí _____ (right away). Me saludó muy cortésmente y me preguntó cómo estaba mi prima Sofía. Le contesté que _____ (unfortunately) la semana pasada se había mudado a otra ciudad, y que fue todo tan rápido que lo supe _____ (by mail). Me dijo que _____ (please) le diera la dirección de mi prima _____ (in order to) ponerse en contacto con ella lo antes posible. Yo _____ (for my part) no tenía ningún inconveniente en darle la información que me pedía, pero _____ (certainly) no quería estar ahí hablando demasiado tiempo sobre mi prima. Así que le dije que había una película de suspense en el cine que estaba _____ (was about to) empezar, que no quería perderme el principio, y que me diera su dirección de correo electrónico _____ (in order to) mandarle las señas de mi prima.

_____ (Apparently) Mario no me oyó, porque continuó hablándome de lo guapa, sexy y simpática que era Sofía, poniéndola _____ (praising her to the skies), repitiéndome _____ (word for word) las conversaciones que había tenido con ella _____ (by phone) el año pasado, y contándome que _____ (in those times) tenía mucho tiempo libre, no como ahora que trabaja _____ (on his own) y es su propio jefe. Aunque también dijo que _____ (for that very reason) tenía que estar _____ (everywhere), y que la semana pasada _____ (almost) le dio un ataque cardíaco _____ (because) no podía con tanto estrés laboral. Mientras tanto la que estaba estresada era yo, que no sabía qué hacer _____ (in order to) Mario dejara de hablar sobre mi prima y _____ (in order to) poder entrar a ver la película tranquilamente. Así que decidí que _____ (like it or not) iba a poner fin a nuestra conversación. Le dije a Mario que _____ (for the love of God) me dejara ver la película de suspense _____ (because), si no, era a mí a quien le iba a dar un ataque de nervios, y que sería _____ (his fault). _____ (Of course), me miró bastante enfadado, y _____ (fortunately) se fue, y _____ (at last) pude entrar en el cine a ver la película.

7 Non-existent words, words with double meanings and other misused expressions

"UN GATO" IS A CAT AND ALSO A ...

It is remarkable how often students take English words and expressions and use them as though they were Spanish. It is important to know which ones they are so that you can steer clear of them. You also need to be aware of a number of common Spanish words that have more than one meaning.

Non-existent words and misused expressions

Below you will find a list of typical mistakes made by English speakers, together with an explanation of why you may be making these mistakes yourself. Note the words and expressions that either do not exist or suffer from serious misuse. They appear crossed out on the page, so that you can cross them out in your mind and learn the correct usage.

1 ✗ al primero

✓ el / al principio

'El principio' means 'the beginning' and 'al principio' means 'at the beginning.' However, 'primero' simply means 'first.'

> Entré **al principio** de la película, pero no me gustó **el principio**.
> (I came in at the beginning of the movie, but I didn't like the beginning)

2 ✗ cinco cientos

✓ quinientos

▶ Although we say 200 (doscientos), 300 (trescientos), 400 (cuatrocientos), we use a different type of compound noun for 500 (quinientos). Also, pay attention to 700 (setecientos and not siete ...) and 900 (novecientos and not nueve ...).

> Tengo más de **quinientos** libros en la biblioteca.
> (I have more than five hundred books in my library)

3 ✗ departir

✓ salir

✓ marcharse

✓ partir (old-fashioned)

▶ The verb 'departir' does not mean 'to depart' but 'to converse' and is not widely used.

> El tren **sale** a la 1:00 de la tarde. ¡No lo pierdas!
> (The train leaves at 1:00 p.m. Do not miss it!)

> Cuando hago un brunch, los invitados **se marchan** a eso de las 2:30.
> (When I make brunch, my guests leave around 2:30)

4 ✗ dependiente de

✓ depender de

▶ The expression 'dependent on' or 'it depends on' in Spanish is 'depender de,' whereas the word 'dependiente' means 'sales clerk' or 'shop assistant.'

> Tu sueldo **dependerá de** la calidad de tu trabajo.
> (Your salary will be dependent on the quality of your work)

5 ✖ ~~embarazado~~
✔ avergonzado

▶ The adjective 'embarazado' (pregnant) is obviously not used in the masculine form. To say 'embarrassed' use the word 'avergonzado.'

¡Qué humillación! Me siento tan **avergonzado**.
(What a humiliation! I feel so embarrassed!)

Mi tía Pepa está **embarazada** de gemelos.
(My aunt Pepa is pregnant with twins)

 (See chapter 4 for more information on this adjective)

6 ✖ ~~facto~~
✔ hecho
Words like ~~facto~~, ~~realistico~~, ~~resulto~~, ~~optimistico~~, ~~pesimistico~~, ~~senso~~ simply do not exist in Spanish.

¡Eres bellísima e inteligentísima! Es un **hecho** incuestionable.
(You are extremely beautiful and intelligent! It is an undeniable fact)

✖ ~~realistico~~
✔ realista

¡Sé **realista**! No puedes trabajar durante el día y también por la noche.
(Be realistic! You cannot work all day and all night)

(Note the same form for both the masculine and feminine: Juan es *realista* y María es *realista*)

✖ ~~optimistico~~
✔ optimista
✖ ~~pesimistico~~
✔ pesimista

Hay que ser menos **pesimista** y pensar de manera **optimista** en la vida.
(You have to be less pessimistic and think about life in an optimistic way)

✖ ~~resulto~~
✔ resultado

Los dos científicos obtuvieron el mismo **resultado**.
(The two scientists got the same result)

❌ ~~senso~~

✅ sentido

Note that the word 'sense' is translated as **sentido**, with various meanings:

> Préstame atención con los cinco **sentidos**.
> (Pay attention with all your senses)

> ¿Cuál es el **sentido** de esta frase? No la sé interpretar.
> (What's the meaning of this sentence? I do not know how to interpret it)

> Tu comportamiento no tiene **sentido**.
> (Your behavior makes no sense)

❌ ~~sensitivo~~

✅ sensible

In Spanish, to say that someone is 'sensitive' we use the word 'sensible,' which is a false friend, since in English the same word means 'having good sense.'

> No seas tan **sensible**.
> (Don't be so sensitive)

  (See chapter 4 for more information on this adjective)

7 ❌ ~~hacer lluvia, nieve~~

  ✅ llueve, nieva, etc.

▶ Remember to use: *llueve* (it rains), *nieva* (it snows), *graniza* (it hails). By contrast, one says: *hace sol* (it's sunny), *hace viento* or *hace aire* (it's windy). But: *hay niebla* (it's foggy).

> Hoy no **llueve** ni **nieva**. **Hace** un sol espléndido.
> (It is neither raining nor snowing today. It is wonderfully sunny)

8 ❌ ~~hacerse enfermo~~

  ✅ ponerse enfermo

  ✅ enfermarse

▶ If you want to say 'to become ill or sick' in Spanish, you can use the reflexive verb 'enfermarse' or the expression 'ponerse enfermo.'

> Con esta humedad uno se **pone enfermo** / **se enferma** con frecuencia.
> (With this humidity, one gets sick often)

9 ❌ ~~dos años pasados~~

  ✅ hace dos años

▶ In Spanish, the word for 'last' is 'pasado' (in the past), e.g. 'la semana pasada' (last week), 'el año pasado' (last year). However, for the word 'ago,' the impersonal expression 'hace' is used to denote time: hace dos días (two days ago), hace dos semanas (two weeks ago), hace dos horas (two hours ago), etc.

Fuimos a Bilbao y a Pamplona **hace dos años.**
(Two years ago, we went to Bilbao and Pamplona)

10 ⊗ ~~insulación~~
  ✅ aislamiento
▶ This word simply does not exist. The right word for 'isolation' or 'insulation' is 'aislamiento.'

La pared tiene un buen **aislamiento**; no se oye el ruido de los vecinos.
(This wall has good insulation; we can't hear any noise from the neighbors)

El ermitaño vive en la cima de la montaña en un **aislamiento** total.
(The hermit lives at the top of the mountain in total isolation)

11 ⊗ ~~Fue muy increíble~~
  ✅ Fue increíble
  ✅ Fue fantástico
▶ One does not say *very fantastic, *very excellent, or *very incredible in English. This is often the case with adjectives which express the maximum degree of something. The same goes for Spanish; one does not need the adverb 'muy' before this type of adjective.

Es increíble pero cierto. El ladrón entró por la chimenea.
(It is incredible but true. The thief came in through the chimney)

12 ⊗ ~~me gusta lo~~
  ⊗ ~~lo me gusta~~
  ⊗ ~~yo gusto~~
  ✅ me gusta
▶ Remember the following structure: 'Tomatoes are pleasing to me' translated as 'Me gust**an los** tomat**es**.' The pronoun 'me' is the indirect object, with 'tomates' as subject agreeing in the plural with the verb 'gustan.' Also, remember that the adverb goes after the verb: 'Me gusta *mucho* el chocolate' = I like chocolate *a lot,* or 'chocolate is very pleasing to me,' and not: *~~me gusta el chocolate mucho~~.

¿Te gusta ese libro? Sí, **me gusta** mucho.
(Do you like that book? Yes, I like it a lot)

¿Te gustan esos libros? Sí, **me gustan** mucho.
(Do you like those books? Yes, I like them a lot)

13 ⊗ ~~muchos tiempos~~
  ✅ muchas veces
▶ The word *tiempo* in Spanish is tricky. It does not always mean 'time.' An example is: *¿Qué tiempo hace?* (What's the weather like?). When there is repetition

involved, e.g., 'How many times have you been to Spain?' you should use the word 'vez,' or its plural 'veces.'

> Para tocar en el concierto tuve que practicar **muchas veces.**
> (To be able to play in the concert, I had to practice many times)

❌ ~~el segundo tiempo~~
✅ la segunda vez

> Ésta es **la segunda vez** que gano el concurso de natación.
> (This is my second time winning the swimming contest)

Note that the expression 'for the first time' does not take an article in Spanish: 'por primera vez.'

❌ ~~por la primera vez~~ / ~~por la última vez~~
✅ por primera vez
✅ por última vez

> **Por primera vez** en mi vida estoy realmente satisfecha con mi trabajo.
> (For the first time in my life, I'm really satisfied with my work)

14 ❌ ~~mixtura~~
  ✅ mezcla

▶ Do not try to tweak the English word 'mixture' to make it Spanish. The correct Spanish word in the majority of cases is 'mezcla,' not ~~mixtura~~ which is rarely used.

> Para hacer el alioli tienes que preparar una **mezcla** de aceite y ajo.
> (To make alioli you have to prepare a mixture of oil and garlic)

15 ❌ ~~similaridad~~
  ✅ similitud
  ✅ semejanza

▶ Many words ending in '–ty' take the suffix '–dad' (e.g. university / *universidad*) in Spanish. But there are exceptions, such as the word 'similarity' which translates as *similitud* (used both in singular and plural) or *semejanza* (more used in the plural form).

> Hay muchas **semejanzas** entre el español y el catalán.
> (There are many similarities between Spanish and Catalan)

Another example of how '–ty' does not always correspond to '–dad':
❌ ~~majoridad~~
✅ mayoría
✅ la mayor parte

La **mayoría** de los ciudadanos apoya las acciones del gobierno.
(The majority of citizens support the government's actions)

 (See chapter 1 for more information on the gender of words that end in –dad)

16 ✗ ~~pictura~~
  ✓ una foto / fotografía (a photograph)
  ✓ una pintura (a painting)
  ✓ un retrato (a portrait)
  ✓ un cuadro (a painting)
  ✓ un dibujo (a drawing)
  ✓ una imagen (an image)
▶ This word does not exist in Spanish. In fact, there are various words to refer to different types of images.

   Me gusta más esta **foto** que ese **cuadro**.
   (I prefer this photograph to that painting)

17 ✗ ~~porque de~~
  ✓ a causa de
  ✓ por
▶ To say 'because of' in Spanish you need to distinguish it from a simple ' because.' In the phrase, *¿Por qué me miras así?* ***Porque*** *estoy enamorado de ti*, the word 'porque' means 'because' and is followed by a verb. However, when 'because' is used to mean 'on account of,' and it is followed by a noun, Spanish uses 'a causa de' or 'por.'

   No fuimos a la playa este año **a causa de** la enfermedad de mi esposo.
   (We didn't go to the beach this year on account of my husband's illness)

   No me gustó el viaje **por** el mal tiempo.
   (I didn't like the trip because of the bad weather)

18 ✗ ~~por mucho del~~
  ✓ la mayor parte
▶ To say 'for most of' use the expression 'la mayor parte de.'

   La mayor parte del fin de semana estuve viendo las Olimpiadas.
   (I was watching the Olympics for most of the weekend)

19 ✗ ~~relatarse~~
  ✓ relacionarse con
▶ This verb does not exist in Spanish. For 'to relate' use 'relacionarse con.'

   Ella tiene muchos amigos porque **se relaciona** bien con la gente.
   (She has lots of friends because she relates well with people)

20 ✖ ~~ridiculoso~~

✔ ridículo

▶ Some English speakers tend to transform the suffix –ous into –oso. While this may work in some cases such as 'miraculous' (*milagroso*) or 'ambitious' (*ambicioso*), it does not work for all words ending in –ous. The correct words for 'ridiculous' and 'serious' are: *ridículo* and *serio*.

> Esa manera de vestirte es **ridícula**. ¡Pareces un payaso!
> (That outfit is ridiculous. You look like a clown!)

✖ ~~serioso~~

✔ serio / a

> Juan es un chico **serio**. Saca buenas notas y es muy **ambicioso**.
> (Juan is a serious kid. He gets good grades and is very ambitious)

21 ✖ ~~tengo ganas de las vacaciones~~

▶ The Spanish expression 'tengo ganas de' or 'I feel like' is always followed by a verb instead of a noun.

✔ **tengo ganas de ir** de vacaciones

✔ **tengo ganas de que lleguen** las vacaciones

> (I am looking forward to being on vacation)
> (I am looking forward to the vacation)

Note that there are many other expressions with 'tener' in Spanish where English does not use the verb 'to have.'

✖ ~~no hace senso~~

✔ no tiene sentido

To say that something 'makes sense' use the expression: *tener sentido*.

> Este texto no **tiene sentido**. ¡Es un arroz con mango!
> (This text makes no sense. It's gobbledygook!)

 (See chapter 6 for a full list of expressions with *tener*)

On the other hand, there are other situations where 'to have' in English is not translated as 'tener.' For example, be very careful with the expression 'to have fun.' In Spanish we use *pasarlo bien* or simply *divertirse*, without using the verb 'tener' (to have).

✖ ~~tener un buen tiempo~~

✔ divertirse

✔ pasarlo bien

> **Me divertí** mucho en la fiesta. Y tu prima Alicia, ¿**lo pasó bien**?
> (I had a good time at the party. And your cousin Alicia, did she have fun?)

(See chapter 2 for more information on the verb 'divertirse')

❌ ~~tener una limonada~~
✅ tomar

Spanish does not use *tener* in the context of ordering a drink in a restaurant. Instead, it uses the verb *tomar* (which means 'to drink' and more generally 'to have something to drink').

¿Y qué quieres **tomar**? **Tomaré** una limonada.
(What are you having? I'll have a lemonade)

22 ❌ ~~un otro~~
✅ otro

▶ Just as one cannot say in English *~~an another~~, it makes no sense in Spanish to say *~~un otro~~. To say 'another' simply use: *otro, otra, otros, otras*, without an article.

Esta toalla está húmeda. ¿Tienes **otra**?
(This towel is wet. Do you have another one?)

23 ❌ ~~los ochentas~~
✅ los ochenta

▶ In English we talk about the decade of the fifties, sixties, seventies, eighties, etc. In Spanish we use the plural article with a singular noun, since the plural article modifies the word *años* which is implicit, e.g., *los (años) cincuenta*, *los sesenta*, *los setenta*, *los ochenta*, etc.

¿De cuándo es este traje tan extravagante? Es de **los ochenta**.
(When does this extravagant suit date from? It's from the eighties)

24 ❌ ~~oír mucho de~~
✅ contar

▶ 'To hear a lot about …' is not translated literally; it requires the verb 'contar' or the expression 'oír hablar de' instead of just 'oír.'

Ellos **me contaron** muchas cosas sobre su viaje a Japón. / **He oído hablar** mucho de su viaje..
(I heard a lot about their trip to Japan)

25 ✅ llegamos en
✅ llegar a

▶ The expression *llegar en* is used with means of transport, such as a plane, train, car, etc., e.g., *Llegué en avión* (I arrived by plane). It is not used to talk about arriving at a place, e.g., *Llegué a Londres* (I arrived in London).

Llegamos a Madrid el jueves y el sábado ya volvimos a casa.
(We arrived in Madrid on Thursday, and on Sunday we went back home)

Llegamos en coche a casa.
(We arrived home by car)

26 ⊗ ~~tomar interés~~
  ✓ tener interés

▶ Note that the verb 'to take' is not always translated as 'tomar.' To say 'to take an interest in something' you use the expressions 'tener interés,' or 'poner interés.'

Tienes que **tener / poner** más **interés** en tus estudios.
(You must take more interest in your studies)

27 ⊗ ~~todos de mis amigos~~
  ✓ todos

▶ To translate 'all of' never use a preposition in Spanish.

Todos mis amigos vinieron a la fiesta de cumpleaños. **Todos** ellos lo pasaron bien.
(All of my friends came to my birthday party. All of them had fun)

28 ⊗ ~~expectaciones~~
  ✓ expectativas

▶ The right translation for 'expectation' is 'expectativas' in the sense of 'hope' or 'prospect.' But 'expectativa' in the singular means 'expectancy.'

Eres muy pesimista. Tus **expectativas** son siempre negativas.
(You are very pessimistic. Your expectations are always negative)

Estamos a la **expectativa** del nacimiento del niño de Andrea.
(We are expecting the birth of Andrea's baby)

The word 'expectación' does exist in Spanish but it means 'anticipation.'

Los fans esperaban a la cantante con mucha **expectación**.
(The fans were waiting for the singer with a lot of anticipation)

The word 'anticipación' is normally used in Spanish with the meaning of 'earliness.' Or in the expressions 'con anticipación' (in advance), 'con anticipación a' (prior to).

Por si acaso, voy a reservar la habitación del hotel **con anticipación**.
(I am going to book the hotel room in advance just in case)

29 ✗ ~~capable~~

✓ capaz

▶ If you want to say 'capable' use the adjective 'capaz.' Not only does ~~capable~~ not exist in Spanish, it sounds like something derived from 'capar' meaning 'to castrate.'

> Ella es una chica muy **capaz**: toca el piano, escribe novelas y pinta.
> (She's a very capable girl. She plays the piano, writes novels and paints)

30 ✗ ~~procedura~~

✓ procedimiento

▶ The right word for 'procedure' is *procedimiento*.

> ¿Cuál es el **procedimiento** para hacer la matrícula?
> (What's the procedure for the registration?)

31 ✓ enfrente de

✓ delante de

▶ Remember that 'enfrente de' means 'across, opposite.' It is a grammatically correct expression that is often misused as a literal translation of 'in front of.' However, to say 'in front of' use 'delante de.'

> Mi mejor amiga vive **enfrente de** mi casa.
> (My best friend lives across from me)

> El maestro regañó al niño **delante de** toda la clase.
> (The teacher scolded the kid in front of the whole class)

32 ✗ para que + ~~indicative~~

✗ para que ~~tengo~~

✓ para que tenga

▶ When you use the construction 'para que' (in order to), make sure you use the subjunctive afterwards.

> Este dinero es **para que** te **compres** lo que tú quieras.
> (This money is for you to buy whatever you like)

However, note that ¿Para qué? ¡Para qué! (what ... for?) do use the indicative:

> ¿Para qué **quieres** la escalera de mano?
> (What do you want the ladder for?)

Remember, the subjunctive is also used after the following expressions

Mnemonic device

The word ¡ESCAPA! will help you remember some expressions that are always followed by the subjunctive.

E	**En** caso de que ...(in case that)
	Voy a llamar a Pedro en caso de que me necesite.
	(I will call Pedro in case he needs me)
S	**S**in que ... (without)
	Organizaremos una fiesta sorpresa sin que lo sepa Juan.
	(We will organize a surprise party without Juan knowing it)
C	**C**on tal de que ... (as long as, provided that)
	Puedes venir con tal de que estés listo a las 10:00.
	(You can come as long as you are ready by 10:00)
A	**A** menos que ... (unless)
	Iremos de vacaciones a menos que no tengamos dinero.
	(We will go on vacation unless we don't have any money)
P	**P**ara que ... (in order to, so that)
	He traído el coche para que lo puedas usar.
	(I have brought the car so that you can use it)
A	**A**ntes de que ... (before)
	Llegué a casa antes de que empezara a nevar.
	(I arrived home before it started to snow)

Mnemonic device

The following mnemonic device, WHEN TO USE IT, will help you remember when to use the subjunctive. Normally the meaning of what the speaker is expressing will determine whether the subjunctive needs to be used (a wish, a recommendation, etc.)

W	Wishes, necessities, prohibitions (desear, necesitar, prohibir, preferir, etc.)
	Mi novio quiere que nos casemos pronto.
	(My boyfriend wants us to marry soon)
H	Hopes, obligations, suggestions (esperar, mandar, sugerir, etc.)
	Espero que llame antes de que vayamos al cine.
	(I hope that he calls before we go to the cinema)
E	Emotions, regrets, consent (estar contento, sentir, lamentar, consentir, etc.)
	Su padre siente que su hermano no pueda venir.
	(His father regrets that his brother cannot come)
N	Negation, doubt, denial (negar, dudar, no creer, no decir, no significar, no tratarse de, etc.)
	Dudamos que llueva o nieve el sábado.
	(We doubt that it will rain or snow on Saturday)
T	Tal vez, acaso, quizás
	Tal vez haga sol mañana.
	(Maybe it will be a sunny day tomorrow)
O	Ojalá
	¡Ojalá nos toque el gordo de la lotería!
	(Let's hope we win the first prize in the lottery!)
U	Unknown, or non-existent antecedent (no hay nadie que, no conozco a nadie que, etc.)
	Aquí no hay nadie que hable japonés.
	(There is no one here who can speak Japanese)
S	Some conjunctions and adverbial clauses (para que, a menos que, etc.)
	Dime la fecha para que pueda reservar el hotel.
	(Tell me the date so I can reserve the hotel)
E	Expressions (impersonal, etc.) (es importante que, es necesario que, etc.)
	Es imposible que llegue a tiempo.
	(It is impossible for him to arrive on time)
I	Imperatives (except tú and vosotros affirmative)
	No mires y no escuches; es una sorpresa.
	(Don't look and don't listen; it's a surprise)
T	To influence another's behavior (insistence, preference, supplication, etc.) (aconsejarle algo a alguien, recomendarle algo a alguien, preferir que alguien haga algo, querer que alguien haga algo, insistir en que alguien haga algo, etc.)
	Te recomiendo que hables con la compañía aérea sobre la maleta.
	(I recommend that you speak to the airline about your suitcase)

Exercises

EXERCISE 1. In the following sentences the underlined word or expression is wrong. Cross it out and write the correct one.

1 Juan es un tipo muy *serioso, no le gustan los chistes.
   _____

2 A María le encanta tener su propio estilo, y se viste como si estuviera en *los ochentas.
   _____

3 ¿Qué te apetece? Voy a *tener una horchata muy fría.
   _____

4 Creo que Pepe no es *capable de torear solo en una plaza de toros.
   _____

5 ¿Podrías traerme *un otro vaso de agua?
   _____

6 José es muy *realistico pero también un poco *pesimistico.
   _____

7 ¿Cuál es el *senso de esta expresión?
   _____

8 Esta tarde voy a conducir el coche nuevo *por la primera vez.
   _____

9 *Tuvimos un buen tiempo porque la música era muy buena.
   _____

10 *Tengo muchas ganas de esquí en Formigal este invierno.
   _____

11 La gente se divirtió muchísimo y la comida fue *muy fantástica.
   _____

12 Estados Unidos y Canadá son países con muchas *similaridades.
   _____

13 Encontramos una *pictura muy antigua de la abuela Dolores.
   _____

14 *Me gusta la limonada mucho que sirven en un bar del centro de La Habana.
   _____

15 Han dicho por la tele que mañana va a *hacer lluvia.
   _____

EXERCISE 2. Fill in the appropriate Spanish expression for the word in parentheses. Make changes accordingly.

1 Ricardo tiene que casarse porque su novia está _____ (pregnant).

2 Decir que la vida es dura es una opinión; no es un _____ (fact).

3 ¿Cuál fue el _____ (result) de mi prueba de sangre, doctor?

4 Ella parece tímida _____ (at first), hasta que la conoces mejor.

5 ¡Las _____ (pictures) de la boda son estupendas!

6 ¡Ay, tengo _____ (five hundred) preguntas que hacerte!

7 Yo no conozco persona más _____ (capable) que mi madre.

8 Los ingleses parecen más _____ (serious) que los norteamericanos.

9 No pudimos llegar a tiempo _____ (because of) el tráfico.

10 _____ (I am looking forward) estar de vacaciones para descansar.

11 Ella ha pasado _____ (most of) su vida en el campo.

12 Creo que ellos _____ (will have fun) durante el viaje a China.

13 Es importante _____ (relate) bien con la gente para tener éxito en la vida.

14 Ella no puede tomar al sol: tiene la piel muy _____ (sensitive).

15 Mucho gusto. _____ (I heard a lot) de tus cuadros.

16 He intentado dejar de fumar _____ (many times). Y siempre vuelvo a fumar.

17 Ella parece tener un sexto _____ (sense) para estas cosas.

18 _____ (All of her) hijos son amables e inteligentes.

19 Nosotros nos vimos en Londres _____ (five years ago).

20 La felicidad siempre _____ (depends) del amor que uno da y que uno recibe.

Words with double meanings

One word in Spanish, two (or more) words in English

Polysemy is the coexistence of multiple meanings for one word or phrase. The following Spanish words have more than one meaning in English. Pay attention to these different meanings, as well as the context in which they are used.

abonar   to fertilize; to pay, to credit

Esa tierra está exhausta; hay que **abonarla**.
(That land is exhausted; it needs to be fertilized)

Tenemos que **abonar** la factura del teléfono.
(We need to pay the telephone bill)

aprobar   to approve; to pass (an exam)

Mis padres no **aprueban** mis actividades políticas.
(My parents don't approve of my political activities)

Si estudias no tengo duda que **aprobarás** el examen.
(If you study you will undoubtedly pass the exam)

arreglar   to fix; to straighten out; to put on makeup, lipstick, etc.
                (arreglarse)

Mi televisión no funciona. Tengo que **arreglarla**.
(My TV doesn't work. I need to fix it)

Tu cuarto está muy desordenado. ¡**Arréglalo**!
(Your room is a mess. Straighten it out!)

La chica se **arregló** antes de salir con su novio.
(The girl put on some makeup before going out with her boyfriend)

el banco   a bench; a bank; a school of fish

Tengo que ir al **banco** a depositar el cheque.
(I need to go to the bank to deposit my check)

El viejito fue al parque y se sentó en un **banco**.
(The little old man went to the park and sat down on a bench)

la banda   a music band; a gang; a sash; a cushion (in billiards)

Yo toco en una **banda** de música, no en una **banda** de ladrones.
(I play in a music band, not in a gang of thieves)

Su vestido tenía una **banda** roja.
(Her dress had a red sash)

el billete   a bus, plane or metro ticket; a money bill

Necesito comprar un **billete** de autobús para Sevilla.
(I need to buy a bus ticket to Sevilla)

Ayer te di un **billete** de cien dólares.
(I gave you a $100 bill yesterday)

blanco   white; a target or bull's eye

Quiero pintar mi piano de **blanco**.
(I want to paint my piano white)

El tirador dio en el **blanco**.
(The shooter hit the target)

la boca   a mouth; an entrance / exit of a subway

¡Sácate el chicle de la **boca**!
(Take the gum out of your mouth!)

Te espero en la **boca** del metro.
(I'll wait for you at the entrance to the subway stop)

la bomba   a bomb; a pump

Una **bomba** explotó en la plaza.
(A bomb went off in the square)

Tenemos que instalar una nueva **bomba** de agua.
(We have to install a new water pump)

la cara   a face; a side (paper); heads (in a coin)

Tengo que empolvarme la **cara** antes de salir.
(I need to powder my face before going out)

Para no desperdiciar papel, favor de escribir en las dos **caras**.
(In order not to waste paper, please write on both sides)

¿Qué escoges, **cara** o cruz?
(Which do you choose, heads or tails?)

la carrera   a race; a career; a degree; a run (in stockings or tights)

Para ganar la **carrera** tuve que practicar mucho.
(To win the race I had to practice a lot)

Él decidió hacer la **carrera** de biología.
(He decided to get a degree in biology)

Tengo una **carrera** en la media.
(I have a run in my stocking)

la cartera   a pocketbook, a wallet, a portfolio, a briefcase

El ladrón me agarró la **cartera** con documentos y salió corriendo.
(The thief grabbed my briefcase with documents and ran off)

Cuando salgo de noche llevo la **cartera** en el bolsillo del abrigo.
(When I go out at night I carry my wallet in my coat pocket)

el casco   a helmet; the hull of a ship, plane, tank

Hoy en día hay que llevar **casco** para montar en bicicleta.
(These days one has to wear a helmet to ride a bike)

El **casco** del Titanic no resistió el choque con el iceberg.
(The hull of the Titanic did not withstand the collision with the iceberg)

contar   to count; to tell

Tenemos que **contar** el dinero que ganamos.
(We have to count the money we made)

¡**Cuéntame** un cuento, mamá!
(Tell me a story, mom!)

la copa   a goblet; an alcoholic drink

Esa **copa** de cristal es de Waterford.
(That's a Waterford crystal goblet)

Vamos a tomarnos una **copa**.
(Let's have a drink)

el cordón   a shoelace; a cord

¿Qué prefieres, zapatos con velcro o **cordones**?
(What kind of shoes do you prefer, those with velcro or laces?)

La policía acordonó el lugar del crimen con un **cordón**.
(The police cordoned the site of the crime with string)

la cruz   a cross; tails (in a coin)

La **cruz** es el símbolo del cristianismo.
(The cross is the symbol of Christianity)

¿Qué prefieres, cara o **cruz**?
(What do you prefer, heads or tails?)

el cubo   a bucket; a cube

Los niños jugaron en la arena con **cubos** y palas.
(The kids played in the sand with buckets and pails)

En geometría hay triángulos, cuadros, rectángulos y **cubos**.
(In geometry there are triangles, squares, rectangles and cubes)

el cuello   a neck; a collar

El cisne tiene un **cuello** largo y elegante.
(The swan has a long and elegant **neck**)

Ese vestido tiene un cuello de encaje blanco.
(That dress has a white lace collar)

el chorizo   a chorizo sausage; a thief (colloq)

Quisiera arroz con **chorizo** italiano.
(I would like some rice with Italian sausage)

Ese **chorizo** me robó las ruedas del auto.
(That thief stole the wheels of my car)

la chuleta   a chop (pork, lamb, etc); a crib sheet

Nos sirvieron unas **chuletas** de cordero deliciosas.
(They served us some delicious lamb chops)

Ese estudiante tramposo llevaba una **chuleta**.
(That cheater had a cheat sheet with him)

el derecho   straight; straight ahead; the study of law; a right

Ese palo no está **derecho**; está torcido.
(That stick is not straight; it's crooked)

Camina **derecho** hasta la esquina; entonces gira.
(Walk straight ahead up to the corner; then turn)

Mi hijo quiere estudiar **derecho**.
(My son wants to study law)

El ciudadano en una democracia tiene el **derecho** de elegir a su gobierno.
(In a democracy, the citizen has the right to choose his/her government)

el diente   a tooth; a clove (of garlic)

El dentista me va a sacar un **diente**.
(The dentist is going to take out one of my teeth)

Para hacer un gazpacho se necesita un **diente** de ajo.
(To make gazpacho you need a clove of garlic)

doblar   to fold; to dub a movie

Voy a **doblar** las sábanas para guardarlas.
(I'm going to fold the sheets and put them away)

En España las películas americanas están **dobladas**.
(American films in Spain are normally dubbed)

encontrar(se)   to find; to meet or rendez-vous; to run into; to be located

Busco mis gafas, pero no las **encuentro**.
(I'm looking for my glasses, but I can't find them)

Me encontré con mi profesor de español en el Café Lalo.
(I met my Spanish teacher at the Café Lalo)

Caminando por la calle 72 **me encontré** con Marta.
(I ran into Marta while walking on 72nd Street)

Mi casa **se encuentra** en la Plaza de Washington.
(My house is located on Washington Square)

la espina   a thorn; a fish bone

Las rosas son bellas pero tienen **espinas**.
(Roses are beautiful but they have thorns)

Ese hombre tiene una **espina** trabada en la garganta.
(That man has a fish bone stuck in his throat)

la espinilla   a shin; a blackhead (pimple)

Jugando al fútbol se lastimó la **espinilla**.
(He hurt his shin playing soccer)

Tengo muchas **espinillas**; necesito ir al dermatólogo.
(I have a lot of blackheads; I need to go to the dermatologist)

la falda   a skirt; a mountain slope

¿Conoces la foto de Marilyn Monroe con la **falda** roja?
(Do you know the picture of Marilyn Monroe in the red skirt?)

Los esquiadores bajaron la **falda** de la montaña con gran rapidez.
(The skiers descended the mountain slope with great speed)

la fiesta   a party; holiday

El sábado estamos invitados a una **fiesta**.
(We are invited to a party on Saturday)

El 4 de julio es día de **fiesta** en los Estados Unidos.
(The 4th of July is a holiday in the United States)

el gato   a cat; a jack

Algunos piensan que los **gatos** negros dan mala suerte.
(Some people associate black cats with bad luck)

Para cambiar la llanta se necesita un **gato**.
(To change a tire you need a jack)

girar   to turn; to send, transfer or issue money

El girasol **gira** siguiendo la luz del sol.
(The sunflower turns to follow the sunlight)

Mi padre me **giró** los $200 que le pedí.
(My father made the $200 money transfer I asked him for)

el hogar   a home; a hearth

Una casa no siempre es un **hogar**.
(A house is not always a home)

Por el frío que hacía nos pasamos todo el día junto al **hogar**.
(Because of the cold we spent all day next to the hearth)

la hoja   sheet of paper; a hand-out; a leaf; a blade; a complaint form

¿Tienes una **hoja** de papel para escribir una nota?
(Do you have a sheet of paper to write a note?)

El profesor de español siempre nos da **hojas**.
(The Spanish teacher always gives us hand-outs)

En el otoño los árboles pierden sus **hojas**.
(In the fall the trees lose their leaves)

El hombre afiló la **hoja** antes de usarla.
(The man sharpened the blade before using it)

El administrador de la compañía recibió **hojas** de los clientes.
(The company administrator received complaint forms from customers)

la manzana   an apple; a street block (remember New York is called the Big Apple or *La Gran Manzana* in Spanish)

Mi **manzana** favorita es la Macintosh.
(My favorite type of apple is the Macintosh)

El atleta corrió alrededor de la **manzana**.
(The jogger ran around the block)

el mono   a monkey; overalls or jumpsuit

El chimpancé es un tipo de **mono** bastante común.
(The chimpanzee is a common type of monkey)

El fontanero vestido con un **mono** tocó la puerta.
(The plumber dressed in overalls knocked on the door)

el muelle   a dock, quay, pier; a spring

Los yates estaban atracados en el **muelle**.
(The yachts moored at the pier)

El colchón tenía muchos **muelles** rotos.
(The mattress had many broken springs)

la nota   a note; a musical note; a mark (on a test)

Me escribió una **nota** diciendo que no venía.
(She wrote me a note saying she wasn't coming)

Do, re, mi, fa, sol son **nota**s musicales.
(Do, re, mi, fa, so are musical notes)

¿Qué **nota** sacaste? Saqué un sobresaliente.
(What grade did you get? I got an A)

el papel   paper; a role

Necesito **papel** y lápiz.
(I need paper and pencil)

Él siempre hace el **papel** de víctima.
(He always plays the role of a victim)

la pastilla   a pill; a bar of soap; a chocolate bar

El médico me recetó **pastillas** antibióticas.
(The doctor prescribed some antibiotic pills for me)

En la perfumería compré **pastillas** de jabón y en la bombonería **pastillas** de chocolate.
(In the perfume shop I bought soap, and in the candy shop—chocolate bars)

el pie   a foot; 12 inches

Tengo los **pies** destrozados de tanto caminar.
(My feet are sore from so much walking)

Mi hermano mide seis **pies** de alto.
(My brother is six feet tall)

la pila   a battery; a sink; a pile of books, dishes, papers, etc.

Tu linterna no funciona; necesita **pilas** nuevas.
(Your flashlight doesn't work; it needs new batteries)

Tengo una **pila** de cosas en mi escritorio.
(I have a pile of stuff on my desk)

la planta   a plant; a ground floor

¡Qué bonitas son las **plantas** que tienes en el balcón!
(The plants on your balcony are so nice!)

Ellos viven en la **planta** baja.
(They live on the ground floor)

el puño   a fist; cuff, a handle

Un boxeador necesita tener **puños** muy fuertes.
(A boxer needs to have strong fists)

Los **puño**s de las camisas se deben planchar primero.
(The cuffs of a shirt need to be ironed first)

la receta   a recipe; a prescription

¿Me puedes dar tu **receta** para hacer paella?
(Can you give me your paella recipe?)

Le traje al farmacéutico la **receta** que me dio mi médico.
(I brought the pharmacist the prescription that my doctor gave me)

la salsa   sauce; a dance

Sirvieron el bistec con **salsa** mexicana.
(They served steak with Mexican sauce)

Bailaron **salsa** en la fiesta.
(At the party they danced salsa)

sentir   to sense; to be sorry, to feel

Siento la brisa del mar en la cara.
(I feel the sea breeze on my face)

Siento mucho lo que pasó.
(I'm very sorry for what happened)

Me **siento** cansada y deprimida.
(I feel tired and depressed)

la sierra   a saw; a mountain range

Para cortar este tronco de madera se necesita una **sierra**.
(To cut this tree trunk one needs a saw)

La **sierra** de Guadarrama se encuentra en el centro de España.
(The Guadarrama mountain range is located in central Spain)

suspender   to cancel; to fail an exam

Tuve que **suspender** la fiesta a causa del ciclón.
(I had to cancel the party because of the cyclone)

Dos alumnos **suspendieron** el examen de matemáticas.
(Two students failed the math exam)

la tapa   a lid; a savory snack; a paperback / hardcover edition

El pianista terminó de tocar y cerró la **tapa** del piano.
(The pianist finished playing and closed the piano lid)

Busco un restaurante de **tapas**.
(I'm looking for a tapas restaurant)

Tenemos el libro que busca en **tapa** blanda y en **tapa** dura.
(We have the book you want in both paperback and hardcover)

el tiempo   time; weather

No tengo **tiempo** para jugar a las cartas.
(I have no time to play cards)

En California hace buen **tiempo** todo el año.
(In California the weather is nice all year round)

el valor   value; courage

¿Cuál es el **valor** de esta casa?
(What is the value of this house?)

El soldado mostró **valor** al salvar a su compañero.
(The soldier showed courage by saving his friend)

vencer   to win, to conquer, to defeat; to expire

Vino, vio y **venció.**
(He came, he saw, he conquered)

Mi pasaporte **vence** a finales de este año.
(My passport expires at the end of this year)

el volante	a steering wheel; a ruffle or frill; a referral note

Conducía con una mano en el **volante**.
(She was driving with one hand on the wheel)

Ella vestía un vestido con **volantes** en el cuello y en las mangas.
(Her dress had ruffles at the neck and sleeves)

El doctor me dio un **volante** para ir a ver a un especialista.
(The doctor gave me a referral to see a specialist)

la yema	an egg yolk; a fingertip

Hay personas que no comen la **yema** del huevo, sólo la clara.
(Some people don't eat the yolk, only the egg white)

Tocó el cristal con la **yema** de los dedos.
(He touched the glass with his fingertips)

> ### Mnemonic device
> By showing the contrast between sound and meaning, these three pairs of homophonic verbs and nouns will help you remember more easily some words with double meanings: **piso el piso** (I step on the floor); **vino el vino** (the wine came); **traje el traje** (I brought the suit). Note that 'el piso' is used more frequently in Latin America, whereas in Spain people normally use the word 'el suelo' to refer to 'the floor.'

Exercises

EXERCISE 3. Complete the sentences using the vocabulary below. As indicated, some of the words need to be used twice.

> • el casco • la banda • manzanas • salsa • aprobar • pastillas • chuletas (x2)
> • un banco (x2) • vencer • la yema (x2) • doblar • la fiesta • los puños • girar
> • una copa • una hoja • papel • un diente • las recetas • cubo • chorizo • el
> volante • unas notas • monos • la sierra • la espinilla • gatos •

1 Muchas personas tienen _____ en casa; en cambio, pocos tienen _____ puesto que viven mejor en la selva.

2 _____ es una herramienta que tiene _____ de metal y se utiliza para cortar madera.

3 En un coche se utiliza _____ para _____ a la derecha y a la izquierda.

4   Ponte _____, coge la bicicleta y ve a buscar _____ al médico.

5   El compositor escribió _____ en un pentagrama y compuso en un santiamén una bonita pieza para _____ del pueblo.

6   Se compró una caja de _____ para la tos, y para no perderse iba contando _____ por las calles de Nueva York.

7   Apretando con _____ de los dedos, el dermatólogo me sacó _____ que tenía en la cara.

8   Peleando sin armas, sólo con _____, el joven logró _____ a su contrincante.

9   Para que esté en su punto, al cocido le falta _____ de ajo y un poco de _____ de cantimpalo.

10 Estaba tan cansado que se sentó en _____ delante de _____ y se quedó completamente dormido.

11 ¿Cómo preparaste esas exquisitas _____ de cerdo? Pues simplemente las freí con _____ de un huevo.

12 Es preferible no _____ un examen, a arriesgarse a copiar con _____ y que te pillen.

13 En el restaurante el camarero sacó el champán del _____ de hielo y me lo sirvió en _____ de cristal.

14 ¿Qué te apetece bailar en _____: mambo, _____ o chachachá?

15 En España empezaron a _____ las películas extranjeras en los años treinta porque la gente no hablaba inglés. Hoy en día los actores son tan buenos que siempre se meten en su _____.

EXERCISE 4. Fill in the blanks with the appropriate word. Make changes accordingly.

1   Robin Hood tiró la flecha y dio en el _____ (target).

2   Tengo que sacar dinero del _____ (bank) lo antes posible.

3   Me encantan los vestidos con _____ (ruffles) de muchos colores.

4   ¿ _____ (Did you pass) el exámen de química?
    – No, lo _____ (failed) porque no había estudiado lo suficiente.

5   Para hacer la torta necesitas cuatro _____ (yolks) de huevo.

6   El fontanero se puso el _____ (jumpsuit) antes de empezar a trabajar.

7   ¡Llueve, truena! ¡Qué _____ (weather) tan malo!

8   ¿Cuántos _____ (notes) de 50€ tienes en la _____ (wallet)?

9   Mi permiso de trabajo para trabajar en EE.UU. _____ (expires) este mes.

10 Ahora es ilegal ir en moto sin llevar _____ (helmet).

11 Adopta a ese pobre niño que necesita un _____ (home).

12 Lo que más se ensucia son los _____ (cuffs) y el _____ (collar) de la camisa.

13 Para encontrar el cine, siga hasta el final de esta _____ (block) y gire a la derecha.

14 En algunos países no se respetan los _____ (rights) humanos.

15 Lo metieron en la cárcel por _____ (thief, colloq.) y estafador.

16 Al terminar de practicar, la niña cerró la _____ (lid) del piano.

17 Después de la lluvia necesitaremos una _____ (water pump).

18 Mi mamá me dio una buena _____ (recipe) de sopa de pescado.

19 Que no se te olvide meter el _____ (jack) en el maletero.

20 En EE.UU. el día de Cristóbal Colón es día de _____ (holiday) nacional.

EXERCISE 5. Choose the most logical ending

1	Decidió no salir a la calle …	a.	corriendo del escenario.
2	Las rosas son hermosas …	b.	y encontrarás el cine.
3	El mosquito giró en el aire …	c.	de ropa y de papeles por todos lados.
4	Hay que tener valor …		
5	Él se sentó a comer su chuleta de cerdo …	d.	en el casco del barco.
		e.	nos invitó a tomar una copa.
6	Después del accidente …	f.	y soplaba una leve brisa de mar.
7	Lo echamos a cara o cruz …	g.	en el maratón de Nueva York.
8	La cantante cantó dos notas y salió …	h.	y no las yemas.
		i.	llegó la ambulancia de la Cruz Roja.
9	Ese chorizo me robó …		
10	Entré en su cuarto y vi una pila …	j.	hay que abonar la tierra primero.
11	La chica llevaba un vestido …	k.	pero la moneda cayó en una alcantarilla.
12	Había un tremendo agujero …		
13	Si quieres que se cueza antes …	l.	pon la tapa.
14	Para cultivar buenas hortalizas …	m.	al verse una espinilla en la punta de la nariz.
15	Tres manzanas más …		
16	Muchos extranjeros participan …	n.	para aterrizar en el brazo de la chica.
17	*Amor en tiempos del cólera* …		
18	Hacía buen tiempo …	o.	es una historia maravillosa.
19	Para celebrar su compromiso …	p.	pero tienen espinas.
20	Para hacer los merengues necesitas las claras …	q.	con hermosos volantes de seda.
		r.	con puré de papas.
		s.	las llantas del carro.
		t.	para nadar entre tiburones.

8 Accents

Accents matter! To miss an accent mark where there should be one, or to write one where there should not be one, constitutes a spelling error in Spanish. We will also see in this chapter that by misplacing or omitting an accent, or adding one where it does not belong, we may be writing something quite different in meaning from what was originally intended. In order to know how accents work, you need to learn certain rules that will help you integrate sound and spelling.

All words in Spanish have **tonal** accents (or stress). Only some, however, carry graphic (or **written**) accents. Accents are extremely important. Whether tonal or graphic, the placement of the accent on a given syllable can change the meaning of a word or the tense (and/or subject) of a verb, e.g.

pú-blico (public) / pu-**bli**-co (I publish) / pu-bli-**có** (he/she/you (formal, singular) published)
ha-cia (towards) / ha-**cí**-a (he/she was doing)

Counting syllables

To correctly place the tonal or written accent on a word, you will need to count the syllables from **right to left**. These syllables are referred to as follows:

tra – ba – ja – **dor**
4   3   2   **1**

1. última sílaba (last syllable)
2. penúltima sílaba (penultimate or second from the end)
3. antepenúltima sílaba (antepenultimate or third from the end)
4. ante-antepenúltima sílaba (ante-antepenultimate or fourth from the end)

It is important to categorize words according to whether the stress falls on the last, penultimate, antepenultimate, etc., syllable and subsequently apply the rules that determine whether the word carries a written accent or not.

Tonal accents and written accents

All words in Spanish have tonal accents, i.e., a syllable that is stressed in a word:

rá-pi-do	**mú**-si-ca	Bru-**se**-las	**lá**-piz	re-**loj**	co-ra-**zón**
3 – 2 – 1	**3** – 2 – 1	3 – **2** – 1	**2** – 1	2 – **1**	3 – 2 – **1**

But as you can see from the examples above, not all Spanish words have a written accent. The existence of a written accent will always depend on:

1. Which syllable carries the stress
2. Whether the word ends in **n**, **s**, or a **vowel**, or not

Words with written accents

Words with written accents are of various types, and they have their own rules which you will need to learn. We will examine written accents on seven different categories of words:

1. Palabras agudas
2. Palabras llanas
3. Palabras esdrújulas
4. Monosyllabic words
5. Interrogative words and exclamations
6. Demonstrative adjectives and pronouns
7. Words that "break" the diphthong

1   Palabras agudas

Palabras agudas are words that carry a stress on the last syllable (first syllable counting from the right).

These words **DO carry a written accent** when they **end in a vowel, n or s**:

tra-ba-**jé**	co-li-**brí**	vol-**vió**	pa-**pá**	a-**sí**	o-ca-**sión**	Pa-**rís**
3 – 2 – 1	3 – 2 – 1	2 – 1	2 – 1	2 – 1	3 – 2 – 1	2 – 1

However these words **DO NOT carry a written accent** when they **end in a consonant different from n or s**.

pa-**pel**	co-**mer**	ro-**bot**	ma-**mut**	Ma-**drid**	re-**loj**	sa-**lud**
2 – 1	2 – 1	2 – 1	2 – 1	2 – 1	2 – 1	2 – 1

2   Palabras llanas

Palabras llanas are words that have a tonal accent or stress on the penultimate syllable (second syllable from the end).

These words **DO carry a written accent** when they **end in a consonant different from n or s**:

cés-ped	i-**nú**-til	**sué**-ter	**Pé**-rez	**dá**-til	**mó**-vil
2 – 1	3 – 2 – 1	2 – 1	2 – 1	2 – 1	2 – 1

However these words **DO NOT carry a written accent** when they **end in a vowel, n or s**.

ca-sa	**Mar**-te	**so**-bre	**tron**-co	**to**-can	in-**gle**-ses
2 – 1	2 – 1	2 – 1	2 – 1	2 – 1	3 – 2 – 1

3   Palabras esdrújulas

Palabras esdrújulas are words that are stressed on the antepenultimate syllable (third syllable from the end).

These words always carry a written accent on the antepenultimate syllable, regardless of the letter they end with, e.g.:

es-**drú**-ju-la	**sá**-ba-do	he-li-**cóp**-te-ro	**prín**-ci-pe	**rá**-pi-do	**Mé**-xi-co
4 – 3 – 2 – 1	3 – 2 – 1	5 – 4 – 3 – 2 – 1	3 – 2 – 1	3 – 2 – 1	3 – 2 – 1

A similar rule applies to words that are stressed on the fourth to last syllable, which is the one that carries a written accent (**palabras sobresdrújulas**), e.g.:

dí-ga-me-lo	**có**-me-te-lo	**dé**-ja-me-los
4 – 3 – 2 – 1	4 – 3 – 2 – 1	4 – 3 – 2 – 1

Exercises

You can listen to the audio files required for the exercises in this chapter on the *Speed Up Your Spanish* website.

EXERCISE 1. The following list contains words that are palabras 'agudas,' 'llanas,' 'esdrújulas,' and 'sobresdrújulas.' Separate the words into syllables and classify each one according to the syllable on which it carries the stress.

1	sílaba	(**sí**-la-ba)	(esdrújula)
2	Pacífico	_____	_____
3	Pérez	_____	_____
4	océano	_____	_____
5	tomate	_____	_____
6	matemáticas	_____	_____
7	tómate	_____	_____
8	composición	_____	_____
9	correspondió	_____	_____
10	perdí	_____	_____
11	tráigamelo	_____	_____
12	público	_____	_____
13	salir	_____	_____
14	publicó	_____	_____
15	lápiz	_____	_____

EXERCISE 2. Listen to the following words and identify the ones that require a written accent by adding one where necessary.

1	lentitud	_____
2	trabajando	_____
3	crater	_____
4	regiomontano	_____
5	pararse	_____
6	bellisimas	_____
7	fuente	_____
8	datil	_____
9	tapiz	_____
10	automovil	_____
11	dificil	_____
12	ventilador	_____
13	precaucion	_____
14	desee	_____
15	reaccion	_____
16	credito	_____
17	desee	_____
18	semaforo	_____
19	catedral	_____
20	limpiabotas	_____

21 leyes _____

22 Gonzalez _____

23 facil _____

24 util _____

4 Monosyllabic words

In Spanish monosyllabic (or one-syllable) words do NOT normally have a written accent, e.g.:

ti la los pie dar fue vi fin dio da pan fe ve vio bien, etc.

However, when two one-syllable words have the same form but belong to different grammatical categories, one of them must carry a written accent to help distinguish its grammatical function and meaning. See the table below for some examples.

Without a written accent	With a written accent
el (singular, masculine definite article 'the') **El** gato está en el tejado. (The cat is on the roof)	**él** (personal pronoun 'he') **Él** no tiene la culpa. (It is not his fault)
mi (possessive adjective 'my') **Mi** tía vive en Brasil. (My aunt lives in Brazil)	**mí** (personal pronoun 'me,' after prepositions) Las flores no son para ti, sino para **mí**. (The flowers are not for you, but for me)
tu (second person singular possessive adjective 'your') Ha llamado **tu** amiga. (You friend has called)	**tú** (personal pronoun 'you') ¿Pero **tú** sabes dónde está? (But do you know where it is?)
se (reflexive pronoun 'self') ¿Sabes cómo **se** llama? (Do you know his / her name?)	**sé** (first person singular of the present indicative of 'to know' or 2nd person singular imperative form of 'to be') No lo **sé**. **Sé** bueno. (I don't know) (Be good)
de (preposition 'of,' 'from') Juan es **de** Sevilla. (Juan is from Sevilla)	**dé** (first or third person singular of the present subjunctive of 'to give' or 'usted' imperative form of 'to give') Quiero que me **dé** un vaso de agua. (I want you to give me a glass of water) **Dé** dinero a los pobres. (Give money to the poor)

Without a written accent	With a written accent
te (personal pronoun 'you')	**té** (noun 'tea')
Te lo preparo en un momento.	¿Quieres un **té**?
(I'll have it prepared for you in a moment)	(Would you like tea?)
si ('if')	**sí** ('yes'; personal pronoun)
Si vienes, te invitaré a un café.	**Sí**, claro.
(If you come, I'll get you a coffee)	(Yes, of course)
	Se preguntó a **sí** mismo "¿debería ir o no?"
	(He asked himself, "Should I go or not?")
	Se lo llevó hacía **sí**.
	(He took it towards himself)
mas (but) (rarely used)	**más** (more)
Quería comer pastel, **mas** estaba a régimen.	Dame un poco **más** de pastel que está muy bueno.
(He wanted to eat cake, but he was on a diet)	(Give me a little more cake, it's very good)

Other frequently used word pairs differentiated only by a written accent are: **solo/sólo** and **aun/aún**. These are not monosyllabic words, but it is important to know the difference between them in written Spanish.

Without a written accent	With a written accent
solo ('alone')	**sólo** ('only,' synonym of 'solamente')
Estoy **solo** en casa, no hay nadie aquí.	Te llamo **sólo** para saludarte.
(I am home alone, there is no one here)	(I am calling only to say hello)
aun ('even')	**aún** ('still')
Siempre apruebas los exámenes, **aun** sin estudiar.	**Aún** es temprano para ir a dormir.
(You always pass your exams, even without studying)	(It is still early to go to bed)

In the case of solo/sólo, the RAE (Real Academia Española) recommends using the accent only when ambiguity can arise as to the intended meaning. However, common usage follows the rules above. The same applies to demonstrative adjectives and pronouns. (See section 6 below.)

Mnemonic device

To remember the difference between 'aun' (even) and 'aún' (still), simply think that the one that means 'todavía' (still) has an accent, just like its synonym.

Mnemonic device

To distinguish between when to put an accent on 'solo,' just remember that the one that means 'alone' (solo) is precisely "alone" because it does not have an accent mark. However the other one, which means 'only' (sólo), does have one.

EXERCISE 3. Put in written accents where necessary to the meaning of the sentence.

1 Tu te vas a casa el lunes con tu primo.
2 El se fue hasta el fin del mundo sin su cartera.
3 Solo quiero pan y paz, nada mas.
4 Para ti, tu perro es mucho mas grande, pero para mi no.
5 No se si tengo mas dinero.
6 Te voy a servir un buen te.
7 Si quieres agua di "si" y si no quieres di "no".
8 No deseo que me de nada, solo lo que me corresponde.
9 Se dijo a si mismo: "ya lo se".
10 A mi me encanta mi casa, ¿y a ti?
11 Dile a el que me de el regalo que te di.
12 Si, ya se que se ha comprado un piso nuevo, pero ella aun no me lo ha dicho.

Mnemonic device

The famous sentence pronounced by the philosopher Socrates, "Sólo sé que no sé nada" (I only know that I don't know anything), will help you remember that you need to pay attention to the accentuation of these words.

5 **Interrogative words and exclamations**

In Spanish, both interrogative and exclamatory words always carry written accents, e.g.: *adónde, dónde, cuál, cuán, cómo, cuándo, cuánto, quién, qué, por qué, etc.*

¿Adónde vas?
(Where are you going?)

¡Qué suerte tienes!
(How lucky you are!)

¿Cuándo llegas?
(When do you arrive?)

¡Cuánto nieva!
(Look how much it's snowing!)

These words also carry an accent mark when they are **indirect** interrogatives and exclamatives, e.g.

No tenía **qué** comer.
(I didn't have anything / what to eat)

Ya ves **qué** calor hace.
(You see how hot it is)

No sabemos **dónde** ir.
(We don't know where to go)

However, when used as **relative pronouns**, these words carry no accent, e.g.

No tenía **que** comer.
(I didn't have to eat)

Dame el libro **que** te presté.
(Give me the book that I lent you)

La casa está **como** la dejé.
(The house is as I left it)

Cuando vengas, llámame.
(Call me when you come)

Me voy **porque** tengo que estudiar.
(I am leaving because I have to study)

Mnemonic device

To figure out when to put an accent on '**qué**' vs. '**que**' and '**cómo**' vs. '**como**,' simply think that if '**qué**' can be translated as 'what' it does have an accent, and when '**que**' is translated as 'that, which, or who' it does not need one. The same rule can be applied to '**cómo**' translated as 'how,' which has an accent, and '**como**' translated as 'as,' which does not have one.

Mnemonic device

To remember the difference you can also recall the sentence: **¿Cómo como?** (How do I eat?), which highlights that only the 'cómo' that translates as 'how' carries an accent mark, while other forms of 'como' like the one that refers to eating, do not.

6   Demonstrative adjectives and pronouns

In the same vein, demonstratives like *este, ese* y *aquel*, and their feminine and plural, require a written accent only if they are **pronouns,** not adjectives, e.g.

> **Ese** libro me gusta, pero quiero **éste**.
> (I like that book, but I want this one)

> **Estas** chicas son más simpáticas que **ésas**.
> (These girls are nicer than those ones)

However, the neuter demonstrative pronouns *esto, eso, aquello* **never** carry a written accent.

> **Eso** no es cierto.
> (That's not true)

> No comprendo **esto.**
> (I don't understand this)

EXERCISE 4. Add accents where necessary.

1   No me gusta nada el vestido que me compraste. ¿Que?
2   Este libro no es el que quiero, sino ese de ahi.
3   Todavia no me has dicho cuando vas a organizar el crucero.
4   ¿Sabes por que ha llegado Juan tan tarde a casa?
5   Aquella es la casa de la que te hable.
6   ¿Que es eso que te compraste en la tienda?
7   A que no sabes a quien he visto esta mañana.
8   ¡Pero por que no dijiste nada durante la comida!
9   Esta tan feliz como si le hubiera tocado la loteria.
10 Dime con quien andas y te dire quien eres.

7 Words that "break" the diphthong

To understand what a **diphthong** is you need to know that there are two kinds of
Spanish vowels: *fuertes* or strong (*a, e, o*), and *débiles* or weak (*i, u*).

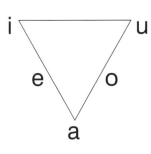

The Hellwag triangle

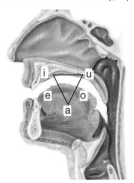

Articulation of vowels

A **diphthong** is a combination in the same syllable of:
– a strong and a weak vowel (the weak vowel must be unstressed) e.g.

    pei-ne a-plau-so sua-ve es-ta-dou-ni-den-se vien-to ra-dio

– or two weak vowels (the first vowel must be unstressed, e.g.:

    ciudad diurno ruido

Breaking the diphthong to make a new syllable

The word **'oigo'** (**oi**-go) has a diphthong. But **'oí'** (**o-í**) has "broken" the
diphthong into two parts, since the written accent has strengthened the weak
vowel such that it can form its own syllable. Other examples where the diphthong
is separated in two, making a written accent necessary, are as follows

    Ma-rí-a / rí-es / ba-úl / rí-o / bú-ho / ra-íz / frí-o / a-cen-tú-a / re-ír / o-í-do /
    grú-a / dú-o / la-úd / ca-fe-í-na / re-ú-no / pa-ís / pro-hí-be / ca-í-da / ma-íz /

> **Mnemonic device**
> The **"burro & búho rule."** A good way to remember whether an **'i'** or a **'u'** in
> a diphthong requires a written accent is to listen to yourself pronounce the
> word. If it sounds like the sound made by a donkey (un burro) (í a–í a) (ba-
> **hí-a**, ca-fe-te-rí-a, etc.), or an owl (un búho) (ú o–ú o) (**bú-ho**, **dú-o**, etc.), it
> needs an accent mark.

Supplementary clarifications

Having outlined the seven basic rules of written accents, we would like to offer several clarifications.

1 Accented diphthongs

Accented diphthongs follow the general rules of accentuation:

- **Interrogatives and exclamatives**: cuál   quién
- **Palabras agudas**: guión bonsái también hacéis adiós después truhán
- **Palabras llanas**: Gutiérrez huésped suéter Suárez
- **Palabras esdrújulas**: miércoles náutico murciélago

You must remember the following specific rules:

- When the diphthong is made up of a strong vowel and a weak vowel, the accent mark generally goes on the strong vowel.
- Diphthong **'ui'** (**frequent error**)

Since we tend to pronounce the **diphthong 'ui'** as though it were broken, many people think that the **'i'** has an accent mark, but **it does not** have one if the diphthong appears in **palabras llanas** or **palabras agudas** that end in a consonant other than 'n' or 's.'

incluido jesuita construido huir

However, the **'i' does get** an accent mark in **palabras agudas** that end in 'a vowel,' 'n,' or 's' or **esdrújulas**:

benjuí cuídate acuífero casuística

2 Triphthongs

Triphthongs are combinations of three vowels. They follow the general accentuation rules and carry the written accent **on the strong vowel**:

habituáis continuéis limpiáis

3 Double vowels

Words with double vowels also follow the general accentuation rules:

albahaca chiita microondas leer

4 Plural words

Many singular words add on a syllable in the plural, which can result in a shift of the tonic accent, all the while remaining subject to the same general accent rules:

lo-bo → lo-bos, ca-sa → ca-sas

(keep their tonic accent in the same place, no additional syllable in the plural)

ma-rro-**quí** → ma-rro-**quí**-es

(keep the tonic accent on the 'i' thus creating a broken diphthong in the plural)

But:

ré-gi-men → re-**gí**-me-nes, es-**pé**-ci-men → es-pe-**cí**-me-nes
(changes the tonic accent but remains **esdrújula**)

ca-**rác**-ter → ca-rac-**te**-res
(changes the tonic accent but remains **llana**)

in-**glés** → in-**gle**-ses, ac-**ción** → ac-**cio**-nes
(goes from **aguda** to **llana** because of the addition of another syllable)

lá-piz → **lá**-pi-ces
(changes from **llana** to **esdrújula**)

5 Foreign words

If a foreign word has already been incorporated into the Spanish language, or has been adapted to its pronunciation and spelling, it will follow the general Spanish accentuation rules:

béisbol   fútbol   bidé   póster   ultimátum   Taiwán

6 Adverbs ending in "–mente"

These words keep the accent mark in the same place as the adjective:

rápido – rápidamente   fácil – fácilmente   lógico – lógicamente

7 Capital letters

Capital letters carry written accents as usual, according to the general rules:

Ávila   PERÚ

8 Compound words

Compound words act as single words, and therefore follow the same rules as discussed above:

pisapapeles   asimismo   décimosexto   cortafríos

However, when two adjectives are joined by a hyphen, each element keeps the written accent of its standalone form:

hispano-árabe   franco-soviético   histórico-geográfico

 Exercises

 EXERCISE 5. With practice you will become very good at knowing when a word needs a written accent. Here are various exercises which will help you develop your skills. As you have seen, putting written accents where they belong is a three-step process:

1. listen for the tonic accent,
2. figure out which syllable the accent falls on,
3. apply the rules of accentuation.

1 Este jarron azul fue mio, ahora es tuyo.
2 Los pajaros tambien hablan mucho, muchisimo.
3 ¿El era mas guapo que tu? Si, afortunadamente.
4 ¿Que es esto? No se. Sera un caiman.
5 Leer frances es tan dificil como cantar en sanscrito.
6 Te buscare un baul verde esmeralda muy elegante.
7 ¿Yo os prohibo que hagais bizcochos solos?
8 A mi me gusto la catedral de Paris con ese jorobado.
9 Nosotros no sabiamos el dia de tu cumpleaños.
10 Si ve el pantalon lila de la señorita Sanchez, traigamelo.

 EXERCISE 6. As you listen to each of the following sentences, add the written accents where required.

6.1. Accent quiz # 1

1 ¿Cuando salio el avion? Pues lo vi despegar a eso de las cuatro de la tarde.
2 Su perrita desaparecio ayer junto con mi gatito. ¡Que calamidad!
3 Ellos aparecieron en la fiesta vestidos de payasos y duendes. ¡Ay que horror!
4 ¿De quienes son estos niñitos? No se, pero los padres se fueron corriendo.
5 Mira que tarta de cumpleaños tan bonita. Voy a comprartela y a cortartela en pedazos.
6 "Conteste el telefono o lo mato," dijo el bandolero con la boca llena.
7 Esa pelicula fue fantastica. Para ti. A nosotros no nos gusto para nada.
8 Cuando mi mama regrese, pidale que se siente en el sillon y que se duerma.
9 Me robaron mi mochila con todo lo que tenia dentro. No seas histerico, solo llevabas un par de bocadillos.
10 Ojala llueva, nieve, truene y relampaguee para no tener que ir al colegio.

6.2. Accent quiz # 2

1 A mi me gusta mi casa, mas ellos prefieren la de Maria Juana.
2 Quiero que usted me de un pedazo de ese pastel de manzana.
3 ¿Que espia salio de la camara frigorifica, el japones o el ingles? No, fue el turco.
4 Ellos no sabian lo que nosotros queriamos. ¿Y tu si?
5 ¡Aun no ha llegado Raul despues de dos horas! ¡Por supuesto que no! ¡Que esperabas!
6 Entre en la universidad en septiembre y me quede un larguisimo tiempo.
7 Le prohibo que entre. ¡Vayase de aqui, y no vuelva nunca mas!

8   ¡Cual es tu secreto! ¡Dimelo o me tiro por la ventana! ¡Pues tirate!

9   ¿Vosotros sabeis en que iglesia, sinagoga o mezquita se caso vuestro tio?

10 Usted tiene un cierto aire quijotesco. ¿Por que? Pues porque va errando por todo el pais.

6.3. Accent quiz # 3

1   No nos hemos visto nunca. ¡Es verdad! Yo a usted no lo he visto jamas.

2   Hablabamos de la politica de esta nacion, que es un autentico desastre.

3   Se le desato el alma cuando le dije cuanto lo queria. ¡Ave Maria purisima!

4   Le mande cortar los arboles. ¿Con que? ¡con un hacha, hombre!

5   Ella nos hizo una suplica al oido, antes de tirarse a la piscina vestida y con zapatos.

6   Los locos del manicomio reñian constantemente y se sacaban la lengua.

7   ¿Y tu creias en el libre albedrio? Yo si. Te equivocaste, estamos en una carcel.

8   Hijo mio, eres un misantropo. Y tu eres un avaro, un codicioso y un charlatan.

9   Melquiades, aqui en este paraiso terrenal creceras sano y fuerte como un roble.

10 Dejame decirtelo antes que se me olvide: estoy embarazada de ti …

 EXERCISE 7. As you listen to each of the following stories, add the written accents where required.

7.1. "Bobby el impaciente"

Eran las tres en punto de la tarde, pero todavia no habia llegado el correo. Impaciente, Bobby salia y entraba en su casa constantemente, dando vueltas y vueltas, cruzando la calle una y otra vez, echandole un vistazo al buzon cada seis minutos. En eso paso un automovil, despues un camion. Un niño lanzo una pelota en la acera, y otro la agarro con su guante. Llego un mensajero que se paro en frente de una casa amarilla y toco el timbre. Una señora pelirroja abrio la puerta, lo saludo, tomo el paquete, le dio las gracias, y cerro la puerta de sopeton. Mas tarde paso un mecanico con sus herramientas, y luego un medico con el tipico maletin negro. Bobby lo observo todo y mucho mas. Pero ese dia el cartero no aparecio.

7.2. "Diálogo de chismosos"

O – ¡Hola Laura!

L – ¿Que es de tu vida, Oscar?

O – Pues aqui, pasandola; ¿y tu?

L – Pues, a que no sabes a quien vi el miercoles en el cafe Lulu.

O – Ni idea. ¿A quien?

L – Pues, me encontre con la novia de Saul.

O –¿Cual, la que le dejo plantado el sabado pasado en la catedral?

L – Esa misma. Pero no fue en la catedral sino en la tintoreria. Y lo mas comico del caso fue que vestia una faldita apretadisima y cortisima.

O – ¿No estara buscando un nuevo novio? A Joaquin por ejemplo.

L – Yo creia eso tambien. Pero despues me di cuenta de que a ella le gustan los pesados.

O – Ah, uno que le da una serenata con violin debajo del balcon cada media noche.

L – Pues si, parece que ese es su tipo de hombre ideal. Cada loco con su tema.

7.3. "El pájaro proactivo"

Tres pajaritos en un nido se quejaban del frio que hacia en la zona norte. Uno decia que no queria pasar un invierno mas como este. Titiritando, el otro emitio un *pio, pio,* y el tercero chirrio un *si, si, si.* Pero en vez de ponerse en accion, los tres comenzaron a picotear un par de gusanitos. De subito el gusanito mas gordo estornudo, y con el ruido azoro a los pajaritos hasta tal punto que uno se cayo del nido. El otro le siguio. Pero el ultimo, bien picaro, logro balancearse con una pata en el borde del nido. De ahi se lanzo hacia una altisima rama del arbol y miro para ver lo que habia a su alrededor. Asi, se sacudio las plumas, tomo aliento, y deseandoles un fantastico "adios" a sus compañeros, emprendio vuelo hacia el Sur.

 ## *Notes*

9 Spelling and punctuation

Since spelling can be a source of difficulty for many students, it helps to become familiar with some key differences between English and Spanish spelling rules.

Spelling

Letter combinations and sounds

Many words in English and Spanish have similar sounds but different spelling. Note that:

1 The following letter combinations **do not exist** in Spanish:

d̶d̶	adición (addition)
ff	diferente (different)
m̶m̶	comercial (commercial)
p̶h̶	alfabeto (alphabet)
p̶p̶	apropiado (appropriate)
s̶s̶	posible (possible)
t̶t̶	atención (attention)

> **Mnemonic device**
>
> To remember all the combinations of double consonants that do exist in Spanish just think of the name **CAROLINE**, which contains all of them: CC—RR—LL—NN.

The –cc– combination is found, for example, in some words ending in *–cción*: colección (collection), infracción (infraction), abstracción (abstraction).

Note that words ending in *–cción* have English cognates ending in –ction:
acción (action), dirección (direction)

Similarly, the Spanish ending *–ción* usually corresponds to the English ending –tion:
adopción (adoption), composición (composition), relación (relation), solución (solution)

Some words with the –cc– combination in English have the same combination in Spanish:
accidente (accident), occidente (Occident), accesorio (accessory), acceso (access), etc.

But remember that there are exceptions:
acento (accent), ocurrir (occur)

2 The letter **k** exists only in words of foreign origin, such as:

kilogramo, kilómetro, kiosco, whisky

(also possible, but less frequently used: quilogramo, quilómetro, quiosco, güisqui)

To make the **k sound**, Spanish typically uses:

qu + e / i as in queso, química, quitar,

c + a / o / u as in casa, coco, Cuba

3 The letter **w** is also only used in words of foreign origin:

windsurf, waterpolo, web

4 The letter **x** is used in words that begin with:

– the prefixes **ex-** or **extra-**

exportar, exfoliar, **extra**er, **extra**ordinario,

– **ex- + -pr-** or **ex + -pl-**

expreso, exprimir or explicar

– note that the prefix '**ex**,' meaning something that is no more, is used without a hyphen, as in:

ex ministro (former minister), **ex** alumno (alumnus), etc.

– **xeno-**, **xero-** or **xilo-**

xenofobia, **xero**grafía, **xiló**fono

– the letter **x** can also be found in the middle of words:

boxeo, conexión

5 The letter **h** is always silent in Spanish:

¡Hola!, habla, hijo, hotel, hospital, alcohol, prohibir

Exercises

EXERCISE 1. Dictation. Here are some practice words. Listen to them on the website and complete the exercise.

1 c _ _ _ _ _	9 _ _ _ _ _ _ _ r
2 a _ _ _ _ _	10 _ _ _ _ _ r
3 _ _ _ o	11 _ _ _ _ _ _ _ _ _ a
4 _ _ _ _ _ _ r	12 c _ _ _ _ _ _ _ _ _ _
5 s _ _ _ _ _ _ _	13 e _ _ _ _ _ _
6 c _ _ _ _ _ _	14 f _ _ _ _ _ _ _ _ _ _ _
7 _ _ _ _ _ r	15 o _ _ _ _ _ _ _ _
8 _ _ _ _ _ _ _ e	16 _ _ _ _ _ _ _ o

17 c _ _ _ _ _ _	26 _ _ _ _ _ _ _ a
18 p _ _ _ _ _ _ _	27 _ _ _ _ _ r
19 d _ _ _ _ _ _ _ _ _	28 a _ _ _ _ _ _ _ _
20 a _ _ _ _ _	29 o _ _ _ _ _ _
21 a _ _ _ _ _ _ _ _ _	30 e _ _ _ _ _ _ _
22 s _ _ _ _ _ _ _	31 _ _ _ _ _ r
23 _ _ _ _ _ o	32 _ _ _ _ _ _ _ _ l
24 _ _ _ _ _ _ d	33 _ _ _ _ _ _ _ _ o
25 _ _ _ _ _ _ _ _ e	

Lower case

Spanish uses the upper case much less than English. Remember to always use **lower case** for the first letter of:

1 Days of the week, months and seasons of the year:
   el martes, el viernes, el sábado
   en enero, en mayo, en julio
   la primavera, el verano, el otoño, el invierno

2 Nationality, ethnicity, culture, religion and language:
   los americanos, los chinos, los sudafricanos, los españoles, los franceses
   los mayas, los incas, los aztecas, los guaraníes, los gallegos, los vascos
   el catolicismo, el judaísmo, el islamismo
   los católicos, los judíos, los musulmanes
   la religión católica, la religión judía, la religión musulmana
   el castellano, el portugués, el inglés, el ruso, el polaco, el japonés

However, note that like in English, geographical names such as cities, countries and continents are written with a capital letter in Spanish:
   América, China, Sudáfrica, España, México, Venezuela, Europa

3 Titles of books, articles, films, plays, short stories, paintings, etc., use a capital letter only for the first word; everything else is written in lower case, except for proper names included in the title:
   Mario Vargas Llosa escribió la novela *La ciudad y los perros*.
   Hable con ella, una película dirigida por Pedro Almodóvar.
   La casa de Bernarda Alba, obra teatral escrita por Federico García Lorca.
   "La siesta del martes", un cuento de Gabriel García Márquez.
   El cuadro *Las hilanderas* de Velázquez se encuentra en el Museo del Prado.

Upper case

Upper case is used:

1 At the beginning of a text and after a full stop, three dots (if they conclude a sentence), a question mark or an exclamation mark:

Cuando por fin llegué al pueblo, me sentí aliviado.

No sé qué … Déjame solo un rato, por favor.

¿Dónde está tu hermana? Hace mucho tiempo que no la veo.

¡Qué bien! Mañana nos vamos de vacaciones.

2 After the greeting in a letter, note, certificate, or before a quotation:

Querida amiga: Te escribo …

Como dice el famoso refrán: "Más vale pájaro en mano que ciento volando".

3 For proper names, such as names of people and places:

la familia Pérez, el Himalaya, Santo Tomás, Zaragoza, Jerez de la Frontera

4 For an article that forms part of a place name:

La Habana, El Salvador, El Cairo

But:

el Caribe, (la) Florida, (el) Perú

5 For names of planets, stars, and constellations:

el Sol, la Luna, la Tierra, Marte, Júpiter

But: in everyday language, we use lower case for the Sun and the Moon:

Hoy hace sol. El sol brilla mucho hoy.

Ese niño siempre está en la luna.

We also use 'tierra' in lower case when it means 'soil' or 'land' instead of the planet Earth:

Esta tierra es muy árida.

Echo de menos a la gente de mi tierra.

6 With respect to God and gods, the convention is the same as in English:

– The monotheistic God is written with a capital letter:

rogar a Dios

– Pagan gods are written in lower case:

el dios de la sabiduría, la diosa de la belleza, los dioses griegos y romanos

– But proper names of gods are, of course, capitalized:

Tláloc, dios de la lluvia

7 Names of commercial brands:

Kleenex, Coca-Cola, Chupa-Chups

8 Titles of nobility, dignity and government, administration as well as institutions, companies and political parties:

Alcalde, Ministro de Asuntos Exteriores, Presidente, el Instituto Cervantes, el Partido Socialista

9 Nicknames of certain people when they are equivalent to the proper name:

Juana la Loca, Iván el Terrible

10 Titles of respect, particularly if they are abbreviated:

D., D.ª, Sr., Sra., Srta., S.A.R. (Su Alteza Real), Excmo. (Excelentísimo)

However, **D. (don)** and **Ud. (usted)** must be written in lower case if they are not abbreviated.

> **Mnemonic device**
>
> A good way to remember when to use lower case or upper case is the sentence: **¿Ellos irán a Irán?** (Will they go to Iran?). It reminds you that country names are capitalized in Spanish (but remember that nationalities and languages are not).

Words or phrases written in capital letters

In Spanish capital letters are used to emphasize words or phrases in the following instances:

1 In Acronyms:

RAE (Real Academia Española), ONU (Organización de las Naciones Unidas), IVA (Impuesto sobre el Valor Añadido)

2 Roman numerals:

Juan Carlos I (*Juan Carlos primero*, not *~~el primero~~ or *~~uno~~), el siglo XXI (el siglo veintiuno), el siglo XV (el siglo quince)

3 In legal and administrative texts, the main verb or noun emphasized in the document:

EXPONE, CERTIFICA, SEÑORES, etc.

CERTIFICA:

Que Dª. Carmen Martínez Valle ha completado satisfactoriamente todos los requisitos del curso …

And remember! You must put accents on all capital letters whenever required:

Ángela, HERNÁNDEZ, Álvaro

 **Exercises**

EXERCISE 2. Choose the correct form in each sentence by crossing out the wrong one.

Example: Voy a visitar (~~madrid~~ / Madrid) con un amigo (francés / ~~Francés~~).

1   El (budismo / Budismo) es la religión de mucha gente que vive en (Asia / asia).
2   Los (Griegos / griegos) tenían muchos (Dioses / dioses).
3   Sara es (chilena / Chilena) y (Judía / judía), pero vive en (el Salvador / El Salvador).
4   ¿Has leído (la novela / la Novela) (*Cien años de soledad* / *Cien Años De Soledad*)?
5   La (Tierra / tierra) siempre gira alrededor del (Sol / sol) aunque hoy no haga (Sol / sol).
6   Hoy es (Martes / martes), (Cuatro / cuatro) de (junio / Junio).
7   En (Tailandia / tailandia) conocimos a (Japoneses / japoneses) que hablaban (Inglés / inglés) y a gente de (mongolia / Mongolia).
8   La ciudad de (La Habana / la Habana) está en (El Caribe / el Caribe).
9   Los (Españoles / españoles) llegaron a (México / méxico) en 1517.
10 Los (Incas / incas) construyeron una gran civilización en (El Perú / el Perú).
11 Las (PYMES / pymes) son pequeñas y medianas empresas que tienen a un representante en el (Ministerio de Trabajo / Ministerio de trabajo).
12 Vimos la obra de teatro (*Bodas de sangre* / *Bodas de Sangre*) el (Domingo / domingo) pasado.
13 Tras la muerte de Carlos II (el segundo / segundo / dos), a comienzos del siglo XVIII (dieciocho / decimoctavo), se produjo un cambio de dinastía en (españa / España).
14 Me encanta hacer experimentos con ácido (phosphórico / fosfórico) en las clases de (física / físsica) y (química / chímica).
15 ¿Eres (Católico / católico), (protestante / Protestante), (budista / Budista) o (musulmán / Musulmán)?

EXERCISE 3. Put capital letters where necessary.

querida amiga:
te escribo desde madrid. he venido a pasar ocho semanas para mejorar el español y mis conocimientos sobre la cultura española. el domingo voy a visitar algunos museos en el centro de la capital de españa. tengo muchas ganas de ver los cuadros de velázquez, *las meninas* y *la rendición de breda*, también

llamado *las lanzas*; *el sueño de jacob* de ribera y *los fusilamientos del tres de mayo* de goya.

me han dicho que todos ellos son lienzos impresionantes. los madrileños son muy agradables y la ciudad está hermosísima en primavera. ayer comí en un restaurante gallego y bebí vino albariño. ¡qué rico estaba todo! vivo con una familia muy simpática. el señor se llama d. jorge y la señora dª. pilar; son encantadores y me tratan como si fuera su hija.

bueno, tere, te dejo por hoy. espero que todo te vaya bien por san sebastián; saluda a la familia iriarte de mi parte.

besos,

natalie

EXERCISE 4. In each but one of the following sentences there is a spelling mistake. Correct the sentences that need it and identify the sentence that is completely correct.

Example: ¿Durante cuántos anos aprendiste chino en China?
Correct form: _____ años _____

1   El profesor siempre dice que tenemos que prestar más attención en clase.

   _____

2   La profesora de Japonés nunca recuerda mi nombre porque en Japón no existen nombres como el mío.

   _____

3   Mi primo vivió en Guatemala y en el Salvador durante diez años antes de irse al Caribe.

   _____

4   El Gobierno tiene que encontrar una solución immediata al problema de la inmigración ilegal.

   _____

5   ¿Te gustó la película de Almodóvar *Todo sobre mi Madre*? A mí me encantó.

   _____

6   El hijo de los Vázquez no es muy efficiente en las tareas domésticas. No sabe cocinar, ni coser ni planchar, pero siempre intenta ayudar en lo que puede.

   _____

7   Angel estuvo en La Habana el verano pasado, pero no pudo entrevistar a Fidel Castro a pesar de tener acreditación de prensa.

   _____

8   Philadelphia es la ciudad más grande del estado de Pensilvania, pero paradójicamente la capital es Harrisburg.

   _____

9   Te recommiendo que leas la novela *El reino de este mundo*, del escritor
cubano Alejo Carpentier.

—————————————

10 Me compré un coche nuevo de segunda mano en verano y tengo que
pasarle la ITV antes de Noviembre.

—————————————

11 ¿Sabes si es possible matricularse el lunes para el curso? No tengo ni
idea. Lo mejor es que preguntes en secretaría.

—————————————

12 El siglo xx se caracterizó por un gran desarrollo técnico e industrial en el
ámbito de las nuevas tecnologías.

—————————————

13 Dicen que lo más difícil de la gramática española es el subjuntivo. Pero
para mí no lo es, porque conozco un recurso mnemotécnico que me ha
ayudado mucho.

—————————————

14 Este verano visitamos Jerez de la frontera con la familia Fontádez Muñoz, y
nos enseñaron el museo y la colección de antigüedades que tienen debajo
de la farmacia.

—————————————

15 El lema de la rae española, «Limpia, brilla y da esplendor» fue acuñado por
el gramático Antonio de Nebrija.

—————————————

Punctuation

1   El punto (.) (period)

The use of a period indicates the end of a sentence, including statements, mild
commands or indirect questions:

> Madrid es la capital de España.
> Consúltalo con tu jefe.

A period is also used:

– After abbreviations:

> Sr. / D. / D.ª / Sra. / Srta. / etc. / a.m. / p.m.

– To separate long numbers into groups of three, counting from the right:

> 1.234   28.730   12.234.565

Note that this is different from English, which uses a comma: 1,234; 28,730, etc.

– To separate the hours from the minutes:

9.15 (although it is better to use a colon: 9:45)

A further difference from English is the use of a period following quotation marks:

La dependienta de la tienda de sombreros le dijo a María que "tendría que esperar".

2   La coma (,) (comma)

Commas are used:

– To separate words in a series:

Lara, Héctor, Laura y Maica fueron los ganadores del premio "Periodistas del Año".

– To separate very brief full sentences:

"Llegué, vi, vencí" dijo Julio César.

– Between a whole number and a decimal, e.g., to distinguish dollars from cents, sterling pounds from pennies, euros from cents, etc.:

El 7,6% de la población / $4,85; £25,67; 78,21€

– To set off a clarification or explanation from the rest of the sentence:

Los vientos, que son muy fuertes en aquella zona, impedían la navegación.

El presidente del Gobierno español, José Luis Rodríguez Zapatero, ha anunciado medidas urgentes para hacer frente a la crisis económica.

– To indicate that a verb has been omitted:

Algunos en la fiesta hablaron de política, otros (hablaron) de negocios.

– To separate a vocative, or direct address, from the rest of the sentence:

Paula, ven aquí ahora mismo.

– Before a conjunction such as a 'y,' 'o' and 'ni' when it precedes a phrase that is not part of the previous sequence:

Los niños eran alegres, juguetones y cariñosos, y todo el mundo los adoraba.

– To set off most introductory elements or separate expressions such as:

Sentence modifier (or parenthetical expression):
pues (since, therefore, so), así pues (so, therefore), o sea (that is), es decir (that is to say), esto es (that's it), sin embargo (however), finalmente (finally), no obstante (notwithstanding, nevertheless), de hecho (in fact), por ejemplo (for example), etc.

pero (but), mas (but), sino (but)

así que (so), con que (as long as), de manera que (in such a way that), de modo que (so)

Por último, nos fuimos a casa a ver la televisión, es decir, a no hacer nada de provecho.

Sabemos muchas cosas, pero aún tenemos mucho que aprender.

Es necesario implantar el voto electrónico, de modo que todo el mundo pueda votar desde su casa.

In a prepositional phrase to indicate an inversion from the logical order of the sentence:
Con esta nevada, no llegaremos nunca a casa para la cena. (or: No llegaremos nunca a casa para la cena con esta nevada)

An absolute phrase:
Habiendo finalizado la carrera, se puso a buscar trabajo.

A tag question:
Eres español, ¿no?

(Note how different from English this punctuation is)

– When the subordinate clause precedes the main clause:
  Cuando salgas, cierra la puerta.

– Between the place and the date at the end of a letter, and the street name and the number of the house or building:
  Lugo, 23 de mayo de 2009
  Calle Rosal, 23

– Between the two parts of a proverb:
  Hombre precavido, vale por dos.

3 **Los dos puntos (:)** (the colon)
A colon is used in Spanish:
– To indicate that an enumeration or series is about to happen:
  Las estaciones del año son cuatro: primavera, verano, otoño e invierno.

– After a greeting at the beginning of a letter, whether formal or familiar:
  Mi querido amigo:
  Te escribo para decirte que llego a Nueva York la semana que viene y …

Note that in English a comma is typically used to introduce an informal letter, while a colon is used only for formal letters.

–In a direct address:
  Señoras y señores:

– To introduce a text, however short:
  Ya os lo dije el primer día: tened mucho cuidado.

– After words or expressions such as: *por ejemplo* (for example), and certain constructions specific to legal documents, such as *declaro/declara* (I declare; he/she declares), *certifico/certifica* (I certify; he/she certifies), *ordeno/a* (I order; he/she orders), *expongo/expone* (I state; he/she states), *solicito/solicita* (I request; he/she requests), etc.

> En España han convivido muchas culturas diversas. Por ejemplo: los musulmanes y los judíos.

– Before a quotation:

> Como dijera Sócrates: "Sólo sé que no sé nada".

– Before a sentence that summarizes or indicates a consequence of the previous statement:

> Perdí la cartera, el móvil, las llaves: fue un auténtico desastre.

4   El punto y coma (;) (the semicolon)

A semicolon is used:

– To separate two complete sentences:

> Tendremos que cerrar el negocio; no hay ventas.

– With conjunctions such as: pero (but), aunque (although), mas (but), if the sentence is long. If it is short, a comma is normally used:

> Se tenían mucho respeto; se llevaban a las mil maravillas, como hermanos; pero, pese a todo, siempre terminaban discutiendo.

– To introduce a sentence that summarizes what has already been said:

> Los niños en el parque, el calor incesante y el camión de los helados; todo parece indicar que hoy es el primer día de vacaciones.

5   Los puntos suspensivos (...) (ellipsis)

An ellipsis is used:

– When something has been omitted, or the sentence has been left unfinished:

> El que ríe último ríe … (mejor)

– For dramatic effect or to indicate doubt, insecurity, fear or surprise:

> Bueno … (well …) en realidad … (in fact …) quizá … (maybe …) es posible … (it's possible …)

6   Los signos de interrogación (¿ ?) y de exclamación (¡ !) (question and exclamation marks)

In Spanish, question marks (¿ ?) and exclamation marks (¡ !) are used both at the beginning and at the end of a sentence. The marks at the beginning are always inverted:

> ¿Dónde has estado? ¡Qué buena cara tienes!

Question marks and exclamation marks are often placed around the specific question or exclamation, and not at the beginning and end of the sentence:

En tu opinión, ¿cómo explicas la popularidad de ese cantante?

Mira lo que hizo Andrés con la pelota, ¡qué desastre!

Eres finlandés, ¿verdad?

Acaban de llamar a la puerta, ¡seguro que son ellos!

Question marks are used:
– After direct questions:

¿Cómo te llamas?

Whenever the question is an indirect one, no questions marks are needed:

Dime con quién andas y te diré quién eres.

Exclamation marks are used:
– After an exclamation:

¡Qué niño tan rico!

– After an interjection:

¡Ah! Perdona. No lo sabía.   ¡Oh! Así de elegante seguro que triunfas.

– After a command:

¡No llegues tarde esta noche!

7   Las comillas ("") (quotation marks)

We use quotation marks:

– To frame someone's words or material from a text, or to enclose direct quotations:

Dijo el presidente: "Yo también soy berlinés".

– To indicate that a foreign language word has been used (italics are often used instead):

El ladrón salió corriendo de la tienda y se metió en un "cul-de-sac".

– To indicate the title of an article or a poem, especially when published within a larger work such as an article, a song, a short poem, etc. To distinguish the larger work, use italics or underline:

Vamos a cantar la canción "De colores" del disco *Cien canciones para niños*.

– To call attention to certain words used in an unconventional way. These can also be written in italics or underlined.

La tecla "Ins" significa "insertar".

– To refer to a nickname or alias:

El cantante José Luis Rodríguez, alias "el Puma", dio un concierto ayer.

– To introduce a dialogue:

"Buenos días. ¿Se encuentra bien?"

8 La diéresis (ü) (diaeresis)

A diaeresis or tréma is used over the "ü" in the syllables "güe" and "güi" to indicate that the "u" is pronounced.

Compare the pronunciation of:

guitarra vs. pingüino, vergüenza, cigüeña, averigüe, lingüística

9 El guión (-) (hyphen)

The hyphen (-) is used:

– To form some compound words (e.g. compound adjectives)

Se trataron temas socio-políticos. Hubo un acuerdo franco-español.

– To connect two dates:

Federico García Lorca (1898-1936).

– To relate concepts that would normally be linked by a preposition:

La relación estudiante-profesor (la relación del estudiante con el profesor)

El guión doble (--) is used:

– To frame a comment or explanation within a sentence:

El mejor museo del mundo --según me han dicho-- es el Metropolitano de Nueva York.

– Introduce dialogue within a text: to separate the speaker's words from those of the narrator:

-- ¿Adónde vas?

-- A casa de la abuelita -- contestó la simpática Caperucita.

-- ¿Y qué llevas en esa cestita? -- le preguntó el lobo.

-- Miel, fruta y unas tortitas para mi abuelita.

10 El paréntesis ( ) (parenthesis)

A parenthesis is used as follows:

– To isolate comments and clarifications within a text:

Los hijos de Pantuflo Zapatilla (Zipi y Zape) no aparecen en esta historieta.

– To give an equivalence in either words or numbers:

Hay aquí un cheque de 1.000 (mil) euros.

– To provide a translation:

Julio César exclamó: "Veni, vidi, vinci" (llegué, vi, vencí).

– To give a personal opinion about what is being said:

Su fama (en mi opinión) será breve.

– To refer to a page, article, book, table, etc.

(véase figura 1.1.)

Exercises

EXERCISE 5. The following two texts require you to give them punctuation, as well as your interpretation. After reading each text carefully and listening to it on the website, proceed to the following tasks:

1. Insert periods where needed.
2. Give the dialogues the appropriate punctuation.
3. Locate any questions and exclamations, and insert question or exclamation marks accordingly.
4. Put in the needed commas.
5. Put the diéresis (or diaeresis, as in naïve or Brontë) on the words requiring it.
6. Hyphenate words if necessary.
7. Insert colons, parentheses or ellipsis as appropriate.

In some cases there may be several punctuation options, so your answers may vary slightly from the answer key.

5.1. "Micaela la limpiabotas"

Una mañana tempranito la tía Pepa que se parecía a un pinguino salió de su casa y como de costumbre se encontró con su buena amiga Micaela la limpiabotas que tenía aspecto de cigueña

Qué sorpresa verte Cómo te va

Pues muy mal replicó la limpiabotas

Por qué le preguntó la tía Pepa

Pues figúrate que ayer me vino un hombre muy bien vestido con corbata chaleco y sombrero que me dijo que era anglo francés y quería que yo le limpiara sus zapatos negros Con mucho gusto le dije y se los pulí hasta que brillaron como espejos Se me pusieron las manos rojas como guindillas de tanto trabajar pero el tipo quedó bien satisfecho Yo le dije Me debe $125 uno veinticinco Con una gran sonrisa él me dijo que en ese momento sólo tenía 4000 cuatro mil euros en el bolsillo pero que iba a ir al banco que queda al doblar la esquina para cambiar el dinero y me lo iba a traer en seguidita Pues aquí estoy esperándolo

Cuándo pasó eso le preguntó la tía Pepa

Pues ayer por la mañana

5.2. "La enamorada"

Qué día más estupendo exclamó la niñita respirando el aire del campo y subiendo la loma Encantada de la vida se sentó en la hierba y sacó de su blusa la carta que llevaba junto al corazón La había recibido esa misma tarde pero no quería abrirla porque sabía que era de su enamorado y quería estar sola en medio de la naturaleza para saborearla al máximo La abrió con mucho cuidado no queriendo romper ese precioso sobre color crema que contenía la carta de su amado un marinero guapo y divertido que había conocido la semana pasada en el puerto cuando acababa de desembarcar de su barco pesquero Ahora estaba en alta mar camino a Goa Asia al otro lado del mundo

Querida Gloria

Apenas te conocí y me enamoré perdidamente desesperadamente de ti de tus ojos negros tu boca de caramelo tu pelo de azabache tu piel de marfil No sabes cuánto te amé Pero ahora que estoy muy muy lejos de ti acabo de enamorarme de otra chica Perdóname pero así es la vida

Saludos

Miguel

Al leer estas palabras escritas sobre el papel la pobre chica no pudo contener las lágrimas lágrimas no de pena tanto como de rabia sinverguenza arrastrado canalla don nadie hijo de así gritaba bajando la loma hasta que tropezó con una piedrecita se cayó por un acantilado y se murió

 Notes

Appendix
Answer key to exercises

Book exercises

Chapter 1

EXERCISE 1.
1. (este) (el) / 2. (una) (la) (la) (las) / 3. (El) (la) (un) / 4. (la) (el) (un) / 5. (un) (el) (una) /
6. (El) (un) (el) / 7. (Este) (la) (del) / 8. (la) (del) (el) / 9. (La) (este) (los mismos) (ése). /
10. (la) (esta) (aquélla). / 11. (ese) (una) (una) / 12. (un) (del)

EXERCISE 2.
1. (el / la) dentista / 2. (el) suelo / 3. (el / la) aguafiestas / 4. (la) motocicleta / 5. (el) barril /
6. (el) agua limpia / 7. (el) dilema / 8. (el / la) estudiante / 9. (el) dogma / 10. (la) rima /
11. (la) mano / 12. (el / la) mártir / 13. (el) carisma / 14. (el / la) guía / 15. (el) paisaje /
16. (el) tigre / 17. (el) naranjo / 18. (la) barca / 19. (el) hada madrina / 20. (el) problema /
21. (el / la) testigo / 22. (la) víctima / 23. (el) Mediterráneo / 24. (el / la) colega /
25. (el / la) poeta / 26. (el) do / 27. (la) actitud / 28. (el / la) amante / 29. (el) martes /
30. (la) muchedumbre / 31. (la) serpiente / 32. (el) delta / 33. (el) tranvía / 34. (la) yegua /
35. (el / la) socialista / 36. (la) serie / 37. (el / la) ordenanza / 38. (el) miércoles / 39. (el)
área / 40. (el) análisis

EXERCISE 3.
1. el gallo / la gallina, 2. el abad / la abadesa, 3. el león / la leona, 4. el poeta / la poetisa,
5. el toro / la vaca, 6. el príncipe / la princesa, 7. el emperador / la emperatriz, 8. el caballo /
la yegua, 9. el héroe / la heroína, 10. el yerno / la nuera, 11. el taxista / la taxista,
12. el padrastro / la madrastra, 13. el joven / la joven, 14. el modisto / la modista,
15. el conserje / la conserje, 16. la ballena (invariable), 17. el vampiro / la vampiresa,
18. la serpiente (invariable), 19. el soprano / la soprano, 20. el barón / la baronesa,
21. el zar / la zarina, 22. el instructor / la institutriz

EXERCISE 4.
1. la cabeza 2. la mano 3. el cura 4. la cama 5. la parte 6. el café 7. el puma 8. el rubí 9. la
salida 10. el análisis 11. el/los aroma(s); el/las agua(s), el/las hada(s), el/las arma(s) 12. la
víctima

EXERCISE 5.

5. 1. Un día de compras
la mañana / la puerta / un rato / la cuadra / del puerto / medio / de la plaza / olivas / pimientos / manzanas / fruta / cerezas / moras / libras / una polea / ternera / una bolsa / la nevera / una parte

5. 2. Valeria y sus amigos
un trompeta / un batería / navajo / a la moda / una torera / la frente / una partida / una apuesta / a la final / torero / un buen partido / un ordenanza / un guardia / a la corte / un banco / una disco / una bolera / el vocal / la policía / la margen / de la capital

5. 3. El novio de Laura
la cólera / la rama / un cerezo / al preso / un pimiento / la terminal / una navaja / media naranja / la punta / del cuchillo / la guía / el editorial / una coma / un punto / la fonda / un cuadro / madera / el llanto / la corte / el capital

EXERCISE 6.

1. la patata / 2. el cuento / 3. la capital / 4. la nevera / 5. la corte / 6. el capital / 7. la cuadra / 8. la disco / 9. el suelo / 10. el pendiente / 11. un rato / 12. el conducto / 13. el fallo / 14. el cuadro / 15. el preso / 16. la loma / 17. la orden / 18. el pez / 19. el derecho / 20. la media / 21. la terminal de autobuses / 22. un muñeco / 23. la manta / 24. el barro

EXERCISE 7.

1. (las libertades) / 2. (los camiones) / 3. (las avestruces) / 4. (los hindús / los hindúes, more commonly used) / 5. (las leyes) / 6. (los caracteres) / 7. (los céspedes) / 8. (los esquís) / 9. (los lunes) / 10. (los pantalones) / 11. (los holandeses) / 12. (los paraguas) / 13. (los ultimátum) / 14. (los faxes) / 15 (las hipótesis)

EXERCISE 8.

1. a solas. / 2. de rodillas. / 3. A sabiendas. / 4. a secas. / 5. a marchas forzadas. / 6. de espaldas. / 7. de puntillas. / 8. a gatas. / 9. De buenas a primeras. / 10. a trancas y barrancas. / 11. en cuclillas. / 12. en brazos. / 13. a oscuras / 14. a hurtadillas / 15. por las buenas o por las malas

EXERCISE 9.

En las escuelas de Seattle hay varias asociaciones estudiantiles, como la asociación de **(1) esquí.** Los chicos se ponen los **(2) suéteres** y salen en **(3) autobuses** hacia **(4) las afueras** de la ciudad todos los **(5) sábados** por la mañana. Es increíble que haya tanta afición por los deportes de **(6) invierno.** En el mismo centro hay una pequeña pista en **(7) un rascacielos.** También durante **(8) las vacaciones** de **(9) verano** los chicos cargados de equipamiento y víveres se van a hacer **(10) camping.** A veces se pierden, y es el guardabosques el que hace sonar la alerta, y la familia **(11) va** a recuperar al chico perdido.

Chapter 2

EXERCISE 1.

1. presumía / 2. chocar / 3. suspendido / 4. presentar / 5. sacar / 6. divertirnos / 7. avisar / 8. disgustó / 9. asistir / 10. contestar / 11. apuntar / 12. se atragantó / 13. dejar / 14. apoyar / 15. relacionar / 16. se entusiasmó / 17. grabar / 18. descansar / 19. se jubiló / 20. desviar / 21. se arrastraba / 22. triunfar

EXERCISE 2.

1. colgar / 2. ayudar / 3. quitar / 4. solicitar / 5. avisar / 6. presumir / 7. fingir / 8. discutir / 9. abusar / 10. demandar / 11. comprometieron / 12. cogió / 13. remover / 14. trato / 15. procurar / 16. mudar / 17. plantar / 18. respaldar / 19. asistió / 20. supongo / 21. pruebes / 22. estrecharon

EXERCISE 3.

1. n / 2. i / 3. p / 4. m / 5. a / 6. t / 7. e / 8. g / 9. l / 10. j / 11. q / 12. h / 13. f / 14. s / 15. r / 16. b / 17. c / 18. o / 19. d / 20. k

EXERCISE 4.

1. aparentaba / 2. presumir / 3. comprometido / 4. frecuentaba / 5. inventó / 6. conduce / 7. patrocina / 8. involucrado / 9. nombrar, ascender / 10. asesorar / 11. disgustada, preocupada / 12. blindar / 13. recurrir / 14. se atragantó

Chapter 3

EXERCISE 1.

1. ejercicio / 2. los globos / 3. la salida / 4. El personaje / 5. víctimas / 6. cuello / 7. universidad / 8. carpeta / 9. ganga / 10. tela / 11. director / 12. el cargamento / 13. una discusión / 14. la culpa / 15. las encías / 16. una copa / 17. el estadio / 18. la tarjeta / 19. un compromiso / 20. El altercado

EXERCISE 2.

1. e / 2. o / 3. r / 4. k / 5. a / 6. s / 7. m / 8. q / 9. l / 10. n / 11. d / 12. i / 13. t / 14. j / 15. b / 16. g / 17. h / 18. c / 19. f / 20. p

EXERCISE 3.

1. la cuestión / 2. el carácter / 3. el argumento / 4. la desgracia / 5. la casualidad / 6. la apología / 7. el bachillerato / 8. la carpeta / 9. la confidencia / 10. la copa / 11. la ganga / 12. el delito / 13. el campamento / 14. el altercado / 15. el cargamento

EXERCISE 4.

1. nudos / 2. jabón / 3. conferencia / 4. la librería / 5. parcela / 6. cuerda / 7. sopa / 8. un suburbio / 9. noticias / 10. tema / 11. un lujo / 12. júbilo / 13. faroles / 14. el desfile / 15. conservantes / 16. un paquete / 17. la receta / 18. un bote / 19. modismos / 20. inquilino

EXERCISE 5.

1. q / 2. t / 3. j / 4. n / 5. s / 6. m / 7. r / 8. k / 9. p / 10. o / 11. h / 12. c / 13. f / 14. d / 15. l / 16. i / 17. a / 18. g / 19. e / 20. b

EXERCISE 6.
1. la librería / 2. el oficio / 3. el suceso / 4. la reunión / 5. los personajes / 6. la lectura / 7. los parientes / 8. la máscara / 9. el jornal / 10. la jornada / 11. la ocurrencia / 12. la trampa / 13. el preservativo / 14. el motivo / 15. el recibo

EXERCISE 7.
1. reunión / 2. desfile / 3. motivo / 4. gripe / 5. parientes / 6. jefe / 7. receta / 8. sopa / 9. queja / 10. receta / 11. atún / 12. tienda de comestibles / 13. conservantes / 14. bote / 15. vaso / 16. jarras / 17. éxito / 18. ilusión / 19. ropa

Chapter 4

EXERCISE 1.
1. sensata / 2. completo / 3. sano / 4. escolar / 5. comprensivo / 6. última / 7. cruda / 8. geniales / 9. entusiasmada / 10. largo / 11. equivocado / 12. en blanco / 13. gracioso / 14. equívoca / 15. colorado / 16. alterado / 17. cómodo / 18. ebrio / 19. emocionados / 20. de color / 21. antigua / 22. asqueroso

EXERCISE 2.
1. k / 2. l / 3. m / 4. g / 5. h / 6. s / 7. n / 8. p / 9. r / 10. o / 11. u / 12. b / 13. f / 14. e / 15. q / 16. t / 17. i / 18. c / 19. j / 20. a / 21. d

EXERCISE 3.
1. estar excitado / 2. una dieta sana / 3. un niño educado / 4. un trabajo eventual / 5. en absoluto / 6. un encuentro casual / 7. pagar en efectivo / 8. estar embarazada / 9. Juan está constipado / 10. una cuestión que es relativa / 11. un hermano fastidioso / 12. actual / 13. un estudiante culto / 14. un tipo peculiar / 15. una última pregunta / 16. una hermana mayor / 17. ponerse colorado / 18. una historia graciosa / 19. una persona indigente / 20. un hecho relevante / 21. una almohada blanda

EXERCISE 4.
1. padres / 2. educados / 3. verdadero, auténtico / 4. antigua / 5. relacionado / 6. culta / 7. sensible / 8. comprensiva / 9. disgustada / 10. despedida / 11. embarazada / 12. envidiosa / 13. cuerda / 14. divertidas / 15. en absoluto, por nada / 16. aconsejable / 17. casualmente / 18. colorada / 19. avergonzada / 20. grandes, maravillosas / 21. de hecho

Chapter 5

EXERCISE 1.
1. (es) (está) / 2. (Estarás) (estoy) / 3. (es) (es) (está) / 4. (es) (Es) (estamos) / 5. (es) (están) / 6. (es) (está) / 7. (es) (está) / 8. (está) (es) (está) (está) / 9. (es) (está) / 10. (estamos) (es) (fuera) / 11. (estoy) (he estado) / 12. (Eres) (soy)

EXERCISE 2.

Margarita, que **(es)** una persona muy viva, **(es)** mi cuñada. El domingo **(estuve)** en su casa y me dijo que últimamente **(estaba)** trabajando demasiado, que **(estaba)** muy cansada, y que por lo tanto le gustaría **(estar)** sin trabajar y sin hacer nada durante un tiempo para **(estar)** un poco más libre y poder disfrutar de la vida. En ese momento pensé que mi amiga **(estaba)** en lo cierto ya que, después de todo, la vida no **(es)** sólo trabajo. Yo le dije que **(estaba)** de acuerdo, que eso **(es)** verdad, y que **(es)** bueno no hacer nada durante un tiempo para darse cuenta de lo que uno realmente quiere hacer. Pues hoy **(es)** martes, **(eran)** las 5:30 de la mañana y Margarita ya me **(estaba)** llamando para decirme que ahora **(está)** aburrida de no trabajar. Yo **(estaba)** medio dormida, no **(estaba)** para bromas a esas horas y colgué y desconecté el teléfono para que no llamara más. Así **(es)** la vida. Unos se conforman con lo que **(son)** y otros no **(están)** nunca satisfechos con lo que tienen.

EXERCISE 3.

1. El profesor de matemáticas es muy aburrido / 2. La puerta está abierta / 3. Esta bicicleta es mía / 4. Aquel señor es abogado / 5. Este niño es muy travieso / 6. El tren está vacío / 7. El bacalao es/está salado / 8. Mi abuela está enferma / 9. Su hermana es/está viuda / 10. Mi móvil es muy ligero / 11. Su bolso es de piel / 12. La conferencia es en el Círculo de Bellas Artes / 13. Hoy es lunes / 14. El libro está encima de la mesa / 15. La televisión está encendida

EXERCISE 4.

1. está / 2. estoy de camarero / 3. es en el aula / 4. Está acostumbrado / 5. Estás de broma / 6. que esté en el examen / 7. Son para mí / 8. Estoy que me muero / 9. correct! / 10. está vivo / 11. está a punto / 12. estaré en Madrid / 13. es de tu hermana / 14. es de plástico - es de cristal / 15. estás

EXERCISE 5.

1. (conozco) (sepa) (sabes) / 2. (conocía) (sabría) / 3. (sabe) (sabe) / 4. (Conocí) (sabía) / 5. (sabría) (conozco) / 6. (sé) (sé) / 7. (sabía) (conocerías) / 8. (conoce) (conozca) / 9. (conozco) (sé) / 10. (conocimos) (sé) / 11. (sabía) (conocías) / 12. (sabía) (conozco) / 13. (Supe) (sabía) / 14. (conozco) (sabía) / 15. (Conoces) (sé).

EXERCISE 6.

1. (Acuérdate) / 2. (comporta) / 3. (deshice) / 4. (se desprendió) / 5. (dedicamos) / 6. (se negó) / 7. (se portaron) / 8. (Te encuentras) / 9. (se va a encargar) / 10. (se le ocurrió) / 11. (se presta) / 12. (acordaron) / 13. (rindieron) / 14. (empeñó) / 15. (te hagas) / 16. (se incorporaron) / 17. (me dedico) / 18. (se comporta) / 19. (Se valió) / 20. (se rindieron)

VERBS AND THEIR DERIVATIVES (Part 1)

1. procedí / 2. acogen / 3. escurres / 4. maldijo / 5. Deduje / 6. diferir / 7. uniformar / 8. rehacer / 9. cohibió / 10. arremetió / 11. omitir / 12. pronunciar / 13. reparte

EXERCISE 7.
1. sucedió / 2. intercedió / 3. concurrieron / 4. discurre / 5. predijo / 6. conduce / 7. recoge /
8. profirió / 9. prefieren / 10. dimitió / 11. conformamos / 12. cometido / 13. rehacer /
14. se encogió / 15. inhibe / 16. entromete / 17. Denunció / 18. deduje / 19. precede /
20. readmitir / 21. Anunció / 22. bendijo / 23. ha traducido / 24. omitir / 25. repártela

VERBS AND THEIR DERIVATIVES (Part 2)
14. exponer / 15. sorprendió / 16. transcribir / 17. seguir / 18. consentir / 19. insistir /
20. sustituir / 21. atenerte / 22. retocarse / 23. extraer / 24. conviene / 25. sobrevivir /
26. provocar

EXERCISE 8.
1. recompuso / 2. sorprendió / 3. aprendí / 4. imponer / 5. suscrito / 6. interpuso /
7. prosiguió / 8. obtuvo / 9. componer / 10. yuxtaponer / 11. conseguirá / 12. asintió /
13. Supongo / 14. contrajo / 15. destituido / 16. predispuesto / 17. prescrito / 18. dispone /
19. conseguir / 20. aprender / 21. depuso / 22. reponer / 23. Persistió / 24. opuso /
25. conviven

Chapter 6

EXERCISE 1.
1. dar una vuelta / 2. echar al correo / 3. cae bien / 4. echado raíces / 5. se echaron atrás /
6. se hacía el sueco / 7. una tormenta / 8. había gato encerrado / 9. dar a luz / 10. hacer
falta / 11. Echo de menos / 12. Échame una mano / 13. echando flores / 14. dar gato por
liebre / 15. enfermo / 16. da de sí / 17. dio la mano / 18. se cayó al suelo / 19. di con /
20. hacen juego

EXERCISE 2.
1. han dado / dieron gato por liebre / 2. echando chispas / 3. echarle flores / 4. hagas el
sueco / 5. dar para / 6. eche las cartas / 7. hacen juego / 8. hacer una pregunta / 9. caiga
quien caiga / 10. dar por hecho / 11. hay gato encerrado / 12. echar a perder / 13. darme
de alta / 14. me caía de sueño / 15. De haberlo sabido

EXERCISE 3.
1. énfasis / 2. se puso / 3. confianza / 4. de Guatemala a Guatepeor / 5. al grano / 6. celos /
7. la culpa / 8. de compras / 9. prisa / 10. miedo / 11. para / 12. sueño / 13. adelante /
14. madera / 15. viene bien / 16. ganas de / 17. un apuro / 18. ¡Vaya! / 19. abajo / 20. en
cuenta / 21. va sobre ruedas / 22. fue corriendo

EXERCISE 4.
1. va por cuenta de la casa / 2. salir pitando / 3. venir de perlas / 4. salió a la luz / 5. tiene
mala cara / 6. tiene un sueño / 7. salir al / 8. venir a buscar / 9. Se le va la cabeza / 10. tengo
sueño / 11. se vino abajo / 12. pongas mala cara - poner la mesa / 13. vamos a medias /
14. pondré al sol / 15. Va de Guatemala a Guatepeor

EXERCISE 5.
1. (para) (por) / 2. (por) (para) / 3. (por) (por) / 4. (por) (por) / 5. (para) (para) / 6. (por) (por) / 7. (Por) (para) (para) / 8. (por) (por) / 9. (Por) (por) / 10. (Por) (por) / 11. (Para) (para) / 12. (para) (Para) (por) / 13. (por) (para) / 14. (Por) (para) (por) / 15. (para) (Para) / 16. (por) (por) / 17. (para) (para) / 18. (Por) (para) (por) / 19. (Por) (por) / 20. (por) (para) (para) (por) (por) (por)

EXERCISE 6.
1. por, por, para / 2. por, por, por / 3. Por, para / 4. para, por / 5. para, por / 6. por, para / 7. para, por / 8. Por, para, Para / 9. para, por / 10. Por, para / 11. para, para / 12. para, para / 13. por, por / 14. Por, por / 15. por, por, para / 16. por, Por / 17. por, para, por / 18. Para, por / 19. Para, por, por / 20. por, por, para / 21. Por, para / 22. por, por, por / 23. para, para / 24. para, por / 25. por, por / 26. para, para, por / 27. por, Para, por / 28. Por, Para / 29. por, por, por / 30. Para, Por, por

EXERCISE 7.
1. por ningún lado / 2. Por lo visto / 3. por escrito / 4. Estamos para / 5. por si acaso / 6. Por supuesto / 7. por desgracia / 8. Para qué / 9. palabra por palabra / 10. para siempre / 11. por aquí / 12. en un dos por tres / 13. Por poco / 14. hablar por mí / 15. Para otra vez / 16. por todas partes / 17. Por difícil que sea / 18. por detrás / 19. por primera vez / 20. para colmo / 21. Por encima de todo / 22. para variar / 23. por correo / 24. Por el momento / 25. Para otra ocasión

EXERCISE 8.
1. por la tarde / 2. por casualidad / 3. por suerte / 4. en un dos por tres / 5. por desgracia / 6. por correo / 7. por favor / 8. para / 9. por mi parte / 10. por supuesto / 11. para / 12. para / 13. Por lo visto / 14. por las nubes / 15. palabra por palabra / 16. por teléfono / 17. por aquel entonces / 18. por su cuenta / 19. por lo mismo (por la misma razón) / 20. por todas partes / 21. por poco / 22. porque / 23. para que / 24. para / 25. por las buenas o por las malas / 26. por el amor de Dios / 27. porque / 28. por su culpa / 29. Por supuesto / 30. por suerte / 31. por fin

Chapter 7

EXERCISE 1.
1. serio / 2. los ochenta / 3. tomar / 4. capaz / 5. otro / 6. realista - pesimista / 7. sentido / 8. por primera vez / 9. Lo pasamos bien - Nos divertimos / 10. Tengo muchas ganas de (ir a) esquiar / 11. fantástica / 12. semejanzas / 13. foto - fotografía / 14. Me gusta mucho la limonada / 15. va a llover

EXERCISE 2.
1. embarazada / 2. hecho / 3. resultado / 4. al principio / 5. fotografías / 6. quinientas / 7. capaz / 8. serios / 9. por - a causa del / 10. Tengo ganas de estar de vacaciones - de que lleguen las vacaciones / 11. la mayor parte de / 12. se divertirán / 13. relacionarse / 14. sensible / 15. He oído hablar mucho / 16. muchas veces / 17. sentido / 18. Todos sus / 19. hace cinco años / 20. depende

EXERCISE 3.

1. gatos - monos / 2. La sierra - una hoja / 3. el volante - girar / 4. el casco - las recetas / 5. unas notas - la banda / 6. pastillas - manzanas / 7. la yema - la espinilla / 8. los puños - vencer / 9. un diente - chorizo / 10. un banco - un banco / 11. chuletas - la yema / 12. aprobar - chuletas / 13. cubo - una copa / 14. la fiesta - salsa / 15. doblar - papel

EXERCISE 4.

1. blanco / 2. banco / 3. volantes / 4. Aprobaste - suspendí / 5. yemas / 6. mono / 7. tiempo / 8. billetes - cartera / 9. vence / 10. casco / 11. hogar / 12. puños - cuello / 13. manzana / 14. derechos / 15. chorizo / 16. tapa / 17. bomba de agua / 18. receta / 19. gato / 20. fiesta

EXERCISE 5.

1. m / 2. p / 3. n / 4. t / 5. r / 6. i / 7. k / 8. a / 9. s / 10. c / 11. q / 12. d / 13. l / 14. j / 15. b / 16. g / 17. o / 18. f / 19. e / 20. h

Chapter 8

EXERCISE 1.

1. (**sí**-la-ba) (esdrújula) / 2. (Pa-**cí**-fi-co) (esdrújula) / 3. (**Pé**-rez) (llana) / 4. (o-**cé**-a-no) (esdrújula) / 5. (to-**ma**-te) (llana) / 6. (ma-te-**má**-ti-cas) (esdrújula) / 7. (**tó**-ma-te) (esdrújula) / 8. (com-po-si-**ción**) (aguda) / 9. (co-rres-pon-**dió**) (aguda) / 10. (per-**dí**) (aguda) / 11. (**trái**-ga-me-lo) (sobresdrújula) / 12. (**pú**-bli-co) (esdrújula) / 13. (sa-**lir**) (aguda) / 14. (pu-bli-**có**) (aguda) / 15. (**lá**-piz) (llana)

EXERCISE 2.

1. lentitud / 2. trabajando / 3. **cráter** / 4. regiomontano / 5. pararse / 6. **bellísimas** / 7. fuente / 8. **dátil** / 9. tapiz / 10. **automóvil** / 11. **difícil** / 12. ventilador / 13. **precaución** / 14. **deseé** / 15. **reacción** / 16. **crédito** / 17. desee / 18. **semáforo** / 19. catedral / 20. limpiabotas / 21. leyes / 22. **González** / 23. **fácil** / 24. **útil**

EXERCISE 3.

1. **Tú** te vas a casa el lunes con tu primo. / 2. **Él** se fue hasta el fin del mundo sin su cartera. / 3. **Sólo** quiero pan y paz, nada **más**. / 4. Para ti, tu perro es mucho **más** grande, pero para **mí** no. / 5. No **sé** si tengo **más** dinero. / 6. Te voy a servir un buen **té**. / 7. Si quieres agua di "**sí**" y si no quieres di "no". / 8. No deseo que me **dé** nada, **sólo** lo que me corresponde. / 9. Se dijo a **sí** mismo: "ya lo **sé**". / 10. A **mí** me encanta mi casa, ¿y a ti? / 11. Dile a **él** que me **dé** el regalo que te di. / 12. **Sí**, ya **sé** que se ha comprado un piso nuevo, pero ella **aún** no me lo ha dicho.

EXERCISE 4.

1. No me gusta nada el vestido que me compraste. **¿Qué?** / 2. Este libro no es el que quiero, sino **ése** de ahí. / 3. **Todavía** no me has dicho **cuándo** vas a organizar el crucero. / 4. ¿Sabes **por qué** ha llegado Juan tan tarde a casa? / 5. **Aquélla** es la casa de la que te **hablé**. / 6. ¿**Qué** es eso que te compraste en la tienda? / 7. A que no sabes a **quién** he

visto esta mañana. / 8. ¡Pero **por qué** no dijiste nada durante la comida! / 9. **Está** tan feliz como si le hubiera tocado la **lotería**. / 10. Dime con **quién** andas y te **diré quién** eres.

EXERCISE 5.

1. Este **jarrón** azul fue **mío**, ahora es tuyo. / 2. Los **pájaros también** hablan mucho, **muchísimo**. / 3. ¿**Él** era **más** guapo que **tú**? **Sí**, afortunadamente. / 4. ¿**Qué** es esto? No **sé**. **Será** un **caimán**. / 5. Leer **francés** es tan **difícil** como cantar en **sánscrito**. / 6. Te **buscaré** un **baúl** verde esmeralda muy elegante. / 7. ¿**Yo os prohíbo** que **hagáis** bizcochos solos? / 8. A **mí** me **gustó** la catedral de **París** con ese jorobado. / 9. Nosotros no **sabíamos** el **día** de tu cumpleaños. / 10. Si ve el **pantalón** lila de la señorita **Sánchez**, **tráigamelo**.

EXERCISE 6.

6. 1. Accent quiz # 1

1. ¿**Cuándo salió** el **avión**? Pues lo vi despegar a eso de las cuatro de la tarde. / 2. Su perrita **desapareció** ayer junto con mi gatito. ¡**Qué** calamidad! / 3. Ellos aparecieron en la fiesta vestidos de payasos y duendes. ¡Ay **qué** horror! / 4. ¿De **quiénes** son estos niñitos? No **sé**, pero los padres se fueron corriendo. / 5. Mira **qué** tarta de cumpleaños tan bonita. Voy a **comprártela** y a **cortártela** en pedazos. / 6. "Conteste el **teléfono** o lo mato," dijo el bandolero con la boca llena. / 7. Esa **película** fue **fantástica**. Para ti. A nosotros no nos **gustó** para nada. / 8. Cuando mi **mamá** regrese, **pídale** que se siente en el **sillón** y que se duerma. / 9. Me robaron mi mochila con todo lo que **tenía** dentro. No seas **histérico**, **sólo** llevabas un par de bocadillos. / 10. **Ojalá** llueva, nieve, truene y relampaguee para no tener que ir al colegio.

6. 2. Accent quiz # 2

1. A **mí** me gusta mi casa, mas ellos prefieren la de **María** Juana. / 2. Quiero que usted me **dé** un pedazo de ese pastel de manzana. / 3. ¿**Qué espía salió** de la **cámara frigorífica**, el **japonés** o el **inglés**? No, fue el turco. / 4. Ellos no **sabían** lo que nosotros **queríamos**. ¿Y **tú sí**? / 5. ¡**Aún** no ha llegado **Raúl después** de dos horas! ¡Por supuesto que no! ¡**Qué** esperabas! / 6. **Entré** en la universidad en septiembre y me **quedé** un **larguísimo** tiempo. / 7. Le **prohíbo** que entre. ¡**Váyase** de **aquí**, y no vuelva nunca **más**! / 8. ¡**Cuál** es tu secreto! ¡**Dímelo** o me tiro por la ventana! ¡Pues **tírate**! / 9. ¿Vosotros **sabéis** en **qué** iglesia, sinagoga o mezquita se **casó** vuestro **tío**? / 10. Usted tiene un cierto aire quijotesco. ¿Por **qué**? Pues porque va errando por todo el **país**.

6. 3. Accent quiz # 3

1. No nos hemos visto nunca. ¡Es verdad! Yo a usted no lo he visto **jamás**. / 2. **Hablábamos** de la **política** de esta **nación**, que es un **auténtico** desastre. / 3. Se le **desató** el alma cuando le dije **cuánto** lo **quería**. ¡Ave **María purísima**! / 4. Le **mandé** cortar los **árboles**. ¿Con **qué**? ¡con un hacha, hombre! / 5. Ella nos hizo una **súplica** al **oído**, antes de tirarse a la piscina vestida y con zapatos. / 6. Los locos del manicomio **reñían** constantemente y se sacaban la lengua. / 7. ¿Y **tú creías** en el libre **albedrío**? Yo **sí**. Te equivocaste, estamos en una **cárcel**. / 8. Hijo **mío**, eres un **misántropo**. Y **tú** eres un avaro, un codicioso y un **charlatán**. / 9. Melquiades, **aquí** en este **paraíso** terrenal **crecerás** sano y fuerte como un roble. / 10. **Déjame decírtelo** antes que se me olvide: estoy embarazada de ti …

EXERCISE 7.

7. 1. Bobby el impaciente

todavía / había / salía / echándole / buzón / pasó / automóvil / después / camión / lanzó / agarró / Llegó / paró / tocó / abrió / saludó / tomó / cerró / sopetón / Más / pasó / mecánico / médico / típico / maletín / observó / más / día / apareció

7. 2. Diálogo de chismosos

O -- ¡Hola Laura!

L -- ¿**Qué** es de tu vida, **Óscar**?

O -- Pues **aquí**, **pasándola**; ¿y **tú**?

L -- Pues, a que no sabes a **quién** vi el **miércoles** en el **café Lulú**.

O -- Ni idea. ¿A **quién**?

L -- Pues, me **encontré** con la novia de **Saúl**.

O -- ¿**Cuál**, la que le **dejó** plantado el **sábado** pasado en la catedral?

L -- **Ésa** misma. Pero no fue en la catedral sino en la **tintorería**. Y lo **más cómico** del caso fue que **vestía** una faldita **apretadísima** y **cortísima**.

O -- ¿No **estará** buscando un nuevo novio? A **Joaquín** por ejemplo.

L -- Yo **creía** eso **también**. Pero **después** me di cuenta de que a ella le gustan los pesados.

O -- Ah, uno que le da una serenata con **violín** debajo del **balcón** cada media noche.

L -- Pues **sí**, parece que **ése** es su tipo de hombre ideal. Cada loco con su tema.

7. 3. El pájaro proactivo

frío / hacía / decía / quería / más / éste / emitió / pío, pío / chirrió / sí, sí, sí / acción / súbito / más / estornudó / azoró / cayó / siguió / último / pícaro / logró / ahí / lanzó / altísima / árbol / miró / había / Así / sacudió / tomó / deseándoles / fantástico / "adiós" / emprendió

Chapter 9

EXERCISE 1.

1. cónsul	12. coleccionar	23. pasivo
2. acento	13. emisión	24. huésped
3. hago	14. fascinación	25. imposible
4. ocurrir	15. ocupación	26. quiniela
5. sensación	16. kilómetro	27. quemar
6. caverna	17. capaces	28. almuercen
7. llover	18. peluquero	29. ocasión
8. inminente	19. diferenciar	30. empiecen
9. prohibir	20. actitud	31. querer
10. llorar	21. anunciación	32. hospital
11. Filadelfia	22. secuencia	33. alfabeto

EXERCISE 2.

1. (budismo) (Asia) / 2. (griegos) (dioses) / 3. (chilena) (judía) (El Salvador) / 4. (la novela) («Cien años de soledad») / 5. (Tierra) (Sol) (sol) / 6. (martes) (cuatro) (junio) / 7. (Tailandia) (japoneses) (inglés) (Mongolia) / 8. (La Habana) (el Caribe) / 9. (españoles) (México) / 10. (incas) (el Perú) / 11. (PYMES) (Ministerio de Trabajo) / 12. («Bodas de sangre») (domingo) / 13. (segundo) (dieciocho) (España) / 14. (fosfórico) (física) (química) /15. (católico) (protestante) (budista) (musulmán)

EXERCISE 3.
Querida amiga:
Te escribo desde **Madrid**. **He** venido a pasar ocho semanas para mejorar el español y mis conocimientos sobre la cultura española. **El** domingo voy a visitar algunos museos en el centro de la capital de **España**. **Tengo** muchas ganas de ver los cuadros de **Velázquez**, *Las* meninas y *La* rendición de *Breda*, también llamado *Las* lanzas; *El* sueño de *Jacob* de **Ribera** y *Los* fusilamientos del tres de mayo de **Goya**.
Me han dicho que todos ellos son lienzos impresionantes. **Los** madrileños son muy agradables y la ciudad está hermosísima en primavera. **Ayer** comí en un restaurante gallego y bebí vino albariño. ¡**Qué** rico estaba todo! **Vivo** con una familia muy simpática. **El** señor se llama **D. Jorge** y la señora **Dª. Pilar**; son encantadores y me tratan como si fuera su hija.
Bueno, **Tere**, te dejo por hoy. **Espero** que todo te vaya bien por **San Sebastián**; saluda a la familia **Iriarte** de mi parte.
Besos,
Natalie

EXERCISE 4.
1. atención / 2. japonés / 3. El Salvador / 4. inmediata / 5. «Todo sobre mi madre» / 6. eficiente / 7. Ángel / 8. Filadelfia / 9. recomiendo / 10. noviembre / 11. posible / 12. XX (capital letters) / 13. correct! / 14. Frontera / 15. RAE

EXERCISE 5.

5. 1. Micaela la limpiabotas
Una mañana tempranito, la tía Pepa --que se parecía a un **pingüino**-- salió de su casa y, como de costumbre, se encontró con su buena amiga Micaela, la limpiabotas, que tenía aspecto de **cigüeña**.
-- ¡Qué sorpresa verte! ¿Cómo te va?
-- Pues muy mal -- replicó la limpiabotas.
-- ¿Por qué? -- le preguntó la tía Pepa.
-- Pues figúrate que ayer me vino un hombre muy bien vestido con corbata, chaleco y sombrero, que me dijo que era anglo-francés y quería que yo le limpiara sus zapatos negros. "Con mucho gusto" le dije y se los pulí hasta que brillaron como espejos. Se me pusieron las manos rojas como guindillas de tanto trabajar, pero el tipo quedó bien satisfecho. Yo le dije: "Me debe $1,25" (uno veinticinco). Con una gran sonrisa, él me dijo que en ese momento sólo tenía 4. 000 (cuatro mil) euros en el bolsillo, pero que iba a ir al banco -- que queda al doblar la esquina-- para cambiar el dinero y me lo iba a traer en seguidita. Pues aquí estoy, esperándolo.
-- ¿Cuándo pasó eso? -- le preguntó la tía Pepa.
-- Pues ayer por la mañana.

5. 2. La enamorada
"¡Qué día más estupendo!" exclamó la niñita, respirando el aire del campo y subiendo la loma. Encantada de la vida, se sentó en la hierba y sacó de su blusa la carta que llevaba junto al corazón. La había recibido esa misma tarde, pero no quería abrirla porque sabía que era de su enamorado y quería estar sola en medio de la naturaleza para saborearla al máximo. La abrió con mucho cuidado, no queriendo romper ese precioso sobre color crema que contenía la carta de su amado, un marinero guapo y divertido que había

conocido la semana pasada en el puerto cuando acababa de desembarcar de su barco pesquero. Ahora estaba en alta mar camino a Goa, Asia, al otro lado del mundo.

Querida Gloria:

Apenas te conocí y me enamoré perdidamente, desesperadamente de ti, de tus ojos negros, tu boca de caramelo, tu pelo de azabache, tu piel de marfil. No sabes cuánto te amé. Pero ahora que estoy muy, muy lejos de ti, acabo de enamorarme de otra chica. Perdóname, pero así es la vida.

Saludos,

Miguel

Al leer estas palabras escritas sobre el papel, la pobre chica no pudo contener las lágrimas, lágrimas no de pena tanto como de rabia: "**sinvergüenza**, arrastrado, canalla, don nadie, hijo de ..." así gritaba, bajando la loma, hasta que tropezó con una piedrecita, se cayó por un acantilado y se murió.

Bibliography

Aaron, Jane E. (1995) *The Little, Brown Compact Handbook*, New York: Harper Collins College Publishers.

Alvar Ezquerra, M. (2003) *La enseñanza del léxico y el uso del diccionario*, Madrid: Arco libros.

Butt, John and Carmen Benjamin. (2004) *A New Reference Grammar of Modern Spanish*, London: Arnold.

Cascón Martín, Eugenio. (2004) *Manual del buen uso del español*, Madrid: Castalia.

García Gutiérrez, María del Pilar and García Iglesias, Jacinto. (1999) *Ortografía Española. Normas Prácticas*, Lugo: Cuaderno I.

Gómez Torrego, Leonardo. (1989) *Manual de español correcto*, Madrid: Arco libros.

Gómez Torrego, Leonardo. (2002) *Gramática didáctica del español*, Madrid: Ediciones SM.

Iribar Ibabe, Alexander. Personal Website. Universidad de Deusto. <http://paginaspersonales.deusto.es/airibar/Fonetica/Apuntes/05.html> (accessed 4 July 2008).

López Nieto, Juan C. and Maquieira Rodríguez, Marina. (2002) *Ortografía práctica de la lengua española*. Madrid: Anaya.

Martínez de Sousa, José. (2004) *Ortografía y ortotipografía del español actual*, Asturias: Ediciones Trea.

Millares, Selena. (1998) *Método de español para extranjeros. Nivel intermedio*, Madrid: Edinumen.

Muñoz-Basols, Javier. (2004) "'An Error a Day Keeps the Teacher Away': Developing Error Awareness and Error Correction as Learning Strategies in the Spanish Classroom," *The Bulletin*. 31-36.

Muñoz-Basols, Javier. (2005) "'Aprendiendo de los errores con la abuela Dolores': el error como herramienta didáctica en el aula de ELE." *Actas del Primer Congreso Internacional de FIAPE*. *RedELE*. Toledo, 20-23 marzo 2005. Online available HTTP: <http://www.sgci.mec.es/redele/biblioteca2005/fiape/munoz_basols.pdf>

Muñoz-Basols, Javier. (2005) "Learning through Humor: Using Humorous Resources in the Teaching of Foreign Languages," *The Bulletin*. 42-46.

Muñoz-Basols, Javier. (with Fernández Tomás, I.) (2006) "*Caperucita en Manhattan*: una invitación a la lectura," *Revista Materiales*. Consejería de Educación de la Embajada de España en Estados Unidos y Canadá. 10: 36-41.

Muñoz-Basols, Javier. (2007) "Creative Learning Strategies in Spanish: Exploiting the Ludic Aspect of Language" in *Recipes for Success in Foreign Language Teaching: Ready-made Activities for the L2 Classroom*, ed. Katharine N. Harrington and Tina Ware, LINCOM Studies in Second Language Teaching (Munich: Lincom Europa), 100-103.

Muñoz-Basols, Javier. (2007) "Mnemonic Devices for Learning Spanish Tenses in a Playful Way," in *Recipes for Success in Foreign Language Teaching: Ready-made Activities for the L2 Classroom*, ed. Katharine N. Harrington and Tina Ware, LINCOM Studies in Second Language Teaching (Munich: Lincom Europa), 149-152.

Prado, Marcial. (2001) *Diccionario de falsos amigos inglés-español*, Madrid: Gredos.

Real Academia de la Lengua. (1999) *Ortografía de la lengua española*, Madrid: Espasa.

Real Academia de la Lengua. (2001) *Diccionario de la lengua española*, Madrid: Espasa.

Real Academia Española: Banco de datos (CORDE) [en línea]. Corpus diacrónico del español. <http://www.rae.es> [12-01-09]

Real Academia Española: Banco de datos (CREA) [en línea]. Corpus de referencia del español actual. <http://www.rae.es> [08-01-09]

Sarmiento González, Ramón. (1997) *Manuel de corrección gramatical y estilo*, Madrid: SGEL.

Seco, Manuel. (1961) *Diccionario de dudas y dificultades de la lengua española*, Madrid: Espasa-Calpe.

On-line dictionaries

http://www.rae.es
http://www.m-w.com
http://www.spanishdict.com/
http://www.wordreference.com/

Index